Studies in European Culture and History

edited by

Eric D. Weitz and Jack Zipes
University of Minnesota

Since the fall of the Berlin Wall and the collapse of communism, the very meaning of Europe has been opened up and is in the process of being redefined. European states and societies are wrestling with the expansion of NATO and the European Union and with new streams of immigration, while a renewed and reinvigorated cultural engagement has emerged between East and West. But the fast-paced transformations of the last 15 years also have deeper historical roots. The reconfiguring of contemporary Europe is entwined with the cataclysmic events of the twentieth century, two world wars, the Holocaust, and with the processes of modernity that, since the eighteenth century, have shaped Europe and its engagement with the rest of the world.

Studies in European Culture and History is dedicated to publishing books that explore major issues in Europe's past and present from a wide variety of disciplinary perspectives. The works in the series are interdisciplinary; they focus on culture and society and deal with significant developments in Western and Eastern Europe from the eighteenth century to the present within a social historical context. With its broad span of topics, geography, and chronology, the series aims to publish the most interesting and innovative work on modern Europe.

Published by Palgrave Macmillan:

Fascism and Neofascism: Critical Writings on the Radical Right in Europe
Eric Weitz

Fictive Theories: Towards a Deconstructive and Utopian Political Imagination
Susan McManus

German-Jewish Literature in the Wake of the Holocaust: Grete Weil, Ruth Klüger, and the Politics of Address
Pascale Bos

Turkish Turn in Contemporary German Literature: Toward a New Critical Grammar of Migration
Leslie Adelson

Terror and the Sublime in Art and Critical Theory: From Auschwitz to Hiroshima to September 11
Gene Ray

Transformations of the New Germany
Edited by Ruth Starkman

Caught by Politics: Hitler Exiles and American Visual Culture
Edited by Sabine Eckmann and Lutz Koepnick

Legacies of Modernism: Art and Politics in Northern Europe, 1890–1950
Edited by Patrizia C. McBride, Richard W. McCormick, and Monika Zagar

Police Forces: A Cultural History of an Institution
Edited by Klaus Mladek

Richard Wagner for the New Millennium: Essays in Music and Culture
Edited by Matthew Bribitzer-Stull, Alex Lubet, and Gottfried Wagner

Representing Masculinity: Male Citizenship in Modern Western Culture
Edited by Stefan Dudink, Anna Clark, and Karen Hagemann

Remembering the Occupation in French Film: National Identity in Postwar Europe
Leah D. Hewitt

"Gypsies" in European Literature and Culture
Edited by Valentina Glajar and Domnica Radulescu

Choreographing the Global in European Cinema and Theater
Katrin Sieg

Converting a Nation: A Modern Inquisition and the Unification of Italy
Ariella Lang

German Postwar Films: Life and Love in the Ruins
Edited by Wilfried Wilms and William Rasch

Germans, Poland, and Colonial Expansion to the East
Edited by Robert L. Nelson

Cinema After Fascism: The Shattered Screen
Siobhan S. Craig

Weimar Culture Revisited
Edited by John Alexander Williams

Local History, Transnational Memory in the Romanian Holocaust
Edited by Valentina Glajar and Jeanine Teodorescu

The German Wall: Fallout in Europe
Edited by Marc Silberman

Freedom and Confinement in Modernity: Kafka's Cages
Edited by A. Kiarina Kordela and Dimitris Vardoulakis

German Unification
Edited by Peter C. Caldwell and Robert R. Shandley

Anti-Americanism in European Literature
Jesper Gulddal

Weimar Film and Modern Jewish Identity
Ofer Ashkenazi

Baader-Meinhof and the Novel: Narratives of the Nation / Fantasies of the Revolution, 1970–2010
Julian Preece

France, Film and the Holocaust: From Génocide to Shoah
Ferzina Banaji

Tribal Fantasies: Native Americans in the European Imaginary, 1900–2010
Edited By James Mackay and David Stirrup

The Balkan Prospect: Identity, Culture, and Politics in Greece After 1989
Vangelis Calotychos

Violence and Gender in the "New" Europe: Islam in German Culture
Beverly M. Weber

Violence and Gender in the "New" Europe

Islam in German Culture

Beverly M. Weber

VIOLENCE AND GENDER IN THE "NEW" EUROPE
Copyright © Beverly M. Weber, 2013.

All rights reserved.

First published in 2013 by
PALGRAVE MACMILLAN®
in the United States—a division of St. Martin's Press LLC,
175 Fifth Avenue, New York, NY 10010.

Where this book is distributed in the UK, Europe and the rest of the world, this is by Palgrave Macmillan, a division of Macmillan Publishers Limited, registered in England, company number 785998, of Houndmills, Basingstoke, Hampshire RG21 6XS.

Palgrave Macmillan is the global academic imprint of the above companies and has companies and representatives throughout the world.

Palgrave® and Macmillan® are registered trademarks in the United States, the United Kingdom, Europe and other countries.

ISBN: 978–1–137–00708–7

Library of Congress Cataloging-in-Publication Data

Weber, Beverly M.
   Violence and gender in the "new" Europe : Islam in German culture / Beverly M. Weber.
      p. cm.—(Studies in European culture and history)
   ISBN 978–1–137–00708–7
    1. Muslim women—Germany. 2. Women—Violence against—Germany. 3. Islam and civil society—Germany. 4. Violence in mass media—Germany. I. Title.

DD78.M87W43 2013
305.6′970973—dc23   2012030677

A catalogue record of the book is available from the British Library.

Design by Newgen Imaging Systems (P) Ltd., Chennai, India.

First edition: January 2013

10 9 8 7 6 5 4 3 2 1

In memorium Charles Weber

Contents

Acknowledgments ix

Introduction: Undoing the Connections between Muslim Violence, "Culture," and Secularism   1

One   A Regime of Gender Violence: Honor Killings, Familial Violence, and Muslim Women's Subjectivities   39

Two   Contentious Headscarves: Cleaning Woman, Forbidden Schoolteacher, Hijab Martyr   77

Three   Troubling Headscarves: Covering, Artistic Reconfigurations of Public Space, and the Muslim Woman's Body   113

Four   Freedom to Imagine the World: Violence and the Writing of Self   137

Five   Violent Authenticities: The Work of Emine Sevgi Özdamar and Feridun Zaimoglu   173

Conclusion   199

Notes   207

Works Cited   213

Index   235

Acknowledgments

I thank Maria Stehle, Ipek Celik, Deepti Misri, and Danika Medak-Saltzman who have read, commented on, and provided invaluable insight on earlier drafts of many portions of the manuscript. Mistakes of course remain my own.

I am grateful for the invaluable friendship and support—intellectual and emotional–of Deepti Misri, Nikolina Dobreva, Enrique Garcia, Yehudit Heller, Kirsten Isgro, Christy McCain, Danika Medak-Saltzman, Britt Nielsen, Peggy Piesche, Tom Schicker, and Maria Stehle. A special thank you to my sometime cowriter Maria Stehle, who has accompanied the writing of this book on every step with patience, humor, and encouragement.

My deep gratitude as well to my family and to G. for their unwavering support and patience.

Thank you to Sara Lennox, whose career, life, and mentoring have been both inspirational and invaluable.

I continue to be inspired by my students. A special thanks to my graduate students, and the students of my Gender, Race, and Immigration course, whose thoughtful conversations in and out of class continue to sustain my work.

Earlier drafts portions of two chapters appeared as: "Hijab Martyrdom, Headscarf Debates: Rethinking Violence, Secularism, and Islam in Germany" in *Comparative Studies of South Asia, Africa and the Middle East*, Vol. 32, issue. 1, pp. 102–115, reprinted by permission of the present publisher, Duke University Press; and "Freedom from Violence, Freedom to Make the World: Muslim Women's Memoirs, Gendered Violence, and Voices for Change in Germany." *Women in German Yearbook*. Eds. Katharina Gerstenberger and Patricia Anne Simpson. Vol. 25, pp. 199–222, reprinted by permission of the present publisher, University of Nebraska Press.

Introduction: Undoing the Connections between Muslim Violence, "Culture," and Secularism

In 2007, a German judge denied a woman an expedited divorce with the words, "The exercise of the right to corporal punishment does not constitute an extreme hardship according to federal law" (Kirschstein; Oswald). The 26-year-old woman filing for divorce had been the victim of domestic violence and death threats at the hand of her husband; under German domestic abuse laws, courts had already awarded her sole access to the apartment and a restraining order against her husband. Yet when she requested a waiver of the required one-year waiting period for divorce, the judge used citations from the Koran to deny the expedited divorce because the petitioner was of Moroccan heritage and was married to a Moroccan man. The judge reasoned that a woman entering into a marriage with a Muslim must already know of the potential for "corporal punishment" within the marriage. The case understandably aroused great protest. For many, the case served as "evidence" of the "quiet Islamicization of Germany" (Bartsch et al.).

Several problems with the judge's reasoning are striking. It runs contrary to German law; it demonstrates ignorance of the realities of contemporary Moroccan law, which since 1962 bans familial violence and in 2003 was amended to explicitly clarify that this ban includes violence between spouses (Hajjar 4–5;8); and it further demonstrates profound ignorance about the range of relationships between the Koran, Shar'ia, and state law in Muslim countries (Hajjar 4). Although the decision itself is not representative of developments in contemporary German law, I open with reference to this case because it illustrates the continued power of a particularly simplistic notion of culture as immutable, and of Muslim culture as necessarily and unchangeably violent. The judge's assumption that Muslim men are oppressive, and Muslim women submissive, prevented the judge from recognizing the petitioner's act of resistance to violence. This case reveals not only the dangers of cultural relativism but also speaks to the ongoing difficulty to conceptualize violence in a way that imagines potential resistance, particularly on the part of Muslim women. Images of covered women, together with stories of honor killings and forced marriages, continue to retain their currency in media representations of Islam and are even more powerful in legal and political representations. After decades of criticism of such representations of Islam and Muslims in Germany, these narratives are now often accompanied by a nod to the "diversity of Islam" or to the fact that "not all Muslim men beat their wives." Yet, despite token complication of discussions on Islam, issues of gender violence continue to play a key role in defining the position of Muslims in the public sphere. Inflected by and related to discourses of security, (multi)cultural crisis, spatial isolation and European Union integration and crisis, discussions of gender violence[1] are important to how Muslim citizens and residents of Europe participate in the public sphere. Muslim men often emerge in public as the perpetrators of violence, whereas Muslim women are often depicted as victims of Islam; both positions prohibit democratic public subjectivities.

Consider, for example, Thilo Sarrazin's bestselling 2010 book *Deutschland schafft sich ab* [Germany Does Away with Itself]. Sarrazin argues that high birth rates among immigrant groups will lead to the destruction of European values, for "whoever multiplies the most, will possess Europe in the end" (Sarrazin 320). Part of his argument relies on generating fear of the presence of women wearing headscarves, for "the headscarf signals at the same time the acceptance of the submission of the woman to the man, that is to say the rejection of the emancipation of women according to the Western model" (Sarrazin 299). The text understands Muslim women who express their religious adherence publicly as a tremendous threat to European democratic values. Although many have been extremely critical of Sarrazin, the text has also had a significant impact on discussions of Islam in Europe.

The lack of possibilities for Muslim women in the public sphere has presented a thorny problem for European studies scholars, particularly those doing feminist work. How can one remain committed to ending violence against women, develop antiracist scholarship, and attend to the complex realities of Muslim women, or women of Muslim heritage, in Europe today? We may best address these urgent, often competing agendas if we consider the persistent power of violence in determining public subjectivities of Muslim Europeans as a regime of gender violence. My notion of a regime of gender violence draws on Michel Foucault's notion of a truth regime, a "system of ordered procedures for the production, regulation, distribution, circulation and operation of statements...linked in a circular relation with systems of power which produce and sustain it, and to effects of power which it induces and which extend it" (Foucault 133). The regime of gender violence is a systematically produced set of statements that insists on the representation of Muslim women as the victims of Muslim violence, while obscuring or excluding their roles as agents in the public sphere and as victims of other forms of violence, particularly racialized forms of violence. This regime thus both produces and is produced by other systems of power, including Islamophobia, xenophobia, heterosexism, and racism. In the German case, the regime of gender violence targets Germany's largest minority population, Turkish Germans, marking them Muslim and defining their public presence according to their relationship to gender violence.

An interrogation of the discourse of gender violence must recognize that it is powerful, but not all powerful. I suggest and practice ways of imagining and analyzing textual figures of immigrant women in Germany that enable new discursive possibilities for representations of Muslims and of Islam. Challenging the regime of violence further requires a politics of radical listening in which the scholar seeks out already existing, alternative representations, often those created by minoritized and racialized groups. In particular, I examine alternatives that insist on the participation of Muslim women and women of Muslim heritage in a democratic public sphere and that locate the experience of gender violence in relationship to a range of forms of violence.

Culture, Multiculturalism, and Racism

Sarrazin's book, and the court case with which I opened, participate in the endless discussions of culture and cultural difference that confront any analysis of the representation of violence in Europe today. I am particularly concerned with the questions inspired by a transnational feminist cultural studies framework, which addresses the imbrication of cultural practices and everyday lives in structures of power, while seeking the possibilities for transformation of those same structures (Grossberg 8). Early calls for a transnational feminist cultural studies challenged liberal multiculturalism, calling for researchers to bring Marxist, poststructuralist, and feminist forms of analysis to bear on one another (Kaplan and Grewal 350; Spivak 255–289). Transnational feminist practices further refuse to choose among economic, cultural, and political concerns (Kaplan and Grewal 357–358; further, see Grossberg 9), while attending "to the linkages and travels of forms of representation as they intersect with movements of labor and capital in a multinational world" (Kaplan and Grewal 357). Inhabiting the position of a cultural studies intellectual, in other words, requires a commitment to radical contextuality (Grossberg 11) that inspires questions such as: How are Turkish Germans and other immigrants from "Muslim" countries represented in relationship to Islam and violence? How do Turkish German texts respond to contemporary and historical discourses of Islam and gender violence as well as to their transnational circulation?

Welcomed to West Germany as inexpensive labor during the postwar economic boom, the second and third generation of Turkish Germans as well as newer immigrants from the Baltic peninsula have long been partially excluded from access to upward mobility, educational opportunities, and meaningful employment (Farrokhzad, "Bildungs- und Berufschancen" 50–51; Farrokhzad, "Erfahrungen" 411). Students with a migration background[2] are less likely to find internships or jobs despite active searches (Beicht and Granato 37). Women with Turkish names, German language proficiency, and equal qualifications are much less likely to be employed than their "German" counterparts; the level of discrimination becomes more severe for better paying work, particularly as white collar professionals (Varela 18–21). People of color in Germany have further been subject to several waves of xenophobially motivated physical violence since unification. As a consequence of the focus on Islam as a primary signal of cultural difference, these other challenges facing immigrants and those of immigrant heritage in Germany are often elided, mirroring developments in many other Western European countries.

A key argument to this project is that the racialized construction of cultural difference as static and absolute, at best, obscures participation by Muslim women in politics, economics and knowledge production and, at worst, limits or even prevents such participation. Race and culture are hardly synonymous terms, nor are discourses around race and culture entirely parallel in their structure. Yet it is imperative that we consider race and culture together, as cultural difference in Europe continues to fulfill the roles played by biological racisms in the first half of the twentieth century (MacMaster 217). In the French context Étienne Balibar has analyzed a post-Cold War shift from race to culture, one that essentializes cultural difference, as a neoracism, centered upon the immigration complex (Balibar and Wallerstein 21). Alana Lentin, alternatively, points out that culturalism in Europe also became a sort of depoliticized postwar response to the racism of the early twentieth century, a desire to create a state of "racelessness" while denying the history of race (Lentin 382); indeed, the construction of Europe as a "race-free" space remains widely accepted (El-Tayeb, *European Others* xv)

Racisms both in Cold War West Germany and in unified Germany, however, differ from those in other Western European countries in at least two significant ways. Firstly, German immigrant populations were not postcolonial citizens or migrants but often guestworkers with minimal familiarity with the language or cultural context. Although Rita Chin argues that this meant that they at least were not exposed to the kind of entrenched racisms in place in postcolonial countries (Chin 27), this also meant that migrants had virtually no access to a path to citizenship. Until the early 2000s, Germany maintained a migration regime founded on *jus sanguinis*, or the law of blood.[3] While Germany did have colonies until the end of World War I and attempted to reestablish a colonial empire in Northern Africa during World War II, West Germany did not recruit from these countries for its guestworkers. Instead, contracts were signed with Spain, Italy, Yugoslavia, Turkey, and Greece. Because of the economic and political insecurity in Turkey, it quickly became the largest sending country, though migration from the former Yugoslav republic dramatically increased during the 1990s. Thus while Germany does share with many other Western European countries a largely Muslim immigrant population, the legal conditions under which immigrants settled and the traditions of democracy and secularism in the sending countries varied quite dramatically.

Germany, like other Western European countries, is heavily invested in promoting an image as tolerant and democratic and, like other Western European countries, tends to equate successful democracy with success in combatting racism (Lentin, "Europe" 488). Unlike other Western European countries, the creation of West Germany in the wake of the Holocaust produced taboos that were tied to the very foundational identity of the state. This coincided with a complex simultaneous "denial and obsession" with race after World War II (El Tayeb, "Dangerous Liasons" 29; Lentin, "Europe" 500). Race is ever present and yet assumed to be a problem that ended with the end of World War II (Chin et al. 5). As a consequence, post-1945 discussions of culture racialize social groups: they set up a clear difference between cultures, produce that difference as unchangeable, and attach a negative value to that difference (Chin et al. 4; MacMaster 2). That negative valuation is not always explicit, or even conscious. The unchangeable difference is sometimes, but not only, linked to the fetishization of certain biological characteristics (Chin et al. 4).

While the current form of cultural difference dominant in Europe relies heavily on the uneven juxtaposition of Islam and Europe, other forms of cultural difference have been similarly mobilized in Germany after World War II. Throughout the Cold War the largest guestworker population, from Turkey, was largely represented as Other via its association with national, class, and educational difference as well as with rural origin rather than racial or religious difference (although these forms of difference were never entirely absent). All these forms of cultural difference make up the landscape of a post World War II "neoracism." This new racism "is a racism whose dominant theme is not biological heredity but the insurmountability of cultural differences, a racism which, at first sight, does not postulate the superiority of certain groups or peoples in relation to others but 'only' the harmfulness of abolishing frontiers, the incompatibility of life-styles and traditions" (Balibar and Wallerstein 21). In the absences of colonial relationships, old, racialized Orientalizing tropes connected to unfulfilled colonial imaginations remained firmly in place and are easily activated in the name of cultural difference. This was rarely addressed in the political sphere, although one German politician suggested in the late 1990s, "It appears that the confrontation avoided by the ending of the Cold War now attempts to establish itself on the level of culture. The buzzwords of global cultural battles, of the battle of civilizations, are used more and more often in an increasingly more targeted manner" (Gerigk 17).

The successes of Samuel Huntington's *The Clash of Civilizations* and a German counterpart, Bassam Tibi's *Krieg der Zivilisationen*, in Germany are illustrative. The process of Othering through the ascription of cultural difference became a form of ethnicization (Lutz and Huth-Hildebrandt 160–163; Pelinka), that also partially determines the forms of communal attachment immigrant subjects can imagine for themselves (Bukow and Llaryora 52). Cultural othering was reinforced in academic studies that took culture as a closed, unchanging system (Çağlar 90) and used "traditional" (often archaic) life forms to explain the lives of Turks in contemporary Germany (Çağlar 99). These tendencies bear structural similarities to Orientalism as Said defined it, in which colonizing powers mobilize notions of tradition and modernity to establish a geographical distinction that translates to forms of geopolitical power (Said 12).

Oddly enough, at first glance the deployment of cultural difference to legitimate societal exclusion has long been accompanied by a sort of uncritical, celebratory multiculturalism—popular festivals such as the famed Carnival of Cultures in Berlin, for example, or in the celebration of the success of Turkish German cinema to make German cultural industries viable in a globalized cultural market (Göktürk 339–340). Uncritical approaches to cultural difference found their intellectual counterpart in the German reception of postcolonial theory, which embraced the "mixing" of hybridity superficially at the risk of depoliticizing the concept (Ha, "Hybridität" 221–222). Although they recognized that theories of "hybridity" may open space for political action, critics argued that a mere celebration of hybridity can hardly serve as effective political strategy (Terkessidis 233). Two important paradoxes are at work here. Firstly, an understanding of immigration as economic necessity to counter the low birth rate in Germany is coupled with inattention to the economic and working lives of immigrants and those with immigrant heritage. The exception: a recent trend that portrays immigrants or those of immigrant heritage as refusing to get jobs or an education (which also plays a role in Sarrazin's book and its reception). Secondly, although immigrant culture is necessary to the economic success of German cultural industries, it is also seen as dangerously other and a threat to "European values." Furthermore, the celebration of hybridity portrays cultural contact as new, obscuring histories of centuries of migration, European colonialism (Ha, *Hype um Hybridität* 14), and the continuities of colonial attitudes in contemporary politics of worker migration (Ha, *Hype um Hybridität* 89–90).

The hidden link between "culture" and "race" thus also exists in notions of multiculturalism. Multiculturalism in Europe emerged as a deeply depoliticized institutional response to early twentieth-century racism, one that ignored racism's role in the trajectory of modernity as well as in the history of the nation-state (Lentin, "Replacing" 381–382). As Slavoj Žižek argues,

> Multiculturalism [...] from a kind of empty global position, treats each local culture the way the colonizer treats colonized people—as "natives" whose mores are to be carefully studied and "respected".... In the same way that global capitalism involves the paradox of colonization without the colonizing Nation-State metropole, multiculturalism involves patronizing Eurocentrist distance and/or respect for local cultures without roots in one's own particular culture. In other words, multiculturalism is a disavowed, inverted, self-referential form of racism, a "racism with a distance"—it "respects" the Other's identity, conceiving the Other as a self-enclosed "authentic" community towards which he, the multiculturalist, maintains a distance rendered possible by his privileged universal position. (Žižek 44)

Liberal multiculturalism often privileges "culture" as marker of difference and marks the "Other" culture as unchanging. It sets up a speaking subject who "grants" multiculturalism while maintaining an abstracted universalized position. A critical approach to multiculturalism remains necessary, and difficult, given the current political climate, in which a vague, popular understanding of liberal multiculturalism is attributed blame for a perceived failure of "integration."

Nevertheless, my project here is conceived of in the spirit of what Gayatri Spivak has called radical multiculturalism—a multiculturalism that can undo, or at least intervene, in transnational cultural racist scripts, in part through deconstruction of the notion of culture itself (Spivak, *A Critique* 334, 353, 397). Textual analyses that question in whose interests cultural difference is defined can reveal the politics of knowledge production (Spivak, "Cultural Talks" 329), whether in popular media or academic work. An examination of how gender violence is talked about in Germany today reveals not only more about Turkish German experience but also about how the possibilities for understanding the Turkish German subject impact the possibilities for her movement in and through the world. I thus seek to widen the field of possibility for "making sense of," for "knowing" European residents of Muslim heritage. While my starting point is the powerful link between violence and Islam that is present in dominant discourses, my work here is also informed by a politics of radical listening that seeks out existing marginalized representations and to imagine other possibilities for more democratic futures. My unusual archive, including popular news media, art exhibits, comedic performance, and literature allows me to more adequately address the circulation of and challenges to the regime of violence, the unevenness and messiness of its manifestations.

Shifting analytical focus from mere cultural difference to the differential impacts of a regime of violence further enables a more ethical humanities scholarship and new representational politics around the figure of the Muslim woman. As Arif Dirlik suggests,

> A critical reading of culture, one that exposes it as an ideological operation crucial to the establishment of hegemony, requires that we view it not merely as an attribute of totalities but as an activity

that is bound up with the operation of social relations, that expresses contradiction as much as it does cohesion. Culture is an activity in which the social relations that are possible but absent, because they have been displaced or rendered impossible (or "utopian") by existing social relations, are as fundamental as the relations whose existence it affirms. (Dirlik 15)

An imagination of a different future, however, takes place not only through such a critical reading of culture, but through a challenge of how culture itself is conceptualized.

The linking of gender violence to an unchangeable Muslim culture and the persistent construction of the Muslim woman as victim prevents an imagination of her intellectual, economic, and political subjectivities. This in turn prohibits scholarship from adequately analyzing the intensely gendered processes of globalization and the experiences of racist violence. Is it possible instead to position textual figures of Muslim women *within* the terrains of democratic politics and economic activity rather than as excluded from them by the violence of Muslim culture? Or, more importantly, is it possible as a European studies or German studies scholar to listen more carefully to the voices of Muslim women to understand how they position themselves in struggles for rights and justice—often, but not solely, through claims to and participation in multiple transnational, national and regional identities and processes? Such questions are part of an ethical reading that insists on a responsibility *to* the other, "an openness toward the imagined agency of the other" (Spivak, *Other Asias* 32). These small steps toward enlarging the discursive fields in which women of immigrant heritage are constituted expand possibilities for alliances across ethnic and cultural boundaries as well—for only when the potential exists for imagining minoritized and racialized women as political and economic actors who produce knowledge does potential exist for wide-ranging political alliances that can organize around economic and political issues that impact women of immigrant heritage and Muslim women in Germany.

The events of 2010 may have provided challenges to the argument, however, that cultural racism has largely replaced biological racism. The success and impact of Sarrazin's book, in which Sarrazin has conflated biological and cultural arguments in ways that demonstrate the similarities between biological and cultural racisms, has been surprising to many—the book has not only been a wild bestseller but has been a touchstone both for the topic and the tone of political discussions about immigration, integration, and Islam since its publication. Sarrazin argues that because Germany's birthrate is dropping, and the largest immigrant populations who immigrate are from less intelligent archaic societies, Germany is at danger of losing the intelligence necessary to compete in a globalized world (Sarrazin 53–58). In particular, migrants from Turkey and from Arab countries have "difficulties in the school system, in the job employment and generally in society [that] derive from the groups themselves, not from the society with which they are surrounded" (Sarrazin 59). Sarrazin assumes an unchanging culture and fears the propagation of that culture by members of the immigrant "lower classes" who have more children than the indigenous German population. Sarrazin's fear of inherited cultural problems that are linked to low intelligence may be a marker of a return to a discussion of biology—even if many public intellectuals seek to "set aside" Sarrazin's biological references to focus on his "cultural" arguments (see, for example, Kelek and Maron). Cultural and biological definitions of race have, of course, often coexisted, but Sarrazin's work and the ensuing discussions could normalize a new understanding of biological race that has remained taboo since World War II.

Gendering Culture and Multiculturalism

Women of color and women of immigrant heritage in Germany, both scholars and activists, have theorized the place of gender in the shifting constellations of culture/race for decades. Yet their work has often been excluded from academic and popular discussions of "multiculturalism" and "integration." Because of these frequent exclusions, it is important to address the overall scholarly trajectory at greater length. Equitable gender relations were already emphasized as a fundamental aspect of the potential for integration in the early 1980s (Chin 140–143). The figure of the unenlightened Muslim woman oppressed by her culture has long played a key role in constructions of cultural difference (Gümen "Die sozialpolitische Konstruktion";

Huth-Hildebrandt *Das Bild*; Lutz and Huth-Hildebrandt; Lutz "Unsichtbare Schatten"). By the same token, even though research on "other cultures" is the one area where gender as a category is constantly employed, its perceived exclusion is constantly lamented: gender has been an indispensable component of understanding minoritized communities in Germany (Lutz and Huth-Hildebrandt 159), creating a complex ethnicization of sexism. The obsession with gender violence as a focus for integration has not improved the economic or political situation of women of immigrant heritage, who remain structurally disadvantaged in terms of access to employment and education (Farrokhzad et al. 19–21).

Despite decades in which immigrant women played a major role in Germany's labor force, and in which gender was a primary focus in academic and popular discourse, careful feminist engagement with the complex issues of immigration (as well as race, nation, and ethnicity) was relatively late in coming. A fixation on gender as the "primary" difference delayed discussions of ethnicity and race by feminist researchers in Germany until the early 1990s (Gümen, "Das Soziale" 220). The focus on gender as a primary difference, together with the resultant lack of research that addressed intersections of racism and sexism, led to ongoing constructions of Otherness that set the Western, emancipated German woman against Turkish immigrant women (Gümen, "Das Soziale"; Gümen, "Die sozialpolitische Konstruktion"). This is reflected in the lack of early research on women who worked in factory positions in textiles, clothing, or electronics. In early guestworker migration, many married women entered Germany as workers with or without their husbands, and immigrant women have consistently been employed at higher percentages than German women (Kofman et al. 142), though prohibitions on spousal employment for guestworkers enacted between 1973 and 1979 eventually made many women economically dependent on their spouses (Kofman et al. 47; 51).

Even early research showing that women made up between 20 percent and 25 percent of postwar labor migration (Booth 197), and tended not to return to their home countries at nearly the rates that their male compatriots did (Booth 194), was interpreted as evidence of a Muslim culture that prevented women from working. The yearly numbers of women workers as a percentage of total female Turkish immigrants in the early years varied only slightly from rates of immigrants from the largely Christian country of Portugal. Yet scholars assumed differences aligned along a Muslim/Christian divide. For example, one scholar suggested that differences between female participation in Spanish, Greek, and Turkish migration existed because fewer Muslim women would migrate as workers than would Christians (Booth 127). The post-Cold War shift in media representations from an emphasis on class and national difference to cultural and religious difference finds a counterpart in 1990s social science discourse on migrant women (Huth-Hildebrandt, *Das Bild* 46; Lutz and Huth-Hildebrandt; Westphal). The "cultural" focus in research on immigrants, particularly the focus on identities, difference, and bodies, masks the material effects of immigration (Kofman et al. 33). The focus on culture became a "straitjacket" (Çağlar) that promoted studies on medical issues and domestic violence while excluding immigrant women from scholarship on education, work, and economics (Chin 140–143; Farrokhzad, "Bildungs- und Berufschancen" 41–42; Gümen, "Frauen"; Huth-Hildebrandt, *Das Bild* 56). Cultural constructions of cultural, ethnic and national difference clearly have material effects, impacting governmental policy and institutional guidelines and determining allocation of funding (Kofman et al. 34–36).

Furthermore, the issues prioritized in activism and scholarship by women of color and women of immigrant heritage in Germany were long ignored in much academic work and in popular media. Since the late 1980s and early 1990s, immigrant, black, and Jewish women together with antiracist white women have vocally critiqued feminist groups in Germany for ignoring the specific concerns related to issues of xenophobia, nationalism, anti-Semitism, and racism, often seeking to make such concerns public via national conferences, as documented in a number of edited volumes (for example, Arbeitsgruppe Frauenkongreß; Lutz, "Sind wir uns immer noch"; Konuk, Piesche, and Gelbin; Kaufman, Jacobsohn, and Ghirmazion). The feminist immigrant group FeMigra similarly sought to create a counterimage of themselves as modern, educated, autonomous, and emancipated in response to the repeated representation of the Muslim woman as the "epitome of women's oppression" (Yurtsever-Kneer).

Scholars of color and antiracist feminists have for decades pointed out the inadequacy of thinking about oppression as additive and hierarchal (Schulz 49), calling for an attention to gender as a category constituted by and constitutive of other categories such as ethnicity, class and race (Gümen, "Das Soziale"; Gümen, "Die sozialpolitische Konstruktion"). This work, calling for attention to diverse intersections of gender with race, nation, and ethnicity, was unfortunately also marginalized by much mainstream feminist academic discourse (Lutz, "Sind wir uns immer noch" 139; Rodríguez, "Fallstricke"; Schulz 48). Much of this scholarly work drew heavily on black and postcolonial feminist academic work emerging from the US and the UK but was further inspired by the writings of antiracist activists in Germany (Erel et al. 240), particularly by the publication of *Showing Our Colors*, a feminist history of blacks in Germany. The nascent Afro-German movement developed in part because of contact with Audre Lorde, who initially met many Afro-German women while teaching a seminar in Berlin. Lorde's own work often called attention to the importance of recognizing how multiple forms of difference inflect experiences as women (114–123); this encounter facilitated academic work in Germany that complicated the way "woman" has been used as a category. Yet mainstream feminism has written a narrative in which the stability of the category of woman is both depoliticized and challenged, primarily by French feminist theory: "The making instable of the category of 'woman' is thematized, but the sociopolitical and historical moment in which this debate was carried out in feminism, remains effaced" (Rodríguez, "Fallstricke"). Thus, a theoretical focus on binary (male vs. female) or hierarchal (gender supersedes all others) forms of difference rather than intersectional differences[4] limited the forms of analysis possible in feminist academic work, whereas the relegation of immigrant women to the realm of culture produced a dearth of research on immigrant women's positioning in Germany in relationship to economics, politics (Lutz and Huth-Hildebrandt 159), and knowledge production. Even in the late 2000s, as the term intersectionality became a new buzzword both in scholarship and in political agendas (Davis), earlier calls for theorizing intersectional positionalities (Gümen, "Frauen"; Varela) and immigrant intellectual agency (Rodríguez,

Intellektuelle) were largely ignored; and the history of intersectionality as a concept that was rooted in antiracist work often disappeared (Erel et al. 240–241).

In North American humanities scholarship, imaginations of the figure of the German Muslim woman have changed dramatically. The early 1990s also brought an important transformation of the fields of literary and textual studies—the avenue by which a large number of German Studies scholars continue to "study Germany"— both in Germany and in North America. With a shift from traditional *Germanistik* to a more interdisciplinary German Studies influenced by cultural studies, a wave of North American German Studies scholarship expressed a commitment to researching culture, particularly literature and film, in relationship to globalization. Because this trend was led in part by feminist scholars, a great deal of attention has been paid to immigrant women's creative and cultural production (Lennox, "Feminisms in Transit" 77). The changing critical attention to Emine Sevgi Özdamar's literary and theatrical production, which I further address in chapter 5, is exemplary of the shifting terrain of literary criticism that takes the writing of immigrant women and women of immigrant heritage as its focus. Since Özdamar earned the prestigious Bachmann literary prize in 1991, amid much Orientalizing praise for her work, (Jankowsky 261–264), an explosion of critical work has examined Özdamar's writing in relationship to how it functions as a hybrid of German and Turkish culture. Two decades of Özdamar criticism demonstrate a larger shift from examining artistic production by foreigners from a sociological perspective both to treating this body of work as art as well as to reading it to examine and problematize notions of multiculturalism and hyphenated German identities. Yet, a focus on identity in scholarship, particularly cultural identity, limits in the same ways that an emphasis on culture in mainstream media does: they prohibit imaginations of Muslim women as democratic subjects, whether as textual or public figures. Leslie Adelson's book *The Turkish Turn* has been groundbreaking in expanding the possible ways of imagining the literary figures of Turkish Germans, precisely because she seeks to shift the focus of literary scholarship from identity to cultural production. Her work on Özdamar's tongue tales, for example, considers the cultural labor performed by such works (Adelson 123–159). She especially emphasizes the ways in which the texts reveal the transnational nature of migrant cultural capital, which in turn reveals shared points of national and transnational histories. Adelson opens new discursive terrain for imagining Turkish German cultural production as participating in the history of Germany, creating new possibilities for reading the textual figures of Turkish German women as active participants in the public sphere.

Although literary studies, then, have partially challenged imaginations of the figure of the Turkish German woman, it has nevertheless remained difficult, even taboo, to consider how to conceptualize violence against women from an antiracist perspective. This is perhaps particularly surprising because an immense amount of North American literary criticism that takes writings by Turkish Germans as its focus is written by feminist scholars. The discourse has become so loaded, the perceived necessary choice between gender justice and antiracist work so binarized, that questioning dominant conceptions of gender violence is a tremendously fraught task. This difficulty intersects with the reluctance of German studies scholars on the Left to address questions about religion. This has at its roots a history of German studies that itself is overdetermined by enlightenment narratives of secularism. A focus on Islam, combined with an openness to addressing the connections between multiple forms of violence in an array of texts, both literary and nonliterary, allows a challenge of the tenacious power of the regime of gender violence in popular discourse. In pointing to the importance of imagining the concerns of women of immigrant heritage that go beyond experiences of violence and cultural difference, I am certainly not suggesting that gender violence does not occur in Turkish German communities. Nor do I wish to deny that there are concerns specific to living in Muslim or Turkish families in Germany. Indeed, a 2004 study, one which provides the first large national study on women's experiences of violence that also does a careful comparative sampling of Turkish heritage and Eastern European-heritage women, does seem to suggest differences in experiences of violence, though not in incidence of violence, between these groups and "ethnic Germans" (U. Müller et al.). Yet, the reception of this study has interpreted it to mean that there are dramatic differences in the incidence of violence. This prevents attention to the fact that women in all groups experience all forms of violence, that the incidence of experiences of violence varies little, and that women from minoritized groups are also subject to gendered forms of racism. Moving beyond assumptions about the immutability of Muslim "culture" enables more careful thinking about strategies for preventing violence in the future. It also allows theorizations of multiple forms of violence (racist violence, familial violence, or intimate violence, for example) together. In turn, one could better understand the full range of violence in relationship to gendered subjectivities. In effect, I am suggesting that reading for this range of violence enables more productive strategies against gender violence. When thinking about women of immigrant and Muslim heritage in Germany, we must also examine sexisms and racisms /culturalisms at work in Germany as contributors to structural discriminations, and provide careful attention to how discursive formations around the culturally other immigrant woman enable particular labor practices, exclude them from educational access, and prevent attention to their economic and political actions as well as to their participation in knowledge production.

The Politics of Speaking and Agency

An ethical humanities scholarship that interrogates the textual figure of the Muslim woman in Europe exists between the commitment to a politics of radical listening and a commitment to an enabling of broader collectivities.[5] These potential collectivities are to be understood differently than those formed under the sign of "global sisterhood" or "global feminism," terms that have functioned in the past as slightly disguised iterations of the "white man's burden" in which white women will save brown women from brown men (Spivak, *A Critique* 284; Grewal). The literary and artistic texts I analyze do not generally provide a concrete politics of collectivity or lay out normative political projects. Instead, I hope to imagine and practice careful readings that approach the (impossible) responsibility *to*, rather than *for*, the other. This requires a leap into tremendous uncertainty for German and European studies scholars: namely, a rejection of Europe's claim to a role as sole inheritor to the culture of Enlightenment, benevolently distributed to the "unreasonable" immigrant or Third World Other (Spivak, *Imperatives* 50; 84). Such a move is an important aspect of the rejection of cultural racism, which would limit immigrant agency to the speaking of victimhood, but not reason, on an intensely gendered discursive terrain where the "enlightened" European defines itself against the trope of the silent immigrant woman oppressed by (the other) culture. Such a politics of reading challenges a politics of identity and alterity, providing a perspective that is carefully attentive to the relationship between the Self and the Other, a relationship of subjects that is mutually constituted though a relationship structured in power. This is a *teleopoetic* project in Spivak's sense, one that understands textual reading as an imaginative remaking (*poiesis*), but one that may reach to the Other (Spivak, "A Note" 13; Spivak, *Death of a Discipline* 30). Particularly because I speak from a position of societal privilege, I must persistently acknowledge that I have no direct access to the Other—but have the right and the responsibility to learn to learn from below. This work requires a practice of "patient reading, miming an effort to make the text respond, as it were, [...] a training not only in poiesis, accessing the Other so well that probably action can be prefigured, but teleo-poiesis, striving for a response from the distant other, without guarantees" (Spivak, "Righting Wrongs" 181). Although I cannot directly access the experiences of someone who faces extensive barriers in accessing education and social mobility, I can attempt a reading of textual representations of the Other. Yet the attempt remains a responsibility, the effort undertaken without guarantees. The act of *teleopoeisis* can be thus understood as simultaneously impossibility and imperative.

Despite the emphasis on self-emancipation that is so important to popular discussions of European enlightenment heritage and immigrant integration, the discussions and controversies surrounding the position of Muslim women in Germany are implicitly linked to the question of who can serve as guardian of human rights—those of Muslims and, in particular, of Muslim women—and how that guardianship is best achieved. In other words, Muslim women are understood as capable of entering into a state of emancipation primarily by claiming a certain paternal guardianship offered up by the German state. The contentious topic of Muslim women's rights is clearly important to the platform of the German Islam Conference (Deutsche Islam-Konferenz; hereafter DIK), for example. The initial version of the DIK's goals included as its first section "Deutsche Gesellschaftsordnung und Wertekonsens" (German societal order and consensus of values): the first point in this section is equal rights for women (Bundesministerium des Innern).

The state's framing of the importance of women's rights has significant similarities to familiar colonialist tropes. When speaking of the British colonialist discourse on *sati*, Spivak famously pointed out that Third World women had to choose between two narratives: one in which "white men are saving brown women from brown men" and one in which Third World widows attained a peculiar sort of agency in choosing a traditional death by self-immolation (*sati*), thus forging an anti-imperial claim to their "nation" (Spivak, *A Critique* 288–289). Ziba Mir-Hosseini, in her explanation of the differing relationships of gender equality to Islamic law, points out structurally similar choices that emerged in a specifically Muslim context. Within a colonial logic that legitimated Western colonization in the name of women's rights, women who were interested in achieving more rights could only express their ideals as a betrayal of their burgeoning national, anticolonial communities (further see Ahmed). In contemporary Germany, similar choices circumscribe the potential imaginations of self. Immigrant women, particularly Muslim women, are often forced to choose between two narratives of self: one in which they might join German women saving Muslim women from Muslim men by rejecting affiliation with a religious or Turkish community, and the other in which they consciously participate in or even desire their own oppression in order to retain a claim to a Muslim community or identity.

The assumption that a "choice" must be made between community and women's rights also belies the wide-ranging discussions about women's rights within Islam (Mir-Hosseini 53–54). These positions vary. Many scholars of Islam move from the assumption that Islamic law itself, properly interpreted, can promote women's rights,[6] whereas others point to the development of explicitly feminist movements in many Muslim countries, often by women who consider their Muslim identity to be primarily cultural rather than religious (Abid 156). Yet, discussions on Muslim women's rights in Germany quickly become limited to gender violence, headscarves, or arranged marriages, evading engagements with racialized violence or structural discrimination against women of immigrant heritage. Access to modernity, then, often becomes bound up in accepting state protection of individual choice while rejecting communal affiliation. The public use of reason or participation in the public sphere is excluded as a potential form of access modern citizenship. The assumption that human rights are the exclusive provenance of a culturally specific *European* heritage is not only inaccurate and problematic but also prevents international cooperation on human-rights issues (Bielefeldt 123; 129–131). By the same token, one might consider the harm done to multigroup alliances against violence within Germany by assuming that only "ethnic" Germans are capable of organizing against violence and claiming rights.

Given such discursive parameters, what potential might exist for a writing of self into political agency? When I argue that both the German government and many mainstream feminists position themselves as guardians of minority women's human rights, I point to the double meaning contained in the German word *erziehungsberechtigt*. While one translation would be "having the right to legal guardianship" (a legal guardian is an *Erziehungsberechtigter*), the word *Erziehung* connotes not only raising but also educating. State and popular discussions on the rights of Muslim women construct a grammar of power between the enlightened German and his/her Muslim Other: one can make legally responsible decisions, whereas the other retains a childlike status in a state of dependency. One can educate and the other can only be educated. One dispenses rights and the other has them or, rather, can regain them via the benevolence of European culture. These dichotomies are rooted in the Eurocentrism of what Dipesh Chakrabarty has called "Western historicism," a perspective from which becoming modern is equated with becoming European (Chakrabarty 33). A western historicist narrative of history contributed to colonial domination, which functioned by constructing "historical time as a measure of the cultural distance (at least in institutional development) that was assumed to exist between the West and the non-West. In the colonies, it legitimated the ideas of civilization" (Chakrabarty 3).

However, the relationship of Western historicism to discourses on Islam in Germany is complex. One must also consider the histories informing the relationship between Turkey and Germany, between Turkish immigrants and Islam in Germany. Atatürk's own project of constructing a Turkish nation-state was premised heavily on precisely this secularist narrative. Where many Muslim countries pursued an anticolonial modernization in which a return to a rational, intellectual Islam could serve as the path to compatibility with the modern technologies and political systems of the West, Turkey sought to "become European" by reducing religion's public role to take on Western political ideals (Mir-Hosseini 67), a process that led to the rejection of Islamic law as well as to the codification of women's equality in the new Western style legal system.[7]

There are a number of important ways in which the history of struggles for women's rights challenges the narrative of an enlightened German secularism that is juxtaposed to a religious, misogynist Muslim Turkish culture. Turkey's own historical commitment to secularism complicates such a narrative, as do movements that seek to inform a feminist consciousness or a position promoting women's rights from a specifically Muslim perspective.[8] Transnational feminist perspectives further question the Western historicist narrative in which secularism is defined as a condition for entrance into modernity and as an appropriate strategy to ending violence. The naturalization of the connection between Western Europe and human rights has divided the "world into those who share Western values, and those who do not" (El-Tayeb, *European Others* 87). Madhavi Sunder argues that within enlightenment discourse, individuals are forced to choose between religious liberty in the private sphere and equality in the public sphere (Sunder 1408). Such forced choices arise from enlightenment strategies to manage religion and other aspects of "culture" by understanding them as part of a natural, unchangeable private sphere. In response, many contemporary transnational feminists contest a notion of human rights that relegates religion and culture to an immutable private sphere. Sunder suggests through her discussion of the emergence of feminist analysis within Muslim communities (in particular, participants in the transnational group Women Living under Muslim Laws) that Muslim women make critiques that both theorize and actively seek change within cultural and religious communities. Their claims teach us that "women's human rights must go beyond *freedom from* violence to *freedom to* make the world" (1413). The right to claim individual rights and to write a self in relationship to those rights is inadequate when women are denied the right to have a voice in the public sphere and thus to participate in the imaginative making of their world.

The freedom to make the world is deeply tied to the potential for imagining self as an actor in the public sphere, whether on the local, national, or transnational stage—or any combination of those. Many groups maintain transnational allegiances without rejecting participation in a national political structure (Asad 310). In today's world, religion is "now also a base for publicly contested identities. As such it is at the very center of democratic politics, from which only the most determined antidemocratic power can keep it out" (311). We might heed Asad's call for understanding multiple modernities by considering the possibility for Muslim women as potential participants in the public sphere without rejecting a public religious identity. How, then, to imagine the place of Muslim women claiming rights *as Muslim women* in a democratic public sphere? This question should not be misconstrued as a call to reject European democratic tradition. In fact, this misreading of my argument would rest on the assumption that the violence of Islamic militants can stand in for the "essence" of a Muslim historical tradition—an assumption popular in Western media (Asad 302); presuming, in other words, that opening space for the voice of the Muslim woman necessarily equates to the rejection of democracy. In particular, I wish to heed Spivak's often used formulation that we also cannot *not* desire democracy, regardless of the way in which it has been appropriated for colonialist or racist narratives.

Nor, I would agree, can we merely dismiss human rights as Eurocentric. As Spivak argues,

> There can be no doubt that "democracy" in the general sense is an unquestioned good. But there can be no doubt either that, in our current predicament, confidence in the formal democratic structures

of civil society as sanctioning a cultural superiority from which to dispense bounty to the migrant, cannot find support. (Spivak, *Imperatives* 66)

The (perceived) uniquely European genealogy of human rights must be challenged to imagine the potential for Muslim women in Germany to write the self as a public subject who can invoke the discourse of human rights against a range of forms of violence. Muslim women in Germany participate in immigrant activist groups that fight to recognize the specific position of Muslim women in Germany but assume that structures of violence are changeable, that there are points of similarity with the lives of ethnic German women, and that gender violence may not be the primary—and certainly not the only—issue facing Muslim women today. Their imagination of work against violence and for a just future is situated in an understanding of violence that begins to approach what Spivak and Butler have deemed a necessary precondition for a politics of nonviolence—namely to conceptualize nonviolence in relationship to an expanded sense of the sacred rather than as the outgrowth of abstract reason (Butler 230).

If we take seriously Sunder's admonition that freedom from violence must be accompanied by freedom to make the world, a feminist approach to combating violence against women in Muslim communities must consider voices of women who might identify with Muslim communities. When the important critiques made by feminists of color in Germany—critiques that admonish feminists to consider the intersections between issues of gender, race, and migration—are appropriated to reconstruct the Muslim woman as Other and to refuse her a voice in public discussions, that freedom to make the world has been denied by the very people who would seek to ensure it.

Violence and Secularism as Path to Peace

Paradoxically, a discussion often conducted in the name of the *protection* of a democratic public sphere serves to *exclude* particular groups from democratic participation in the public sphere. A prevailing assumption in debates about multiculturalism, citizenship, immigration, and democracy in Europe is that beginning with the Enlightenment, the changing role of religion sparked the creation of the modern public sphere by transforming the relationship between the public and the private (De Vries 2), thus setting Europe on the path to peace (Asad, *Formations* 6–7). Discussions of Islam's place in contemporary Europe conducted on these terms present a theoretical difficulty. If the public sphere is to be a realm outside the influence of religion, then discussions of religion itself should only have a marginal role in how the public sphere is defined and redefined (De Vries 2). However, positions articulated in support of the removal of headscarves from the schools, for example, often argue that Christian or Jewish symbols can and should remain. When discursive association with Islam becomes the means to effect exclusion of targeted groups (for example, when Islamic headscarves are banned for schoolteachers whereas Christian symbols are permitted in public school classrooms), religion *has* defined the public sphere by marking its boundaries: "Muslim organized collective identities and their public representations become a source of anxiety not only because of their religious otherness as a non-Christian and non-European religion, but more importantly because of their religiousness itself as the 'other' of European secularity" (Casanova 77). Discourses of gender violence participate in these exclusions by producing the Muslim subject as necessarily undemocratic.

Forms of managing the relationship between religion and State vary throughout Western Europe. Countries with official state religions, such as Great Britain, Denmark, and Greece, tend to accord Islam the same rights granted to other religions, though this is not implemented evenly. For other countries, such as Belgium, France, Italy, and Spain, equal rights hinge on an official recognition of the religion (Jocelyne Cesari 65–74). Unlike France, for example, which banned relationships between the church and the state in 1905, Germany maintains an institutionalized relationship between the church and the state via the recognition of religious communities as "public law corporations." The Evangelical Church and the Catholic Church in Germany, as well as several smaller Christian communities, each have the status of public-law corporations under the constitution; their relationship to the state is governed by a series of treaties. Members of participating congregations in the church structure pay a tax to the state, which is distributed back to the churches and often serves as a marker of official membership. The provinces oversee the training of religious educators, which takes place in public; most provinces further offer Protestant and Catholic religious education in the public school (Ewing 38–40). In all cases religious education is considered the purview of the individual provinces, as culture is an area of provincial mandate, although the public law corporations are organized nationally and maintain a relationship to the national government as well. The Central Council of Jews, an umbrella organization, has been recognized in a similar role as a public law corporation that can represent the interests of Jewish communities to the State; it signed its first state treaty establishing this status in 2003.

There is no such Muslim organization in Germany, though the Central Council of Muslims in Germany (Zentralrat der Muslime in Deutschland; hereafter ZMD), an umbrella organization, sought such status. Furthermore, the vast majority of Muslims in Germany are not affiliated with an organized Muslim community. In 2010 the ZMD was also excluded from theDIK, a multi-year conference of several working groups consisting of Muslim individuals, representatives of Muslim organizations, and representatives of the German State. This is significant insofar as the DIK seems to be the likely route for the creation of a similar relationship between the state and Islam in Germany—that is, via the construction of an nonstate organization that will be tasked with working with the individual provinces to oversee the creation of religious education and the training of educators and to potentially regulate other aspects of Islam in society. The DIK's goal is to facilitate the integration of Muslims into German society; but until now no formal steps have been taken toward forming an organization that can be granted the status of public law corporation.

The Coordinating Council of Muslims (Koordinationsrat der Muslime; KRM) was formed from the four existing umbrella groups initially taking part in the DIK (including the ZMD) and came under heavy criticism because it represents only the most religious Muslim groups in Germany, and is recognized by less than 5 percent of Muslims ("DIK—Muslimische Verbände"). Nevertheless, it has become the official partner of North Rhine-Westfalen, the first state to formally establish a partnership to create a curriculum for Muslim religious education.

The forms of secularism present in Germany clearly do not exclude religion from any relationship to the state, though the relationship is regulated in a particular way that is designed to minimize religious impact in the political sphere and to set clear boundaries for state oversight of religion. Yet, secularism is often understood as the creation of a public sphere from which all religion and, indeed, all forms of cultural difference, must be excluded. Jürgen Habermas's early elaborations of the public sphere conceptualized it as an emancipatory space that emerges from rational deliberation on common issues, which ideally result in polices that will serve the common good. An effective public sphere must remain inclusive and guarantee access to all citizens, but to do so it transcends and brackets out difference to seek the common good (Habermas 49). Even many cultural critics of forms of racism in Germany reproduce the assumption that difference can only be "productive" in the private sphere (see, for example Terkessidis, "Wir selbst" 204).

In the interceding decades since Habermas's early theories of the public sphere, a number of critiques have emerged. A large body of research argues that in bracketing out difference, the public sphere works against the common good by excluding women and other groups (see, for example, Young 381–383; Fraser 61–63). The early modern public sphere actually functioned to enable a very specific group to claim a status as universal, and the public sphere continues to exclude large groups that are produced as Others. Chantal Mouffe has argued that the notion of the public sphere may go so far as to relegate all dissension to the private (Mouffe 134–135). The most radical critiques seek not to amend a normative public sphere to be more inclusive but suggest that the public sphere actually *produces* exclusion that is based on relations of dominance and power. "Difference," in other words, does not exist outside the public sphere, nor can it be restricted to an abstracted private sphere. Difference is in fact *produced* by the public sphere (Çınar, "Subversion" 892–893); the expulsion of that which is viewed as "difference" by necessity privileges the dominant groups, who serve as the norm against which difference is defined. Indeed, the public sphere, by seeking to exclude certain forms of difference, produces marked bodies in opposition to an abstracted, disembodied subject of the public sphere (further see Berlant 26–27; 176; Çınar, "Subversion" 893–895).

Mouffe has further argued for considering difference as necessary to the public sphere. A desire for reconciliation, or for elimination of difference, renders liberal conceptions of the public sphere untenable (Mouffe, "Religion, Liberal Democracy, and Citizenship" 320). The drive to homogeneity derives in part from the tendency to conflate the separations between church and state, religion and politics, and public and the private, and in part from the conflation of *politics* with *state politics*. If what is truly at stake is the separation between religion and *state power*, there is no reason to prohibit religious groups or individuals from intervention in the larger political arena (Mouffe, "Religion, Liberal Democracy, and Citizenship" 325). Rather, the problem emerges when certain religious communities are allowed to appear in public space while others are not. Recent laws that ban Islamic symbols from German classrooms, while permitting Judeo-Christian symbols in several German provinces, provides an excellent example, one that will be further examined in chapter 2. As Joan Scott suggests, "Indeed, if secularism were understood as a platform for the negotiation of difference instead of as its erasure, national unity based on shared values might still be the result" (Scott 104).

Many contemporary public discussions illustrate the importance of visual regimes for constituting the public sphere, making any distinction between public space and public sphere difficult. Bans on face veiling (often mistakenly dubbed "burqa bans")[9] in France and Belgium and an overturned ban in Spain, as well as the minaret ban in Switzerland, reveal a desire to remove visual markers of Islam from public space. The Turkish headscarf debates over a ban of headscarves in university further demonstrate that we should also understand the public sphere both as productive of power difference and as partially visually constituted; the public sphere is

> no longer a site of emancipation or liberation that comes through debate and dialogue but a field of visuality that subjugates through controlled silences, performative acts, speech acts, and visual displays. It is a visually constituted field of power relations where subjugation operates through the ongoing marking and categorization of diverse visibilities and subjectivities by the public gaze. (Çınar, "Subversion" 895–896)

In a visually constituted public sphere, images quickly function as replacement for and repression of political citizenship (Çınar, "Subversion" 910). That is to say, representation in the form of *Darstellung* (depiction) often replaces representation in the form of *Vertretung* (substitution, political representation)—particularly of any political representation where Muslims might be perceived as the representatives rather than as merely the represented.

The visually constituted public sphere functions differently in Germany (and, I would argue, in much of Western Europe) than in Turkey, however. In Western Europe, images of Muslim women serve to exclude them from the public sphere by marking them in relationship to a regime of gender violence. Although a visually constituted public sphere did gain importance particularly during the period of the headscarf debates, women are constituted as public subjects primarily through their relationship to a perception of Muslim violence. In Western Europe, the headscarf became a symbol of victimhood through its association with familial violence, a development that obscured the complexities of the headscarf as an embodied practice embedded in a context of structural disadvantage. Emphasis on Muslim violence as domestic violence has distracted from experiences of other forms of symbolic, structural, and personal violence that continue to exclude immigrants from political participation. Thus, visual elements are powerful, but not all-determining: texts produced by activist groups and the DIK, together with the pages of newspapers, parliamentary debates, and even books such as Sarrazin's bestseller, remain powerful components of the public sphere.

Habermas himself has recently sought to rethink the relationship between religion and politics in what he (with ambivalence) has called a "post-secular" Europe. His remarks have been important departures from his earlier work in their willingness to articulate a productive place for religious language in public political discussions. They consequently also challenge his earlier understanding of a public sphere as an abstracted space unmarked by difference. Habermas replicates, however, a traditional narrative of secularism in Europe, which is understood as a path to peace after the confessional wars (Habermas, "Notes on a Post-Secular Society"). Secularism, in this narrative, is a strategy for ending the violence of religious conflict by managing the relationship between religion and the public sphere (particularly the State) by relegating religion specifically to the private. Whereas Habermas has sought to acknowledge the role that the violence of colonialism and "failed" decolonizations have played in constructing recent emergence of religious movements, particularly Islamic "fundamentalism," (Habermas, "Religion" 1) he fails to incorporate these forms of violence in his theorizing of secularism and modernity.

Habermas revisits his conception of the public sphere to emphasize that it can only succeed with the mutual recognition of citizens of differing religions and worldviews (Habermas, "Notes on a Post-Secular Society"). In this age there must be, for Habermas, a place for religious language at the political table. Debates on religion provide a space in which people become participants in democracy—in finding common political ground, the individual cultural identities can be maintained even as people see themselves as participants in a common political community. This can work for Habermas, even if religious language is allowed to play a role in political discussions, so long as those who are representatives of the state insist on framing their justifications for policy in secular terms (Habermas, "Religion" 8–9). In that sense Habermas has challenged the common discourse on the Left in Europe, which often dovetails with xenophobic and liberal-feminist critiques of Islam to produce a totalizing discourse on Islam as antimodern and undemocratic (Casanova 80).

Yet, Habermas's theorizations remain inadequate for the European situation. He has focused on organizations and individuals wishing to articulate policies that are based on a religious identity. His conceptualization of the public sphere cannot, however, aid us in understanding the representation of Muslim women who are permitted to emerge in the public sphere, first and foremost in their relationship to familial and intimate violence, and secondarily, as victims of human-rights abuses. It is particularly interesting that Habermas, who championed Germany as part of the "avantgardist core" that should lead a Europe that was committed to human rights (Habermas and Derrida 6), is then unable to deal with the controversies about women's rights and violence against women that have been such an important part of the debates on integration, Islam, and Europe. This may be prohibited in part by his definition of secularism, which he seems to measure by the numbers of people participating in religious communities. Such a definition cannot account for state institutionalization of forms of Christianity in many Western European countries—via management of religious education, for example. Perhaps, more importantly, Habermas's focus on language and identity as informing public-sphere participation tends to elide the importance of embodied practices such as covering practices. A more adequate understanding of a functioning public sphere today might thus theorize embodied participation and its relationship to forms of difference.

Embodied Secularisms: Rethinking Violence, Religion, and the Public Sphere

Feminist criticism has long criticized the notion of a disembodied, abstract subject of the public sphere, which effectively works to exclude specific groups of people while granting other groups universal status—historically, white, male, Christian Europeans. The history of the secular subject reveals similar problems. The calling into existence of the subject of human rights—of the subject as human—occurred through techniques of bodily discipline. An examination of the epistemological assumptions of the secular reveals the importance of pain and torture in constituting the subject as human during enlightenment Europe (Asad, *Formations* 25). As Talal Asad suggests, the emergence of secularism and human rights rests on questions of what forms of pain were made acceptable and not acceptable. The subject of human rights today is policed according to logics of exclusion that determine who is capable of interrupting pain and violence.

Whereas the traditional narrative sees secularism as an important means to tolerance and peace, Asad suggests that "a secular state does not guarantee toleration; it puts into play different structures of ambition and fear. The law never seeks to eliminate violence since its object is always to regulate violence" (8). Influenced by postcolonial theory, Asad's narrative of European secularism highlights the premodern violence of Europe's religious wars. Religious violence was not erased by the onset of secularism and modernitiy but was instead displaced to the violence of national and colonial wars (7). Secularism issues from a modernity that is intimately bound up in the processes of colonialism. The "violence lying at the heart of a political doctrine that has disavowed violence on principle" (59) exists only through the cultivation of an other (Asad, *Formations* 59). This violence sustains liberal notions of tolerance (Asad, *On Suicide Bombing* 144).

Asad's discussion reveals a tradition that led to an understanding of the enlightenment subject and of Europe as free of violence except for that which invades from "outside." Asad further questions a secular viewpoint held by many—that there is only agent (representing and asserting self) and victim (passive object):

> Those who think that the *motive* for violent action lies in "religious ideology" claim that any concern for the consequent suffering requires that we support the censorship of religious discourse—or at least the prevention of religious discourse from entering the domain where public policy is formulated. But it is not always clear whether it is pain and suffering as such that the secularist cares about or the pain and suffering that can be attributed to religious violence because that is pain the modern imaginary conceives of as gratuitous. (Asad, *Formations* 11).

What pain and suffering is conceptualized as "gratuitous" in the twenty-first century? Gender violence, certainly. That fact is to be celebrated. Yet, forms of pain and suffering that could be attributed to specifically Christian or Eurocentric ideologies tend to cause less concern (with the exception of extremist neo-Nazi ideologies).

Furthermore, the attribution of suffering to religious violence in Europe today is predicated on a slippage between familial violence and Muslim violence, a slippage that ignores the existence of familial or intimate violence in larger German society. Whereas domestic violence has received tremendous attention over the decades, at the moment in which Islam enters the discussion, domestic violence is spoken of as a Muslim problem. Why, then, to borrow Asad's phrasing, does precisely *this* form of suffering become excessive, while other forms of suffering are ignored? A focus on the pain and suffering within the Muslim family, for example, might allow other forms of suffering, such as that caused by economic disadvantage, racialized violence, or precarious legal status to disappear—these are not perceived of as gratuitous pain but rather as suffering, which is allowed in the name of the preservation of the German nation-state or European Enlightenment heritage.

Turkish Secularism, German Politics

The history of Turkish secularism inflects discussions of secularism in Germany in complex and often contradictory ways. Many public figures of Turkish heritage draw on Turkey's trajectory of secularism to argue for the exclusion of Muslim presence both in public space and in the public sphere. The Kemalist project envisioned a nation state based on Western European models, in particular that of France, and conceptions of modernity. This produced a particular relationship between religion and the state, considered a "laicist" relationship. Although *laïcité* is often used to denote an extreme separation of church and state, in connection to France the term often emphasizes the goal of nearly total exclusion of religion from any state institution, while in the Turkish context, laïcité is sometimes used to emphasize a separation of church and state that includes constitutional regulation of religious institutions (Keyman 222). German officials often explicitly reject a French model of laïcité as being too restrictive of religious freedom, even though the German provincial governments maintain control over the education of teachers of religion. Though French laïcité served as a model for Turkish approaches to secularism, whereas France eventually gave up state control of religious institutions, Turkey maintains state control of the education of Turkish religious clerics, who then become state employees. The government branch responsible for this oversight, the Diyanet, also has sponsored religious communities in Germany through the organization DİTİB, the Turkish-Islamic Union for Religious Affairs. This is similar to German national oversight of funding of the largest Christian churches, which receive funding through state-levied taxes that in turn define church membership.

The nation-building mythologies that were supported in the early years of the Turkish Republic relied on notions of religious and secular homogeneity. Western European countries approved the authoritarian path to secular modernity that was set in the 1930s (Özyürek 10). Those mythologies of homogeneity, together with those of ethnic and linguistic homogeneity, have been challenged from the very beginning of the republic, but that challenge intensified in the 1980s as a consequence of Kurdish resistance and growing Islamist movements. The military intervention of 1984 drew on Islam as a source of identity that could combat the fragmentation seen on the Left (Yavuz and Esposito xxiv–xxvi). The recent success of Islamic parties can be seen as a re-Islamization of a secularized public space, rather than as a form of Islam that has retained power throughout Turkish history, and as a consequence of the Islamist parties' pluralist approach upon recognition that an Islamic monopoly on party politics was impossible (Roy 54–55; 93). M. Hakan Yavuz has termed these changes, which occur as a result of urbanization, industrialization, and increased access to education, an attempt to "vernacularize modernity" (Yavuz and Esposito viii). Ironically, the ongoing criticism of the Turkish state by the European Union (EU) meant that by the 1990s, Islamist politicians were those most in favor of EU participation (Özyürek 11).

Women's participation in these parties, is, in turn, "the outcome of a new interpretation of the Islamic religion by the recently urbanized and educated social groups who have broken away from traditional popular interpretations and practices," paradoxically claiming newly acquired class and educational status to construct a collective identity against modernity (Göle 5). From the beginning, the Kemalist project used women's bodies to symbolize a relationship to modernity, constructing a precarious female body that was endangered by antimodern forces that could best be challenged by revealing the body, thus making it available for salvation by the new Turkish state (Çınar, *Modernity* 55; 59–74), a process mirrored by the Islamist Refah Party's emphasis on reveiling women's bodies in its 1990s campaigns (Çınar, *Modernity* 75–76). The early regulation of the female body in public images found its male counterpart codified in the Hat Law, which regulated men's headwear to signify entrance into modernity.

Further complicating an understanding of these discourses is the complex path by which Islamism has increased in recent decades in Turkey: an anti-Western Islamism propagated by external forces in Turkey had an impact, as did the contradictory folk Islamic traditions that moved to the cities with the citizens from rural Turkey as the economic gap between urban and rural Turkey widened (Filiz and Ucuç 35–37). Turkey's long history of turning to or considering itself part of Europe deeply informs the conversations about Islam in Germany today, yet now the early days of the public are often also viewed nostalgically as the beginnings of a non-Western modernity that has not yet been achieved (Özyürek 9–11). These trends also emerged partly as a response to ongoing Western European opposition to Turkey's bid to join the EU. Germany has exerted a great deal of power over decisions about who else could join: although it was a staunch supporter of the integration of Eastern European countries into the EU, it was for a long time the country that was most opposed to Turkey's membership (Onis 135–36). Although initially those concerns were framed in terms of economics and modernization, objections later tended to rely on cultural division and political reasons (Onis 106–107; 115–116).

Violence in the Name of Germany, in the Name of Europe

The competing narratives of secularism I've described above occur at an important moment of European imagination. In the early 2000s, leading Western European figures intensified their fight for a European constitution, a campaign that failed when two countries voted down the first proposed constitution in 2005. In response and in reaction to accusations that the EU was an elitist institution with little mandate from its "people," EU institutions intensified their promotion of a European civic identity that would serve as the community legitimating the EU institutions. Those identities in part construct an often utopian Europe which can protect or enact peace. At the same time that Germany seeks to gain and consolidate its power within the EU, the EU seeks to consolidate its power by constructing a European history, an antiviolent tradition that can serve as corrective to the violence of the Holocaust.

This tradition often lauds tolerance as an effect of secularism, seen in turn as a specifically European tradition. Tolerance, understood as the means by which peace can be achieved between religious and ethnic groups, is itself violently structured (Žižek, *Violence* 41; W. Brown, *Regulating Aversion* 11–12). In reinforcing a relationship of power between the tolerant and the tolerated, discourses of tolerance may circulate racial hatreds at the same time that they claim to alleviate racist violence. Mobilizations of tolerance may even legitimate racist state violence (W. Brown, *Regulating Aversion* 11–12). Particularly when a regime of tolerance requires that a marginalized group reject its affiliation with a particular culture, "the subject of 'free choice' in the Western 'tolerant' multicultural sense can emerge only as the result of an extremely *violent* process of being torn out of a particular lifeworld, of being cut off from one's roots" (Žižek, *Violence* 146).

In light of a tolerance that seeks to mitigate some forms of violence at the same time that it continues to perform others, it is perhaps not surprising that an EU seeking to construct an antiviolent tradition does so in part through the deployment of a discourse of security. Violence performs an ordering function in the conceptualization of security, one which in turn reproduces culturally and historically specific subjects and narratives of violence (Shepherd 248). These discourses of peace and security compete within the EU, and the regime of violence informing the place of Muslim women in the public sphere plays an important role in this tension. I explore this further in chapter 1.

I caution, however, against narratives that would see the path to a European identity, or even a European public sphere, as a fairly linear path that is markedly intensified by anti-Islam reactions to 9/11. As my analysis in chapter 1 shows, certain Islamophobic discourses were deeply entrenched before 9/11, and in the German case, unification may have played a much more dramatic role in their emergence than did 9/11. Furthermore, the European public was resistant to the US response to 9/11 and, as a consequence, was somewhat cautious about anti-Muslim rhetoric. Instead, terrorist attacks in the UK and in Spain and the murder of Theo van Gogh in the Netherlands sparked new waves of anti-Muslim sentiment.

One of the most important difficulties posed by the task of a critique of violence, and of the regime of gender violence is: How does one represent violence in such a way as to work to oppose it? More specifically, given my focus on gender and representations of women, how can one represent and oppose forms of violence against women without reinforcing cultural racist discourses on Turkish and Muslim minorities in Germany? We may find that what emerges as a strategy from the first problem becomes a response of sorts to the second. An interrogation of the regime of violence, its constitution and effects—particularly in terms of limiting public subjectivities available to women of immigrant heritage in Germany—leads to a politics of radical listening. A politics of listening to and for political, economic, and intellectual subjectivities reveals the often hidden work that women do to fight violence in German society as well as the importance of placing violence in a context of European forms of violence. This politics of listening enables imagination of forms of violence as contestable and allows for alliances across the ethnic, religious, and national boundaries drawn by the regime of violence.

Žižek argues that in making the opposition to all forms of violence their main preoccupation, "tolerant liberals" use an "SOS call" that drowns out all other approaches. He calls for changing the topic—from the obsession with subjective violence and the urgency of ending violence to an investigation of the interaction between subjective (the obvious violence that takes place with clear agents), objective (anonymous, systemic violence), and symbolic violence (ideology that is so total that it becomes the invisible backdrop of everyday life) (Žižek, *Violence* 10–11; 36). At times, he seems to suggest that action against violence is necessarily impossible, even harmful. However, the careful analysis for which he calls does not have to be in contradiction to action against violence. There is no reason to assume that analysis of the intersecting forms of violence is somehow truly valid action whereas other forms of action are invalidated. That rhetorical move reinforces an unnecessary and unproductive divide between activism for social justice and academic analysis of forms of marginalization. The analyses of these different forms of violence, in fact—the symbolic, objective, and subjective—have already been an important project of transnational cultural studies for quite some time. What perhaps has been less a part of transnational cultural studies is a careful consideration of how the popular conception of violence *itself* informs these other forms of violence. I take that as the subject of this project here. In examining how violence is imagined, portrayed, and challenged in Germany, we might also learn much about how conceptions of what violence is determine strategies for action.

In the first part of this book I seek to explore and analyze the regime of violence in public discourse. In chapter 1 I elaborate on my notion of the regime of gender violence by examining the representations of violence against women as Muslim violence in popular print media from the time of unification to the present. In chapter 2, I turn to the public sphere as visually constituted via the headscarf as the symbol of violence. I juxtapose the discussions of the headscarf debates in popular media, legal discourse, and political discourse with the representations of Marwa el-Sherbini as "hijab-martyr."

The second section of this book represents a project that emerges from a politics of radical listening. In this section I more specifically focus on self-representations and artistic interventions, largely those of Turkish heritage or Muslim heritage artists and writers. In chapter 3, I examine artistic representations of the headscarf. I'm interested here in the possibilities raised for reconfiguring public space as a space where Muslim women are visible, present, and active as participants in democracy. These interventions, many of which are critical of Islam, nevertheless provide opportunities for recognizing the power of the regime of violence and imagining Muslim women in public spaces. Chapter 4 examines autobiographical pieces by Muslim women. The most popular of these works allow certain

Turkish women to claim an expert status by reifying the regime of violence and rejecting affiliation with Islam—and by requiring all Muslim women to do the same to enter into European modernity. However, other, generally lesser known works provide more complex, often humorous negotiations of communal and familial affiliations while representing women of Muslim heritage in relationship to economic activity, democratic participation, and intellectual production. In chapter 5, I consider the work and careers of Emine Sevgi Özdamar and Feridun Zaimoğlu, who have at various times been constructed as authentic voices or as Orientalizing voices. Özdamar was long the face of Turkish German literature via much Orientalizing attention that ignored her engagement with the history of the 1960s, whereas Zaimoğlu has a problematic relationship with the notion of authenticity that has contributed to his immense popularity as representative of the "new" Turkish German literature. By exploring their representations of violence and their relationship to the literary critical apparatus, we learn much about the histories that were obscured by the regime of violence—including the ways by which the reception of these two authors has obscured representations of political violence committed in the name of secularism (in the case of Özdamar), and the representations of racialized violence (in the case of Zaimoglu). By way of conclusion I explore the fear of violence and its relationship to secularism, considering what the discussion of the regime of violence thus far might mean for how we consider representations of violence against women. In particular, I focus on the alliances for combating gender and racialized violence that may be enabled by a shift away from "culture" and toward the differential impacts of a regime of violence.

CHAPTER ONE

A REGIME OF GENDER VIOLENCE: HONOR KILLINGS, FAMILIAL VIOLENCE, AND MUSLIM WOMEN'S SUBJECTIVITIES

In 2005, 23-year-old Hatun Sürücü was standing at a bus stop in Berlin when her youngest brother, Ayhan, shot and killed her. This act not only tragically ended Hatun Sürücü's life but also led to a new chapter in representations of Islam and violence in Germany and Europe. Her death sparked massive national and international attention, accompanied by sensationalist headlines such as "Strangled, Stabbed, Drowned—the 'Honor Killings' in Berlin Pile Up" (Müller-Gerbes 61). Sürücü's story is often framed as an example of a successful integration against all odds, which was violently interrupted by her murder; in the years since her death, her murder has become a touchstone haunting discussions of Islam, immigration, and integration—any cursory reference to her death instantly evokes the specter of "failed integration."

Sürücü, who was raised in Berlin, was married to a cousin in Turkey at age 17. She fled the relationship and returned to Berlin with her small son, Can. There, now estranged from most of her immediate family, she found an apartment and began training as an electrician. Ayhan Sürücü was 18 at the time of the murder. At trial he claimed that he had wished to restore "order" to the family, an order disrupted when Sürücü left her husband, stopped wearing the headscarf, and began dating German men (Wahba). Two of his older brothers were accused of aiding and abetting in the murder by supplying the weapon and serving as lookout. The two older brothers were found guilty, then released, based on problems with the collection of evidence. They escaped to Turkey along with their father before they could be retried, though proceedings for a new trial were initiated. Ayhan Sürücü was found guilty and is serving his sentence in Germany; because he was considered a minor at the time of the crime, he received a reduced sentence.[1] A fourth brother, a lawyer, has been estranged from the family for some time.

Sürücü's murder is unquestionably a tragic reminder of the ongoing need to recognize and strategize against violence against women. In this sense the extensive media coverage has been quite effective. Sürücü's murder was considered the fifth in a series of Berlin "honor killings" (Seils 4), though her murder received much more immediate and widespread attention than the other four, continuing to elicit media coverage years later. Every major newspaper, both national and regional, has devoted significant space to covering her murder, the trial of her brothers, and the controversies surrounding an organization founded in her name. International media have also been surprisingly responsive; pieces on Sürücü's death appeared in *El País, Le Monde, The New York Times, The Guardian, The Economist,* and *The LA Times* as well as in many regional newspapers.[2] International coverage has portrayed the murder as being exemplary of the experiences of Muslim women in Germany and as demonstrating the limits of tolerance and the failure of multiculturalism. A book and a television movie are based on her life, and Feo Aladağ's feature film *Die Fremde* [The Stranger] was inspired by Sürücü's story. As has frequently been the case in the last two decades whenever an honor killing makes the news, stories insist that there has been a lack of willingness to talk about violence in minority communities in Europe. Indeed, despite extensive international coverage of the Sürücü death, conservative columnists, who are normally antagonistic to feminism, have used the issue of domestic violence in Muslim families to suggest that because "multiculturalism trumps feminism," the US media refuses to write about honor killings (see, for example, Steyn). In this way Sürücü's murder is easily appropriated for a range of Islamophobic, racist, or anti-immigrant agendas throughout the West; the media coverage served to create and stabilize boundaries between the majority community and minority Muslim groups (Korteweg and Yurdakul 229–233).

The massive media attention has thus had ambivalent effects; although it has opened up another dramatically public discussion about violence against women and the position of women of immigrant heritage in German society, it has continued to obscure potential voices against violence from the Muslim community while implicitly imagining an ethnic German community that is largely free of gender violence. In this chapter I argue that the representations of Sürücü's murder participate in a script that imagines Muslim women as necessarily being victims of Muslim men. Here I consider the Sürücü case both in the context of the post-1989 trajectory of media representations of violence against Muslim women as well as in terms of the breadth of coverage of the case itself in a range of popular media representations.

I explore the changing regime of gender violence through an analysis of media representations of domestic and familial violence during three periods: from 1989 to 1993, when a number of articles were published in the weekly newsmagazine *Der Spiegel,* which focused on immigrant women; from 1997 to 2003, the time of Germany's first headscarf controversy and a time of renewed attention to the plight of immigrant women in Germany; and from 2005 to 2010, a time in which Sürücü's death becomes a primary referent for discussions of failed integration. To provide both an analysis of the change over a longer period and an in-depth analysis of the Sürücü case, I generated two sets of samples. For the first, I examined articles from *Der Spiegel,* a weekly news magazine, by identifying (from the tables of contents from 1988 to 2010) all articles that focused on immigrant women. I then generated a sample of articles relevant to the Sürücü case by performing a keyword search for Hatun Sürücu in Factiva and Lexis-Nexis databases of print news media; I also independently searched the *Frankfurter Allgemeine Zeitung* as this is the only major German daily not included in these databases.

The intense attention to honor killings in this media coverage reveals a regime of gender violence operating in the public sphere, in which a discursive construction of a violent Islam is used to order public space. My analysis suggests a public imagination of Muslim women in which victims of familial violence are easily imagined, whereas Muslim women as participants in public democracy and victims of racialized violence are often largely unthinkable in the public sphere. There are, however, clearly changes in these representations over the two decades I address, as well as important challenges to this regime. Here, the three periods I identify are times when the discourse around Muslim violence intensifies, and they reveal the changing parameters of this discourse since German unification.

My goal here is certainly not to deny the forms of violence experienced within the families, relationships, or communities that include people of immigrant heritage. Rather, my intervention shows that the recent crisis calls for attention to "honor killings" and to forced marriages actually prohibit effective activism against violence against all women by locating experiences of violence primarily within the Muslim home and contextualizing them in histories and traditions located solely outside Europe. The preoccupation with Muslim gender violence prohibits an intersectional understanding that considers how Muslim women residing in Germany exist in complex circumstances that expose them to a *range* of forms of violence, including racialized violence. My critique of the regime of violence should thus be understood as an investigation of the conditions of the construction of violence, an "interrogation of how violence is circumscribed in advance by the questions we pose of it" (Butler, "Critique, Coercion" 201), in the hopes of enabling better strategies against violence.

I consider the regime of gender violence as a discourse, a systematically produced set of statements that insists on the representation of Muslim women as the victims of Muslim violence while obscuring their roles as agents in the public sphere and as victims of racialized forms of violence. The regime of gender violence genders and racializes Muslim women or women of Turkish or Kurdish heritage in such a way that their public subjectivities are often reduced to positions as victims of violence. When Islam is conceived of as necessarily violent, and that violence is particularly thought to be enacted in forms of intimate and familial violence targeting women, it becomes impossible to imagine Muslim women as participants in the German public sphere or as activists against domestic violence. Sürücü's life story, as well as the story of her murder, have been deployed to uphold this gender order, which often operates to exclude Muslim women from full cultural and political citizenship.

The discourse of gender violence works in conjunction with a newly reemerged global regime of "tolerance" (W. Brown, *Regulating Aversion* 2), as well as with a conception of modernity as being confined strictly to European enlightenment heritage, to produce a public sphere that ultimately excludes the participation of Muslim women who do not explicitly reject communal or religious attachments to Muslim and Turkish communities. Conceptualized in theory and practice as strategy to maintain peace in the face of difference, tolerance can effectively function to exclude the Other from the public sphere by "[regulating] the presence of the Other both inside and outside the liberal democratic nation-state, [often forming] a circuit between them that legitimates the most illiberal actions of the state" (W. Brown, *Regulating Aversion* 8; further see Žižek, *Violence* 41). Wendy Brown has pointed out that contemporary discourses of tolerance are structured in power; those who are tolerated are inherently already presumed to be unable to attain the status of those who tolerate. Tolerance itself can function to obscure processes of colonialism and racism, as well as their effects, for

> the valuation and practice of tolerance simultaneously confirm the superiority of the West; depoliticize (by recasting as nativist enmity) the effects of domination, colonialism, and cold war deformations of the Second and Third Worlds; and portray those living these effects as in need of the civilizing project of the West (W. Brown, *Regulating Aversion* 185).

The regime of gender violence and the regime of tolerance are mutually constitutive: Germany's claim to superiority is enacted through a "civilizing project" that includes the education of the Other into European modernity through a gendered disciplining of the Muslim body. This process creates an untenable set of circumstances for Muslim women in Europe in which they are forced to "choose" between a position from which they can reject racist speech and claim a communal or religious affiliation with Islam and a position from which they can openly criticize violence against women while rejecting communal or religious ties to Islam. This discourse on violence consequently ignores the activism against violence by women who continue to identify as Muslim and, indeed, works to reject any public participation by such women, who cannot be "made sense of" in the context of this regime.

Gender Violence, the Secular Subject, Crimes of Honor

The role of domestic and familial violence within the public imagination of Muslim women must be understood at the complex intersection of histories of secularism and anthropological notions of honor. The dominant understanding of a public sphere in Europe and its relationship to religion provides a set of discursive conditions within which Christianity's presence is normalized as a secular path to peace, whereas Islam is seen a force that is opposed to secularism and that must be excluded. Furthermore, violence is located within Islam and is viewed as being outside Europe and European tradition, via a discourse that considers European secularism the sole path to nonviolence.

Ironically, the successes of German feminisms have made it difficult to effectively theorize about violence against Muslim women in Germany. Gender equality has emerged after World War II as a key ideological site for the articulation of a democratic identity in the Federal Republic of Germany (Ewing, *Stolen Honor* 3). Yet, success in normalizing the goal, if not the reality, of gender equality often comes at the cost of expelling the racialized Muslim Other: "The national subject of a modern democracy based on equality and respect for human rights stands as the antithesis of an abjected subject whose sense of belonging must rest on violence and the abuse of women" (Ewing, *Stolen Honor* 3). The abjection of the Other from a position of democratic subjecthood also occurs through a sexualization of the Muslim woman's body, in particular through the obsession with revealing the Muslim woman's body during the headscarf debates (Weber, "Cloth" 46). Women's rights have become an essential part of the definition of (Western) European democratic identity, which is performed against a construction of Europe's Others as being unable to support women's rights. Differing modes of gender organization and bodily discipline in Germany and Turkey are thus easily interpreted and appropriated to legitimate the assumptions that Islam is incompatible with the principles of democracy and the

German constitution, obscuring forms of discrimination that continue for Turkish and Muslim minorities in Germany today (Ewing, *Stolen Honor* 5–6).

As a consequence, Muslim women continue to be thought of as in need of saving via the civilizing project of Western enlightenment. Such a civilizing project occupies an ambiguous position and is simultaneously considered both necessary and impossible. Access to enlightened modernity is foreclosed by the assumption that Muslims are inescapably caught in a violent culture as evidenced by gender violence, in at least two ways: (1) the Muslim woman is unable to function as a subject of democracy because her body is never her own property; and (2) the Muslim woman is unable to critique the conditions of gender violence because such critique can only take place through a rejection of Islam and an entrance into secularism.

If one considers the notion of the body as property that is so central to enlightenment thought, this becomes clearer. Personal possession of one's body, and by extension the ability to claim to be the origin of its actions and the forms of speech articulated by it, are key to the constitution of the liberal subject. Women were not only traditionally excluded from such possession but also became the object of a male gaze enabled by this new conceptualization of bodily possession. Once this (male) subject had emerged into the secular, it could also be capable of critique, as a form of criticism that can reveal the conditions that produce and require false consciousness (W. Brown, "Is Critique?" 12). Throughout the German intellectual tradition, the notion of critique is grounded in the presumption that critique can both explain and supplant the religious (W. Brown, "Is Critique?" 13). A double impossibility is thus produced by a discourse of gender violence as inherent to Islam: Muslim women can never critique that violence because they are within Islam and therefore nonsecular, and furthermore, they can never attain the status of a public subject because they are unable to "possess" their own bodies in the face of the violence of Islam. Paradoxically, only as a secular individual in full possession of one's body could become the abstract possessor of rights, which were disembodied from the particularities of social relationships.

The regime of gender violence further relies heavily on the notion of a regional honor-shame complex that emerged within anthropology in the 1960s and became the defining aspect of understandings of gender relations in the Mediterranean (Ewing, *Stolen Honor* 30). The honor-shame complex, which reductively defines "Mediterranean" gender relations and identities solely in terms of an expression of values of honor and shame, has been largely discredited within anthropology over the decades. Challenges to the honor-shame complex arose almost simultaneously with the emergence of the concept itself. Whereas honor as a concept certainly played a role in the behavior and choices of young men in Turkey at the time, scholars pointed out that everyday practices must be understood as embedded in the context of other—contradictory—values and practices that are negotiated by young men in Turkey, and of Turkish background in Germany (Ewing, *Stolen Honor* 30–33). Nevertheless, many academic studies in Germany long continued to focus on the honor-shame complex as having explanatory legitimacy in the Turkish context, even as it lessened its hold as the defining characteristic of other Mediterranean societies. No longer "Mediterranean," but "Turkish" or "Muslim" honor, as a value in village life, became a metonymy for "Turkish values" in all of Turkey, to explain the values of Turkish-heritage communities in Germany (see, for example, Baumgartner-Karabak and Landesberger, an MA thesis published by Rowohlt and cited frequently in the media during the 1990s). This simplified understanding of gender relations in the Mediterranean retains tremendous currency in popular publications today as well, playing a major role in bestselling books such as *The Foreign Bride,* by Necla Kelek.

As a consequence of the continued power of the honor-shame complex in popular media, domestic and familial violence are often framed as culturally specific "honor crimes." This has several consequences. In a public sphere at least partially visually constituted by the image of the headscarf, domestic violence becomes one consequence of a perceived "slippery slope"—if headscarves are permitted in schools, honor crimes will be one tragic result. Furthermore, within a discourse of honor crime, Muslim women are represented as victims confined to the private space of the home. Assumptions about women's spatial confinement and physical violation at the hands of Muslim men reify the association of male violence with Islam that already exists within discussions of terrorism and suicide bombings, which in turn are also considered eventual effects along the slippery slope of tolerating a Muslim presence in public. Finally, discourses of Muslim violence, with the emphasis on domestic violence, produce a history that locates the sources of violence outside Europe.

The German discussion can benefit from the interventions made by women of South Asian heritage in Europe and North America, who have long interrogated how violence against women is constructed in European and Eurocentric ways. As Purna Sen has pointed out, the massive international attention to crimes termed "honor crimes," particularly honor killings, has opened up valuable space for the formation of international alliances to combat this form of violence. Yet, "identifying Islamic cultures as deeply imbued with backward approaches to gender relations, associating Islam intrinsically with honour killings, and highlighting Islamic cultures as therefore inherently problematic" has also complicated action against honor crimes (Sen 42). Indeed, as honor crimes become nearly automatically linked to discourses on Islam and terrorism, an activist agenda against honor crimes is endangered by its imbrication with Islamophobic discourses (Sen 42). This argument has affinities with postcolonial scholar Uma Narayan's discussion of "death by culture" (Narayan 84). Representations of domestic and familial violence in minoritized groups offer cultural explanations for fatal violence against "third-world" women, whereas violence against "first world" women remains strangely resistant to such cultural explanations (Narayan 83–117). Few question how Western culture contributes to specific forms of gender violence, although "third-world" women are constantly defined as victims of culture. Considerations of women's rights today, and the emphasis on culturally specific forms of violence, continue to be impacted by colonialist discourses that legitimated Western superiority and colonialist intervention via desires to "save" third-world women from becoming victims of culturally determined gender violence (Spivak, *A Critique* 288–289; Narayan 80) or the veil (Ahmed 42–46). Women of color and those of immigrant heritage in Europe today often find their choices similarly circumscribed, making it particularly difficult to develop antiracist activism against violence. Instead, they are faced with a choice between an affiliation with a Turkish or a Muslim community, or with a feminist one. Cultural Otherness, as an explanation for violence against women, prohibits truly effective alliances across perceived ethnic, national, or cultural boundaries. Effective alliances would further require critical positioning vis-a-vis one's "own" cultural location and a rejection of the primacy of culture's explanatory power (Sen 43).

A frustration at such limitations is clearly evident in the documents written for the founding of Bundesverband der Migrantinnen in Deutschland e.V./Göçmen Kadınlar Birliği [the Federal Organization of Migrant Women in Germany]. Founded in 2005 as an organization of Turkish and Kurdish heritage women to advocate for the *range* of issues facing them in Germany–including employment access, job discrimination, domestic violence, and forced marriages– the organization today also emphasizes its antiracist work. Their original mission statement read: "We work against every attempt to represent migrants of Turkish heritage as 'women who cannot stand on their own two feet'" (Bundesverband der Migrantinnen in Deutschland). In response to the media coverage and political discussions that ensued after the murder of Sürücü, the group argued:

> The contemporary debate on honor killings and forced marriages unfortunately does nothing to help those who are impacted. A believable and constructive political strategy is missing. Migrants are understood across the board as perpetrators or victims, and stigmatized as culturally backwards. This denies the life realities of migrant women. (Göçmen Kadınlar Birliği–Bundesverband der Migrantinnen in Deutschland e.V)

This organization's work remains largely invisible in the popular public media, perhaps precisely because it takes this complex approach to violence. The activist group imagines complex subject positionings for women who are impacted by honor killings or forced marriages, as women who have agency and are capable of participating in the public sphere to resist violence, without necessarily rejecting their complex and multiple cultural or religious affiliations. Because the public sphere is organized around an assumption that activists against violence cannot identify as Muslim, a notion of antiracist activism by Muslim women against violence in all forms has remained unthinkable.

Both Sen and Narayan seek to open space for conceptualizing positions that are both anticolonial and against gender violence, much as the Federal Organization of Migrant Women in Germany seeks an antiracist position against gender violence. Sen and Narayan enable this theoretically by undoing the explanatory power of culture. They further challenge histories and memories of forms of violence against women, and in doing so, they allow parallels to emerge between violence against women in India and the United States (Narayan) as well as between Middle Eastern and European countries (Sen). Narayan and Sen illustrate that honor is neither historically, nor in contemporary times, an exclusively non-Western concept; crimes in the name of "honor" or "pride" exist in Western contexts as well. By acknowledging the multiple manifestations of honor crimes as well as their location in a spectrum of violence against women, Narayan and Sen can imagine more productive alliances against violence.

Gendered Scripts of Victimhood

The tendency to locate the origins of violence in Islam and outside Europe is layered with a problem facing feminists who discuss domestic violence regardless of context: how can one address the experience of violence and end a culture that legitimates violence against women, without imagining a subject bound by her position as victim? Given the thorny political and legal implications of challenges to how one conceptualizes violence against women, gender violence has become in some ways virtually untheorizable. Indeed, even in a period during which the body became a primary topic of feminist theory and analysis, developments in theorizing violence against women stagnated (Mardorossian 744). Critiquing how violence against women is discussed is difficult, not least because such critiques are easily appropriated to place blame on the victim or to undermine legal action against perpetrators of gender violence.

Feminist scholar Sharon Marcus's examination of the language of rape, and of rape as language, provides one possible intervention into the regime of gender violence in Germany today. Marcus grapples with the scripts that determine the field of possibility for responding to sexualized violence, and rape in particular. Although the forms of violence against Muslim women represented in the popular media are deeply sexualized, they are not generally linked to rape. Yet Marcus's discussion of "rape scripts" allows us to question the power of a discourse of victimhood of gender violence in other contexts. Marcus argues for limiting the impacts of rape by lessening the power of its narrative. She considers how feminist theory has shown the ways in which women come into being as subjects through already existing social meanings which, despite their tremendous impact, do not have to determine our lives completely. In other words, by thinking of rape as both scripted and scripting, Marcus suggests that we can subvert a grammar of violence predicated on woman as object, which constructs a notion of woman as inherently rapable. This script also partially determines a woman's response to rape—produced as a subject of fear, the woman cannot see herself responding to defend herself against rape (Marcus 172–176); as a consequence, self-defense advice often advocates against active forms of defense (176), focusing instead on passive forms of resistance.

The rape script coincides with a power differential that takes the woman's body as an object that is at the mercy of the superior strength of the male body and a spatial construction of the woman's body as immobile: "A subject of violence acts on an object of violence to define her as the boundary between exterior and interior, which he crosses, and as the immobilized space through which he moves" (Marcus 180). A radical interruption of rape culture must support a notion of female sexuality that undoes its construction "as an object, as property, and as an inner space" (Marcus 181). Resistance to rape (and, I argue, other forms of gender violence) can be effective only by enacting new visions of female sexuality as well as new imaginations of embodied female subjectivities.

Marcus's work has been criticized, often by feminists who fear that her challenge to the rape script and antirape activism may focus activism exclusively on the victim. In particular, Carine

Mordorassian is concerned that Marcus's work displaces the site of rape activism from culture or from the social to the individual victim's psyche (Mardorossian 755–757). Bringing Marcus's intervention to a discussion of other forms of violence against women suggests otherwise, however. Considering and analyzing how gender violence is scripted as Muslim allows us to find ways to interrupt that script. Although we may find that those interruptions emerge from individual challenges to the construction of violence, Marcus's argument implies that alternative discourses must occur at multiple levels. Indeed, to reduce intervention into a culture of gender violence to the level of the individual, or to the individual family, would reinscribe the very same problems that hinder action against violence. The script of violence here must not merely be addressed at the level of individual, individual family, or "Other" culture, but but also to regional, national, and transnational institutions and discourses that contribute to or enable violence.

The racialized regime of gender violence at work in the German public sphere constitutes an iteration on the rape narrative Marcus describes. The body of the Muslim man, rather than just the penis, is scripted as a weapon used by Islam against the Muslim woman. The Muslim woman, then, often becomes scripted in the public sphere primarily as the victim of male violence, the victim, to use Narayan's terminology, of "death by culture." The gendered ascription of violence limits her access to cultural citizenship by assuming that voiceless, the Muslim woman simply cannot participate. Her participation in politics against racist and sexist violence is obscured because it is unthinkable without her explicit and public rejection of affective attachment to Islam or to an ethnic community understood as Muslim. Thus through a strange slippage, Muslim women are understood both as Other to Europe and as evidence of Islam's violence against Europe. Conversely, within this grammar of violence, the emergence of the Muslim male subject is often (though not always) limited to a position as the agent of violence—against women, within criminality, or as terrorist. The constructions differ in the consequences for a relationship to the state—men's bodies are to be disciplined by imprisonment, whereas Muslim women's bodies are to be protected and removed from any community that is defined by a relationship to Turkish heritage or to Islam. These positions are articulated in the German case within a larger European discussion about the place of Islam in Europe, as well as within a German discussion about immigration, integration, and the protection of "German" identity.

Though the representations of violence I discuss in this chapter rarely include rape, except in the form of forced marriages, discourses around Muslim women are acutely sexualized. They suggest that violence against Muslim women emerges from a desire to protect honor, which is predicated on the sexual purity of a woman. Although the violence itself may not take the form of rape or sexual assault, the powerful script which portrays Muslim violence against women as inevitable remains a script of sexualized violence. Yet, the strategies that dominate public media and government discussions are rarely strategies for enabling the construction of new sexualities or new subjectivities for Muslim women that could also refigure constructions of Muslim masculinity. Instead, they often rely on the rejection of communal attachment and religious ritual or markers, a rejection deemed necessary for Muslim women to find refuge in a secular "European" or "German" community. New forms of sexuality are often framed in terms that suggest a necessary sexual availability of the woman, in particular by revealing herself through the removal of the headscarf while asserting a sexual autonomy by dating German men or women.

Islam and Domestic Violence in the German Media
Tracing the Figure of the Immigrant Woman in *Der Spiegel*, 1989–1993

Domestic violence has long played a role in media representations of Muslim women in Germany. Cultural products that represent Muslim women as the victims of familial violence are not only particularly successful in Germany but have have played a major role in the successful global marketing of German popular culture (Terkessidis, "Globale Kultur"; Göktürk, "Kennzeichen"). Despite the repeated statements over the decades that honor killings and forced marriages are "just now" receiving attention, these forms of violence have received significant and ongoing media and scholarly attention for at least three decades (Lutz and Huth-Hildebrandt; Huth-Hildebrandt, *Das Bild*). Particularly immediately before and after unification, and then again around 1997, immigrant women and women of immigrant heritage received renewed attention as victims of a violent Islam. In the following section I use the weekly news magazine *Der Spiegel* as my archive to illustrate these shifts.

Der Spiegel is the most respected German weekly news magazine and is modeled on *Time magazine*; it was founded after World War II. Although the second-most widely read magazine in this genre, it is generally considered the most reliable weekly and reaches a large mainstream audience that cuts across class, regional, and educational boundaries. The importance of *Der Spiegel* to public debates in Germany is well illustrated by a 1997 incident. A cover story entitled "Dangerously Different/Other [fremd]" declared the failure of multiculturalism and sparked a nationwide discussion in the media, which impacted public policymaking (Sarıgöz 9). *Der Spiegel* figures prominently in work that is critical of representations of minoritized groups (see, for example, Lutz, "Rassismus Und Sexismus, Unterschiede Und Gemeinsamkeiten" 66; Terkessidis, "Globale Kultur" 224–225). Ironically, *Der Spiegel* has also been roundly criticized for ignoring women's issues (Huhnke 249–250)—rendering the number of articles that focused on immigrant women and women of immigrant heritage as being particularly important.

This period of media coverage from 1989 to 1993 must be understood in the context of a larger shift, noted by scholars, in the representation of immigrants from an emphasis on class and national difference to one on religious and cultural difference (Balibar and Wallerstein 21; Lutz and Huth-Hildebrandt 161; Huth-Hildebrandt, *Das Bild* 46; Westphal 20–22). Discourses on race and culture continue simultaneously, though the emphasis on how culture is defined has transformed. Culture became important as a foil for race immediately after World War I, producing a simultaneous "denial and obsession" with race (El Tayeb 29). In the shift to an emphasis on cultural difference that ensued upon the advent of labor migration, the UK, Germany, and France exhibit, racializations both silent and "profoundly embedded in the discursive architecture of political debate" (Eley 147; further see Lentin, "Europe" 497–500). Indeed, post World War II German media culture had, until this point, constructed difference primarily in terms of an uneducated, working class Other that had emerged from rural Turkey, though these tropes could draw on (and coexist with) centuries of racialized and Orientalizing discourses. Unification, however, marked a move to difference that was constructed as cultural difference, which was increasingly described in terms of Islam.

Given the well-researched historical propensity to portray women as the emblem of (national) culture while denying them access to political power as citizens (Kaplan, Alarcón, and Moallem 5–7), it is not surprising that the intense attention to nation during unification coincides with the increasing importance of the figure of the abused Muslim woman. This began, however, a few months before the fall of the Berlin Wall. At this time, *Der Spiegel* began a series of articles focusing on gender violence against immigrant women. These articles coincided with one that sought to dismantle stereotypes about male immigrant criminality outside the home, ("Wenn je"), but the figure of the Muslim woman remains a surprisingly stable signifier of difference. When immigrant women or women of immigrant heritage are the primary focus of *Spiegel* articles, a rhetoric of violent Turkish or Muslim masculinity and passive femininity is established, naturalizing violence as endemic to Islamic culture and ensuring a dominant narrative of a violent Muslim male.

Two articles published in 1989 and 1990 focused specifically on immigrant women in Germany. The 1989 article, "He Could Not Have Acted Differently: Violence in Immigrant Families: Motive: Culture Shock," describes violence against women in Turkish and Muslim communities as natural and inevitable. It reports a long list of crimes of familial violence within Muslim immigrant communities in Germany, including: a Moroccan carpetweaver who stabs his daughter to death for wearing lipstick and fingernail polish; a Turkish teenage girl murdered by her brother after she fled the physical abuse of her father; and a Turkish woman who attempts to kill her daughter for moving out, starting a job, refusing to wear a headscarf, and generally rejecting "Islamic laws" ("Er Konnte" 96). This list is used as evidence for the argument that "the culture shock experienced during the transition from the strict, traditional Orient to the permissive West frequently leads to familial violence" ("Er Konnte" 96).

In 1990, "Club to the Back, Baby in the Belly" describes a Turkish man who stabs his pregnant daughter for resisting an arranged marriage ("Knüppel"). Perpetrators of crimes against immigrant women are described in this article as "so often" male family members, who are "so often" motivated by medieval codes of honor. The article points to old Turkish proverbs such as "The man is the seed, the woman the earth—and of the earth there is much," or that women need a "club in the back and a baby in the belly" as evidence of contemporary Muslim backwardness ("Knüppel" 103). The men are understood to be profoundly incapable of acting differently, existing in a contradictory space in which they are both victim of culture and perpetrator of crime. The women, alternatively, are understood as victims of the male Muslim violence that is rooted in traditional Turkish culture.

Thus, even as there is a challenge to the portrayal of Turkish men as being responsible for criminality in Germany, the representation of Turkish women remains surprisingly consistent. Several popular fictional films of the time are referred to as a sort of evidence for Muslim women's victimhood. References to Hark Bohm's *Yasemin* (1988) and Tevfik Başer's *40m² Germany* (1986), which respectively relate the stories of a Turkish teenager kidnapped by her father and a Turkish (im)migrant woman confined to her apartment by her male family members, are used throughout the 1990s as common cultural references. *Der Spiegel* participates in a larger discursive production of Germanness as the progressive heir to enlightenment reason and as potential savior of the backward Turk by referring to these films ("Knüppel" 96; "Er Konnte" 103; 105). In *Yasemin* the ethnic German boyfriend "saves" the Turkish German Yasemin from being kidnapped by her father and returned to Turkey: the German boyfriend brings freedom to Yasemin, who in the course of the film is increasingly imprisoned, literally and metaphorically, by her family. *Yasemin* had wide appeal, was promoted internationally by the Goethe Institute, and was by far the most popular German film of the 1980s to thematize the experiences of women migrants (Göktürk, "Migration und Kino" 335). Like many films of the time, supported by federal public funding in a tradition of a sort of "cinema of duty" that had already been established throughout the 1980s, this film draws on stereotypes of the archaic Turkish Other, suggesting that the only hope for the future is a radical break between generations (Göktürk, "Migration und Kino" 335–336). Deniz Göktürk argues:

> The films of Hark Bohm and Tevik Başer arise from the same circumstances of production and subsidy and are ideologically quite similar. Both [...] draw on an arsenal of popular assumptions, images and narratives and ultimately confirm the superiority of German culture. The rhetoric of authors, directors, and artists of foreign heritage is not necessarily more authentic; often they understand quite well how to satisfy the expectations of the native Germans [*Inländer*]. (Göktürk, "Migration und Kino" 336; further see Ewing, *Stolen Honor* 52–93).

Yasemin and *40m2 Germany* thus provide a powerful set of statements that determine how the German public "knows" about Muslim women, namely, as victims of violence. *Der Spiegel* uses these films to invoke and reinforce a discourse in which the Western European subject "knows" Muslim women quite literally as "the middle ages in the middle of Germany" ("Knüppel" 98). These juxtapositions parallel comments about "prudish Muslims" who consider Germany to be a "godless world," clearly delineating Muslim immigrants as the cultural Other and Other to secular society via their treatment of women. Germany is, in fact, so enlightened that crimes of domestic violence, when committed by immigrants, are "incomprehensible" ("Er Konnte" 96). The use of the word incomprehensibility is paradoxical here—it is precisely their incomprehensibility as victims of violence that makes these women recognizable to the German public. Thus contemporary Germany is figured as a modern, enlightened space that is relatively free of violence against women until the arrival of immigrant communities.

In contrast, Turkey is associated with traditional norms, patriarchy, and moral rigidity ("Er Konnte") that explain why relations between men and women are always structured in violence. Women are constructed as victims on several levels:

> Inside their own four walls the helplessness against the violence of the men—certainly no population in the FRG lives a more miserable existence than Turkish women and girls. They are terrorized and beaten, they live in constant fear of violent husbands, brothers, or male relatives, who have complete power over everything in the family that wears a skirt. ("Knüppel" 99).

The very discourse of victimhood is also used to rob the Muslim woman, victim of an "archaic code of honor," ("Knüppel" 98) of any sexual agency, whereas Turkish violence against women is naturalized: "As is so often the case, when the blood flows among the Turks, Fikyre's execution also was enacted following the traditionalist conceptions of honor. And as is so common, it wasn't the young man who stole Fikriye's innocence who had to die. The victim was, as it goes without saying, the girl" ("Knüppel" 100–101). The language here locates violence as explicitly and naturally Turkish. The imagined alternative to the current scenario does not construct an autonomous sexual subjectivity but rather suggests punishment for the man with whom she slept. The regulation of violence here is imagined then in terms of state control over the Muslim body rather than as the emancipation of public female agency.

The appropriation of women's issues to define Germany as more enlightened is particularly disturbing in light of the court cases that rely on the cultural drive to kill for honor to minimize punishments (Hauschild). In prosecutions of violence against immigrant women, the courts, to varying degrees, exercise leniency on the basis of the "culture shock" experienced upon entry into the liberal, permissive Western society in Germany. This implicates the state in enforcing a Germanness that ironically understands Germany as the protector of human rights, the promoter of women's rights, and the bearer of enlightened tolerance at the very moment it refuses to punish violence against women. The circulation of representations of women as always already victims of culture produces concrete effects on their recourse to the German courts for crimes committed against them. This is a particularly crass example of why, as Susan Okin has provocatively suggested in another context, multiculturalism might very well be "bad for women" (Okin 7–25). Forms of multiculturalism that rely on a notion of culture as unchanging, and of cultures as essentially different, produce differential sentencing in the courts.

This period from 1989 to 1993 is fundamental for establishing the terms of the discourse of violence that is most common today, though it has been reconfigured in some ways by later events. It is also a time of unusual consistency in terms of how Muslim women are represented in the public eye. Both earlier and later discussions will provide much more contradictory representations. Yet in this period, when cultural difference displaces discourses of class and nation, when unification provides a dramatic set of challenges to the notion of nation, a relationship to domestic violence becomes the primary discussion through which Muslim women emerge into the public eye. The regime of violence is used to mark Islam and the largest German immigrant group as unable to participate in modernity or secular democracy. At the same time the regime of violence itself excludes women of immigrant heritage from politics broadly understood by defining them so clearly as victim that they cannot participate in resistance to violence.

The Headscarf as Domestic Violence: 1997–2003

Turkish and Muslim women become an important media topic again in 1997, coinciding with Germany's first controversial "headscarf case," in which schoolteacher Fereshta Ludin sought placement in a public school while wearing hijab. In conjunction with this case, the perceived threat to German civic society was somewhat displaced from the oppressive Muslim male to the dangerous Muslim woman who enters public spaces—the public school in particular—wearing a headscarf. The covered Muslim woman serves a deeply contradictory function both as victim of and as perpetrator of violence. As an upwardly mobile woman entering a particularly important space for the reproduction of German citizenship, and therefore as a woman who desexualized the headscarf to make it a symbol that is partially unavailable to a male Orientalist fantasy for consumption, Ludin's case disturbed understandings of Muslim woman victimhood in a way that was experienced by the public as particularly threatening (Terkessidis, "Globale Kultur" 6; Weber,

"Cloth" 50). The now-dangerous Muslim woman remained a victim of violence and continued to be linked to a dangerous culture threatening the perceived integrity of German and European culture. This case occupies the public so completely that media representations of Muslim women shifts dramatically to focus on headscarves.

This case came to construct the headscarf as a symbol of domestic violence at a time when Muslim women again became increasingly visible in public media. The headscarf discussions provide a visual ordering of the public sphere via its reference to confined space and its relationship to domestic violence. Ludin's case sparked a new wave of articles that use the figure of the Muslim woman to demonstrate "failed integration" and the dangerous mystery of Islam on the covers of a 1997 *Spiegel* and a 1998 *Spiegel-Special*. The covered woman becomes publicly visible via her role in demonstrating the "limits of tolerance" in German society (Sorge 126). Any acceptance of veiling practices in public schools would be evidence of a naïve tolerance that would require Germans to say "goodbye [to] Germany and Europe" (Sorge 125–126). Indeed, the Muslim woman proves an enormous threat to the values of the constitution itself (Bednarz 112).

During the headscarf case, media coverage of issues pertinent to immigrant women is increasingly visually constituted and organized. The contemporary public sphere is often visually organized as "a field of visuality that subjugates through controlled silences, performative acts, speech acts, and visual displays. It is a visually constituted field of power relations where subjugation operates through the ongoing marking and categorization of diverse visibilities and subjectivities by the public gaze" (Çınar, "Subversion and Subjugation" 895–896). Domestic violence finds a new form of visual representation in the public sphere, as the headscarf case links the confining space of home, the space of the "Turkish ghetto," and the confining space of the headscarf. Media stories discuss the Muslim family as a special space of violence, but the violent space of the home is now mirrored by the headscarf's limitation of bodily space. For example, one notable politician argued that a teacher wearing a headscarf would encourage students to conform to the restrictive edicts of their parents (Henkel-Waidhofer). A particularly sensationalist *Spiegel* article titled "The Cross of the Koran" links the headscarf to a long list of incidents that are perceived as being related to Muslim integration: familial violence—the rape of a Turkish girl by her uncle; the so-called "Camel fatwa" issued by a self-named caliph in Germany, which argued that a girl cannot be further away from her home than a camel can travel in a day; the ghettoization of Germany's Muslim populations; the low educational level of immigrants; and the fact that some of the 9/11 terrorists were living in Hamburg. These forms of violence are conflated with the headscarf merely through the fact that all have something to do with Islam. The images in this article further emphasize threat and danger: a picture of animals being slaughtered, full of blood; two activists wearing burqas with signs reading "end it before it's too late;" girls in a Koran school captioned as "Islam's real fighters;" and a scantily clad woman dancing in a club, captioned "Turkish disco—understanding for the camel-fatwa" (Cziesche et al. 85–86). The caption seems to indicate that clubbers support the restriction of women's travel.

This last example is particularly interesting in that it verbally evokes a spatial restriction of the woman to the home at the same time that it visually depicts the sexualized body of a woman who is clearly comfortably present in public space. The bare back of a dancing woman, marked as "Turkish" by the caption, is clearly visible; her face and those of the people dancing around her reflect a joy that makes no sense in the context of the caption, "Understanding for the Camel Fatwa," which in the text actually refers to a judge who considered the "camel fatwa" when allowing parents to keep a child home from a school trip. The images, even though they actually depict a public space, superficially connect that familial violence to a range of dangers seen as inherent to Islam. Through the conflations of violence with Islam, Germany's commitment to an egalitarian society as part of its democratic identity is presumed to be already achieved, a civilization to which Muslim "culture" is understood as necessarily opposed. This is the overall effect of the article despite an included discussion of the incomplete nature of Germany's secularism, as evidenced by the fact that the Catholic Church retains a status as a "public law corporation" despite the fact that women are not allowed to become priests (Cziesche et al. 87). Though this discussion might lead to the conclusion that enlightenment secularism has not necessarily meant equal rights for women, the article frames the mention of the Catholic Church differently—its discrimination against women could provide additional legitimation to Islamist groups to oppress women (86).[3]

The image of the woman in the disco, then, contains a contradiction, then, that disturbs readers and challenges them to rethink questions about the public presence of Turkish German women, but only in an extremely limited way: her "visibility" is quite literal and is dependent on her exposed back. This period from 1997 to 2003 differs from the first period I've discussed, however, in an important way—the media representations of Muslim women do begin to diversify, if not as visibly so, in the pages of *Der Spiegel*. The association of headscarves with domestic violence occurs most clearly in *Der Spiegel*, though other media outlets also linked the headscarf to domestic violence and honor killings (see, for example, Langenbach). However, other print media responses to this case focused more on the headscarf as a generic symbol against the emancipation of women (Weber, "Cloth" 51–53) but with fewer specific references to domestic violence. Even though *Der Spiegel* continues to have tremendous influence over how questions of integration and immigration are perceived, the more diverse representations in other forms of media provide new, though limited openings for imagining the Muslim woman as democratic subject and German citizen (Weber, "Cloth" 56–57).

The Subject of Suffering: Hatun Sürücü

The murder of Hatun Sürücü in 2005 impacted the representations of violence and Muslim women in crucial ways. It marked renewed focus on honor killing as a marker of Islam's inherent violence but consolidated discussion around a single life story that could easily be appropriated for a particular script of violence. The representations of her murder in the public media reveal and constitute important shifts in public understanding of Muslim women in Germany. Throughout this discussion, the voices of women of Turkish immigrant heritage become important for the first time. However, the voices most valued are often those that can fit into a dominant narrative of German secularism, often by explicitly or implicitly rejecting Islam or affiliation with a Turkish or a Muslim community.

Thousands of articles in online and print German press have covered Sürücü's murder. A review of the articles reveals several dominant themes. In particular the articles focus on the details of the crime itself; the conviction of her youngest brother, who shot her; the declaration of a mistrial for two older brothers due to evidentiary issues; and the elder brothers' escape to Turkey before they could stand trial again. Several memorials to Sürücü have also contributed to keeping her story in the press years after her death. The establishment of "Hatun und Can" to help Turkish women who are victims of familial violence gained extensive attention, particularly after the famed feminist Alice Schwarzer won 500,000 Euros on the German television show *Who Wants to Be a Millionaire* and donated it to the organization (Plarre). When Schwarzer questioned how the funds were being spent, a criminal investigation began; the criminal misuse of funds by the head of Hatun und Can provided the backdrop for continued reference to Sürücü's murder. Feo Aladağ's 2009 debut film project *Die Fremde*, inspired by Sürücü's death (though not based on her story) and starring Sibel Kekilli, won numerous awards in Germany and abroad and is continually brought together with Sürücü's death in the coverage (see, for example, Kappert; Schulz-Ojala; Ranze); it was also chosen as Germany's entry into the competition for the Academy Award. In 2010 a debate began about whether a Berlin street should be named after Sürücü (Fietz; "Die Unvergessene Tat"); the Greens officially requested this name change in December 2010.

The coverage of Sürücü's death constitutes a significant shift in the relationship of Muslim women to the ordering of the public sphere. As domestic violence emerges as the major issue through which immigrant women and women of immigrant heritage are represented, the visual power of the headscarf diminishes somewhat. The murder also sparks a renewed debate about the failure of multiculturalism and integration, a debate that imagines an increasing assault on the values of Europe. A discourse of domestic violence asserts dominance in the public sphere, which is all the more powerful because of its recourse to real, horrifying physical violence. However, this was also a moment of increased diversity of representation of violence against Muslim women as well, as scholars and activists critical of the discussion of domestic violence also responded in the pages of mainstream newspapers. I wish to examine this moment, then, as a moment that opens up many possibilities and forecloses others in thinking about the role of Muslim German women.

Certainly, horror in response to murder is appropriate, as is outrage at all forms of gender violence. However, it is important to remain attentive to how difference is produced via this response, what the consequences of that production are, and what issues might be obscured in the crisis moment that is experienced through response to this horrific event. Anthropologist and ethnologist Werner Schiffauer has pointed to the ways in which the response to Sürücü's murder demonstrates a "desire for horror" [eine Lust am Schaudern] (Oestrich and Am Orde). Like the rape discourse Marcus analyzes, the contemporary discourse of domestic violence, framed as culturally specific "honor killings" and "forced marriages," scripts a role for a Muslim woman as a victim.[4]

The case of Sürücü also sparked mentions of the "long ignored" problem of honor killings in Muslim families (Bruns; Bullion), an assertion repeated in international press stories that claim that honor killings rarely make the newspapers (Fleishman). Sürücü becomes the exemplar of a well-integrated woman of Turkish heritage, whose integration is performed as a participation in a modernity defined by escape from Turkish space, escape from her Turkish marriage, escape from community attachments, and attainment of sexual freedom marked by the revelation of her body to the public eye and her involvement with a German man.

Yet this integration is often imagined as both necessary and impossible, and Sürücü's murder inevitable—she "had to die" (Laninger and Banse; "Ehrenmord-Prozess"). The inevitable fact of her death is considered a consequence of her being "too modern" or "too German" (Bakirdögen and Laninger, "War Hatun"; Laninger and Banse; Bakirdögen and Laninger, "Lebte Hatun"; Bullion, "Mord im Namen der Ehre"; Schiffauer; Wahba). This modernity is linked partly to her clothing—she is described as being unlike other Turkish women because she wore modern clothing (Laninger and Banse), and the fact that she stopped wearing the headscarf was repeatedly emphasized (Kelek; Wahba; Deckwerth; Lau; Schiffauer). The markers of participation in modern German life, including her navel piercing and her "German boyfriend," make Sürücü a target of violence within her family (Ataman; Deckwerth, "Ein angekündigter Tod"; Leveringhaus). There is even an odd suggestion of a sort of postmortem punishment that occurs when her family denies her "modernity" after her death by giving her a traditional burial in a Muslim cemetery (Lau). The struggle to claim an enlightened Europeanness against a notion of Islam as backward, conducted on the body of the Muslim woman, extends here in a strange way even to her buried body.

The murder of Sürücü further became evidence of the "clash of cultures," (Bullion, "In den Fängen"), or even the need to defend the values of civilization against the threat of Islam (Kelek, "Anwälte"). Necla Kelek suggests, for example, that

> we are dealing with a completely different view of humanity and the world in Muslim communities in Germany. These people do not live according to the ten commandments or the principles of the constitution. These values are unknown to them and contradict their culture. They live in a Muslim-Archaic parallel world in which they follow what they see as the laws of Sharia. (Kelek, "Anwälte")

Whereas Kelek, who is of Turkish heritage, generally presents herself as nonreligious, here she points to Christian traditions as aligned with the constitution, in contradistinction to Muslim values.

The power of this discourse is visible in the reaction of a noted public intellectual, the Turkish German poet, novelist, and media critic Zafer Şenocak. Although Şenocak is generally critical of the essentializing descriptions of cultural difference in the media, the light sentences given to Sürücü's older brothers, who are assumed to have participated in the planning of the murder, evoke language that is remarkably similar to Kelek's:

> [Woman] is more or less a continuation of her man, clearly submissive to him. Muslims must finally begin to at least discuss this antiquated view of women. It is inadequate to claim that Islam legitimates neither forced marriage nor honor killing. The traditional

Muslim image of women is not compatible with gender equality. (Senocak, "Ganze Stadtteile")

Şenocak does not equate Islam per se with violence against women, which is an important distinction. A later text is critical of the role that violence against women plays in German discussions of Turkish integration, pointing out that these same acts are illegal and considered archaic in Turkey aswell (Şenocak, *Deutschsein* 118–119). Immediately following the trial, however, his response to the Sürücü case, in its focus on "traditional images" of gender roles in Islam, fits easily into the discussions which collapse Islam with gender violence, demonstrating how tremendously powerful the media discussion of Sürücü had become and reducing the possibilities for an effective portrayal of the situation of Muslim women.

The existence of domestic violence among communities with immigrant heritage is depicted as in fact a barrier to the safety of German life, for "with forced marriage and honor killings, there can be no tolerant living together [Zusammenleben] in Germany" (Bruns). The assertion of cultural conflict and the need to defend civilizational values also becomes important in American press coverage. An *LA Times* article cites the rhetoric deployed by the right-wing *Republikaner* party, which appropriated Sürürcü's murder for their own xenophobic agenda, stating that "Along with Hatun Surucu [sic], the dream of multiculturalism has died. The death of this young woman must convince the last multicultural romantic that the dream of a peaceful coexistence of different cultures and religions is over. Islam is and remains incompatible with the values of our constitution" (qtd. in Fleishman). Mainstream and right-wing rhetoric converge here to imply that domestic violence has been essentially absent in German and Western society except in immigrant families, or that the forms of domestic violence existing in Muslim families are so pervasive and fundamentally different that they exclude potential productive Muslim participation in German life.

The figure of Sürücü exists in an uneasy space, then, where she has become "German" but can only have done so by removing herself from Turkish culture and, by doing so, condemns herself to death. Repeatedly, headlines and quotes consider why she "had to die" and find an easy answer, repeating the reason given by her murderer: for living Western, living European, living modern, or living German. This constellation of identities and lifestyles are then both attached to freedom and deeply sexualized. By becoming German, she has also become a prostitute: "What is really going on in the heads of young Turkish men, for whom the 'German woman' is clearly a synonym for a whore?" (Lau; further, see Deckwerth, "Opfer oder Bruder"). Sürücü emerges as a subject in public space firstly through her status as a victim of murder and secondly, or secondarily, as "German"—a Germanness achieved in turn largely by the degree to which her body conforms to perceived signifiers of modern dress (the lack of headscarf, navel piercing, etc.). Sürücü is seen as "becoming" German through her sexual availability. Is this an alternate sexuality that is posed as a strategy against familial violence? If so, this comes at the cost of imagining a political position in the public sphere. The Muslim woman's emergence into European subjecthood appears to come only to the degree to which she "frees" herself from Muslim control by exposing herself to the German gaze.

The threat posed by Turkish culture and domestic violence is often framed in terms of cultural difference, which is experienced as spatial invasion. This is not entirely new; Maria Stehle has argued this in her analysis of feminist press and media references to immigration in the 1970s: "Feminist press evoked a nightmare of the Americanized, patriarchal, and violent city that is no longer safe for women and children; *Der Spiegel* focused on racialised fears that such a comparison to the US triggered" (Stehle 50). What has shifted, however, is an explicit linking of a racialized space of the Other to an antidemocratic tradition that is incompatible with women's rights (further see Stehle 60–61), as we see for example in the following excerpt from an article on Sürücü's death:

> Can it be that we are making giant leaps backwards in the integration of Turkish immigrants? Are Turkish families in the middle of Germany a justice free [rechtsfrei] space for thousands of young girls and women? Is the conception of woman within Islam incompatible with our system of values and law? (Lau).

Schiffauer also deploys spatial metaphors of separation when he argues that this case has "little to do with Islam and much to do with self-isolation" (Schiffauer). Sürücü's murder is said to be indicative of the spatial division existing in Germany—indeed, the Berlin district in which the Sürücü family lived is described as not really being a part of Germany, due to its large Turkish German population (R. Müller). The spatial metaphors, then, which marked much early German popular culture addressing the situation of immigrants in Germany, have reemerged here to mark a clearly bounded antidemocratic space that is marked by a lack of women's rights. Within the logic of this discourse, although Sürücü was able to escape this space, she was killed for leaving.

These discussions can be seen as an example of what elsewhere has been termed elsewhere in the German context as a "culture trap" (Weber, "Beyond the Culture Trap"), in the Indian context "death by culture" (Narayan 89–117), or in the Turkish context as the "tradition effect" (Kogacioglu). Rather than examining the complex societal, historical, and institutional contributors to violence and considering violence against women as changeable, the "culture trap" constructs an essentialized culture that is beyond redemption because it is unchangeable. This happens through the deployment of the notion of "honor killing" to specify a culturally specific form of domestic violence, conceived of as mere effect of tradition, without naming it domestic violence, which would align the phenomenon with violence that also occurs in ethnic German culture. Instead, the secular German state is seen as ethically tasked with the salvation of violent Muslim culture (see, for example, Franck). Even those who might be willing to acknowledge the presence of gender violence in German society locate this violence firmly in the past: "We were not willing to recognize [domestic violence in immigrant groups], because it isn't long ago that similar actions belonged to our majority culture. That which was overcome in long, strenuous battles over freedom and emancipation now comes to us from other countries, other cultures" (Bruns).

The difficulty of challenging a notion of "honor killing" is clear when one journalist points to the importance of questioning the concept—not to suggest a critical approach to the use of the term but to naturalize it by placing it in a binary of "our laws" and "their violence": "It is good that Judge Poulet also is thinking about the concept of honor killing. For it cannot be honorable, to kill a young woman. And because it is high time to let those who think that they are beyond our notions of right and custom to know it" (Müller-Gerbes). In other words, the potential for a challenge to the notion of honor exists only by insisting that murder is not honorable—not by questioning whether this is an adequate conceptual framework for understanding violence against women in Muslim families living in Europe.

Activists and public intellectuals hoping to dispel associations of Islam with honor killings often contrast "tradition" and "Islam," to argue that such violent acts have "nothing to do with Islam" but rather are the remnants of pre-Islamic Middle Eastern culture (see, for example, Schirrmacher). This form of argumentation is problematic. So long as we assume that either Islam *or* "Middle Eastern" cultures are *necessarily* connected to violence, we ignore the efforts of Muslims to combat violence against women, as well as ignore the violence against women that has existed and continues to exist in European cultures. We further close off the potential to imagine alliances with others who are fighting a range of forms of violence. Effective reimaginations of culture that make violence against women unacceptable require more than condemnation of honor killings. It is also necessary to consider a context that includes not just a history of Islam and a traditional understandings of gender roles but also a trajectory of change within Turkish culture and the ongoing experiences of violence in Germany. So long as Islam is considered necessarily and fundamentally violent, and so long as "Turkish" or "Muslim" culture is considered both backward and unchangeable, action for change remains impossible, and imagining Muslim women as participants in change remains unthinkable.

Emerging Political Subjectivities in the Sürücü Media Coverage

There are some important exceptions to the power of the regime of violence and its prohibition of the emergence of political subjectivities among women of immigrant heritage. This coincides with the arrival into the public sphere of two women in particular, who have attained the status of experts on violence and Islam—Seyran Ateş and Necla Kelek. Their positions on violence against Turkish and Muslim women in Germany have accorded them credibility not only in Germany but internationally as well (Poggioli, "Muslim Women"; Poggioli, "Reporter's Notebook"; Poggioli, "Muslim Activist"; Snyder; Schneider; "Turkish Honor Killings in Germany"; Marion; Fleishman).

Ateş is a feminist, activist, and lawyer who has been forced to temporarily close her practice due to threats on her life. Her public statements focus on sexualities in response to the Sürücü murder, though at a complex level. She seeks to desexualize the discussion by calling for a sexual revolution. In the wake of Sürücü's murder, Ateş expressed ideas that are more fully articulated later, in her 2009 book *Der Islam braucht eine sexuelle Revolution* [*Islam Needs a Sexual Revolution*]. She argues that Turkish women live under a moral double standard that ended for Western women with women's emancipation—namely, that men were naturally sexual, whereas women's sexuality needs to be controlled and repressed (Leveringhaus). She further argues that the "dream of a false tolerance" has contributed to a Islamicization of Germany's immigrant groups (Fleishman). However, Ateş's discussion remains confined to a need to address individual sexual freedoms, which reinforces a reading of secularism that simply opposes Western freedom to Muslim victimhood. Ateş occasionally does address forms of structural discrimination that may impact Muslim men. She suggests, for example, that Muslim men have been put "into a box" by a situation that combines a lack of employment opportunities with experiences of discrimination after 9/11 (Fleishman). However, she ultimately subordinates that argument to her call for a rejection of Islam and false tolerance.

Kelek, a writer and activist with a PhD in sociology, takes a more extreme position. Although she too is concerned with access to sexual freedom (Buchbinder), she sees little chance for reform either within Turkish culture or within Islam. To the contrary, she argues that attempts to "understand" Turkish or Muslim culture, together with an "irrational fear" of being racist, have led to the tolerance of violence against women (Kelek, "Eure Toleranz"): "Never has the difference between archaic, religiously determined culture and enlightened society become so visible as through this honor killing: it reveals the well-intentioned looking away as a deadly tolerance" (Kelek, "Reifeprüfung. Der Fall Sürücü wird neu verhandelt"). For her, Islam is itself unavoidably archaic and indivisible from traditions that enable violence against women (Lau).

Kelek and Ateş achieve their status as experts in several ways.[5] They've both written autobiographical books on violence against Turkish women, are well educated, and are outspoken. However, they are as susceptible to the same discursive restrictions as Other Turkish women. Their own experience as victims of violence is constantly repeated in articles and interviews, though their work as activists, and (in the case of Ateş), as a lawyer is also mentioned. Kelek, for example, is sometimes labeled an expert, not because of her education or her activist work but because of her experience as a Turkish woman (Lau). Their Turkish heritage is deployed as proof that the discussion of honor killings has "nothing to do with Islamophobia or xenophobia" (Lau, "Kulturbedingte 'Ehrenmorde'").

Other Turkish-heritage women who are active as politicians also emerge in the story's context. In response to the murder, Emine Demirbüken, the first Turkish German woman in the Center Right party, the Christian Democratic Union (CDU) leadership, argued that this case shows that "Juvenile law, with its mild punishments—a maximum of ten years for murder—becomes an incentive for families to commit an honor killing in Germany, rather than the intended deterrence" (Lau, "Wie eine Deutsche"; Müller-Gerbes). Lale Akgün, a parliament member of the center left Social Democratic Party (SPD) was also quoted occasionally. A piece she authored argues that the use of honor in the German public is simplified and ignores the migrants' situation. In particular, she suggests that the specific manifestation of honor as a value today may occur partly because of the emphasis on individual achievement in German society (Akgün)—in other words, honor is not merely inherited from Turkish culture but dovetails with an emphasis on individual achievement in German culture. Yet whereas Akgün gestures to a context for domestic violence that includes its relationship to the experiences of globalization rather than one that is located solely in traditional village mores, her complex views are dramatically simplified in other articles. For example, she was extensively interviewed in a story in the left-leaning daily, the *Taz*, in which she suggests that one should not address this issue by demonizing men, but also should consider the role of women, particularly mothers, in encouraging honor killings: "We are thinking incorrectly. We say, 'The Turkish men, they are the perpetrators, the place where we must start.' But it is the women who often raise their sons with these thoughts. Often they are the driving power behind an honor killing–they turn their sons against their stepdaughters" (Schmitt). The focus and editing of the interview leaves the reader to assume that Akgün merely expands the culture of violence within Turkish or Muslim cultures to include women as perpetrators.

The use of Turkish-heritage "experts" in the discussions of Sürücü's murder thus largely serves to reify rather than challenge the regime of violence. The members of the activist group Göçmen Kadınlar Birliği–Bundesverband der Migrantinnen in Deutschland e.V (the Federal Council of Migrant Women in Germany), on the other hand, who were openly critical of the parameters limiting public discussions of Sürücü's death, are excluded from media coverage. Kelek emerges as an expert largely on the basis of her own experience as a victim of violence as well as her rejection of Turkish and Muslim communities (both of which aspects were incorporated into her best-selling book). She assigns blame for violence to those communities as well as to those members of the majority society who tolerate honor concepts, forced marriages, and domestic violence in the name of a misguided multiculturalism, "robbing girls of their sexual freedom" (Buchbinder; Kelek, "Eure Toleranz"). Ateş's case is more contradictory and complex—she alternates between a rhetoric that imagines change from within immigrant, Muslim communities and one that presumes such change as impossible. However, her reimagination of sexuality is limited here as she is caught up in the rhetoric of freedom and choice that excludes identity as Muslim from that choice. And her imagination of a different place in society for Turkish or Muslim women is limited to—a place of sexual freedom. Akgün's more complex views, in which she considers honor in a globalized context that includes German mores, are unfortunately reduced to a slight variation of the usual narrative of Turkish violence in which Turkish women are now equally culpable as are men. Although Akgün is introduced as a former parliamentarian and "Islam" expert, the only policy she concretely mentions in conjunction with the Sürücü case is the criminalization of forced marriages. In concrete terms, this criminalization has only taken place in terms of immigration limitations—one now has to be 18 years of age to immigrate as a spouse.

Whereas my analysis here has been on the dominant discourses, as circulating in the pages of popular news media, there are important additional challenges to the discourse of gender violence, though they are generally made using other media. Media critics Patrick Bahners and Kay Sokolowsky have both published books targeted at a general audience, which are intended to be "critical of the Islam critics" (Sokolowsky; Bahners). Both Bahners and Sokolowsky condemn the contemporary discussion of Islam and briefly criticize the reliance on Ateş and Kelek as experts on "honor killings" (Bahners 194) and the plight of the Turkish German woman (Sokolowsky 112–132). Also, sociologist Elisabeth Beck-Gernsheim has published two editions of a book, *Wir und die Anderen* [We, and the Others], which summarizes academic research but targets a general audience. Her section on victim stories argues that the production of sympathy with female victims of violence becomes dangerous when it leads to reductionist understandings of Muslim culture, and along with that, the exclusion of Muslim women from German society (Beck-Gernsheim 81–82). She further points out the problems with past sociological research, both in terms of the assumptions that have informed it and the outdated and unreliable studies that often frame it (Beck-Gernsheim 51–73). Reception of these books has been mixed. They are generally considered controversial, and the authors are frequently accused of trivializing the everyday experiences of violence that many face, as when one reviewer argues that Beck-Gernsheim ignores the plight of Turkish girls who face the "sword of forced marriage waving over their head" (Weickmann). Nevertheless, though they have not garnered the immense attention that other authors like Kelek and Ateş have, these books have been important vehicles for further challenging the obsession with Muslim women as victims of violence.

Reimagining Domestic Violence, Approaching the Future

To challenge the power of a script that naturalizes violence against women in Muslim families and excludes Muslim women from participation in the public sphere, gender violence must be rethought, in terms of careful attention to the construction and interpretation of empirical studies, the critique of cultures of violence, and the analysis of violence as a historically and socially specific process.

Shortly before Sürücü was murderd, the first major comparative and comprehensive study examining forms and impacts of violence against women in Germany was completed.[6] This study, which was released just months before Sürücü's death, provides the most comprehensive and complex look available at forms of violence against women in Germany. Nevertheless, certain assumptions impacted the interpretation of the data within the study itself and guided the media coverage.

The study, funded by the federal government, found that women of Turkish heritage,[7] who were defined as women who had Turkish citizenship or had two parents who had immigrated from Turkey, were likely to experience violence in their lives at a higher level than women in the general sample. Interestingly enough, however, the newspapers widely reported this difference as significant without addressing the already high percentage of experiences of violence among the general sample (40 percent versus 49 percent among women of Turkish heritage) (U. Müller et al. 118–119), which are also significantly higher than Europe-wide averages (U. Müller et al. 31). Turkish-heritage women were also more likely to experience more intense forms of physical violence (U. Müller et al. 125) and significantly more likely to experience violence at the hands of their partners (U. Müller et al. 121). Left largely unreported was the fact that Turkish-heritage victims of violence were more likely to utilize the available institutionalized forms of help than victims of other backgrounds (U. Müller et al. 133), demonstrating an ability to negotiate German institutions, which suggests an understanding of and a willingness to participate in public life. The fact that women of Turkish heritage who have become victims of violence are more likely to seek forms of help also questions the study's assumption that women of Turkish heritage are less likely to report their experiences of violence. Also largely unreported in the media was the fact that Turkish-heritage women experienced sexualized xenophobic violence, suffered almost identical rates of psychological and sexual violence as women of German heritage, similar rates of violence before the age of 16, and were less likely to experience sexual harassment than German heritage women (U. Müller et al. 120–123; 130). Women of Turkish heritage were also shown to experience higher levels of psychological violence from strangers, often for xenophobic reasons (U. Müller et al. 130).

Although the study points to the fact that Turkish women are much more likely to experience violence within relationships than the general sample, data on the heritage of the perpetrators was not collected (U. Müller et al. 122, fn 98). The summaries also tended to point to the difference in experiences of violence within immigrant groups, without considering the fact that the incidence of violence against German women was already quite high. Thus the suggested explanations for the high rates of violence against women of Turkish heritage continued to revolve around cultural explanations. Assumptions about agency and involvement in the public sphere in the study may also explain why the analysis expressed such surprise that women of Turkish heritage would report violence to the police at high rates. An important exception, however, lies in a brief follow-up article by Monika Schröttle, a coauthor of the study, who has since also argued that the attention to violence against Muslim women ignores larger questions of violence in German society (Schröttle 269). While this analysis seems relatively isolated in contemporary research of domestic violence, Schröttle's ongoing activity in this field suggests that new attention might be forthcoming in contextualizing violence against Muslim women in Germany in relationship to overall forms of violence.

The coverage of Sürücü's death, together with the interpretation of the study's results, suggest some important impacts of the way that violence against women is talked about in Germany today. The regime of violence orders the public sphere by largely limiting emergent political subjectivities for those women associated with Islam to their position as victims of domestic violence. One consequence of such limitations is the inability to link those forms of violence experienced by women of immigrant heritage, particularly partner or familial violence, to those experienced by German-heritage women. This promotes an inability to form important alliances and constructs an artificial and unnecessary segregation in the battle to end rape culture and violence against women. It also covers up a crucial aspect in ignoring the strategies that Muslim women deploy to combat violence, including finding and availing themselves of institutionalized structures. Framing "honor crimes" as a particularity on a larger continuum of violence against women is a key strategy in addressing the issue of the specificity of honor crimes. This would allow an understanding of the complexities of Muslim women's subjectivities without resorting to an inappropriate discourse in which Muslim culture necessarily leads to violence against women (Sen 53–55). It also can combat the tendency toward domestic violence in "Western" families to emerge on the international stage as evidence of Western hypocrisy, which in turn becomes a justification for addressing gender violence in non-Western countries as legitimation for agendas that have little to do with violence against women.

The heavy emphasis on the assignation of blame to immigrant communities and their culture for the incidence of domestic violence precludes research and activism that might more successfully address the multiple causes of these forms of violence. From the study it is clear that women of German heritage also experience violence at high rates, though the forms and degrees of violence differ. For women living in Germany, regardless of heritage, then, what are the multiple factors impacting violence? How do they interact? What role might the "scripts" of violence actually play in enabling and normalizing violence? In enabling lesser sentences for convicted perpetrators? How is access to education and employment impacted by these violence scripts?

Sürücü's murder thus teaches us much more than merely to attend to the fact of domestic violence among Muslims in Germany today. A regime of gender violence expressed in representations of domestic violence, which was established during unification, reconfigured during the headscarf debates, and consolidated in the wake of Sürücü's murder, has important implications for how we understand violence in Germany today. Sürücü's case gained such public attention in part because it so perfectly fit the dominant narrative. Women of Turkish, Kurdish, or Muslim heritage, such as Kelek and Ateş, who are able to emerge into the public sphere partially outside a position of victimhood, are largely able to do so because they confirm this narrative, in particular the incompatibility of Islam with women's rights.

To understand domestic and familial violence in the context of historical and social processes, we must acknowledge how a particular narrative of secularism that attributes a peaceful nonviolence to Europe and an antidemocratic violence to Islam is reinforced in the aftermath of Sürücü's murder. The discussions following her death reveal that the "Mediterranean" honor-shame complex that emerged in the 1960s has been reconfigured in popular discourse as a "Muslim" or "Turkish" problem with honor. Residents of largely Christian Mediterranean countries, who are now also European Union member countries, appear to have at least partially "arrived" into Europeanness and whiteness, given their disappearance from the script of violence. In turn, Germans of Turkish heritage have been redefined via their association with domestic violence, which is used as marker of their inability to enter into a secular democracy.

The victim of domestic violence in this script is also removed from the "secular" public sphere. As in the rape script analyzed by Marcus, she is constructed as an object to be violated, but one that embodies a complex layering of boundaries. If she is the "immobile space" through which the perpetrator moves, as Marcus suggests in the rape script, she also becomes simultaneously the boundary between the uneven pair of Europe and Islam—much as the woman wearing a headscarf does, as I will further explore in the next chapter. By rejecting Islam, certain women are allowed to become "experts" on the subject of Islam in Europe and its relationship to violence against women; in this way they are comfortably accommodated within Europeanness without evoking the danger of a Muslim Otherness. Other women who claim a religious identity may appear in public imaginations, largely as victim, but are clearly excluded from the agonistic space of the public sphere. Sürücü's murder inspired fears about Islam in Germany all the more effectively because she had "become" German, Western, and European in the public media coverage. She thus doubly serves as boundary crossed by and violated by Islam while she also serves as the embodiment of fear of Muslim violence. At the same time, she herself no longer poses a threat to norms of Europeanness—because she has been silenced as victim.

Chapter Two
Contentious Headscarves: Cleaning Woman, Forbidden Schoolteacher, Hijab Martyr

> *In particular, external behavior that would evoke the impression by students or parents that the teacher is against human dignity, the equal rights of people according to Article 3 of the Basic Law, basic freedoms, or the liberal democratic order, is not permissible. The fulfillment of the educational mandate [...] of the constitution, and the relevant representation of Christian and Western educational and cultural values or traditions, do not infringe on [this] dictate.*
> —Text of the Baden-Württemberg Law Instituting a Provincial Headscarf Ban (Drucksache 13/3091. Gesetz Zur Änderung Des Schulgesetzes)

The immense and ongoing attention received by Sürücü's murder stands in stark contrast to coverage of the xenophobically motivated murder of another Muslim woman, Marwa el-Sherbini, in a German courtroom in 2009. The incident began when el-Sherbini, wearing a hijab, asked Alex Wiens to make space for her three-year-old son on a playground swing. He responded by accusing her of being an Islamist. She brought charges, and Wiens was subsequently fined by the local authorities for xenophobically motivated speech. Upon appeal, el-Sherbini testified again against Wiens, who demonstrated in court that he was an open sympathizer of the right-wing party, the National Democratic Party. Immediately after her testimony, Wiens stabbed el-Sherbini to death in front of her husband and son. Media coverage of and political response to el-Sherbini's death in the Dresden courtroom were notably muted. Although the murder quickly gained attention in Egypt (el-Sherbini's home country) and Iran, followed by stories published in the United States and the UK, German officials and press did not react to the case for nearly a week. By the time they responded, el-Sherbini was being referred to as a "hijab-martyr" in the Islamic world, and her death was acknowledged as the first Islamophobic murder in Germany. Once a governmental and media response finally appeared, it was short-lived, and el-Sherbini's murder quickly disappeared from the public eye.

It is nearly impossible to discuss the contemporary questions surrounding diversity in Germany without addressing the contentious responses garnered by forms of Islamic headcovering in public space, in particular the debates generated by Fereshta Ludin's attempt to obtain a public teaching position while wearing a hijab.[1] Yet it is quite easy to enter into a discussion about Islam in Germany without discussing the xenophobically motivated murder of el-Sherbini, who was dubbed by many as the "hijab martyr." The radically different responses to the violent deaths of Sürücü and el-Sherbini, the former murdered in the name of a gendered "Muslim" code of honor, the latter murdered when she challenged a particular understanding of the "Muslim woman," are revealing. They suggest a public imagination of Muslim women in which victims of familial violence are easily imagined, whereas Muslim women as participants in public democracy and victims of racialized violence are largely unthinkable in the public sphere. The story I tell here is partly about how the visibility of the headscarf and the invisibility of forms of racialized discrimination are reflective of the larger discussions about Muslim violence in Europe. It is equally important to examine how Ludin and el-Sherbini, as two women who explicitly sought to claim their rights in the public sphere while wearing the headscarf, contradict the pervasive narratives in which Muslim women are unable to both demonstrate their affiliation with Islam in public and productively participate in European democracy.

The epigraph above was taken from one of several provincial laws that had been passed in response to a 2003 German Federal Constitutional Court that ruled on the constitutionality of preventing public schoolteachers from wearing hijab. The decision resolved little; it stated that the regulation of headscarves in public schools would fall under the purview of provincial, not federal, law. Furthermore, provincial law would need to more clearly regulate the relationship between church and state to provide a legal basis for banning headscarves (BVerfG, *2 BvR 1436/02*). This ruling, the only ruling by Germany's highest court in Germany's headscarf debates, opened the path for a number of controversial provincial laws banning headscarves for public schoolteachers.

The ongoing contentious conversations around the presence of Islamic headcoverings in public space have coincided with Germany's championing of the expansion and integration of the European Union (EU). While the image of the headscarf has served as an important marker of cultural difference throughout Western Europe, it has been particularly, and perhaps surprisingly, controversial in Germany; other nations that have similar forms of secularism, such as the Netherlands and Austria, have actually been relatively tolerant of the headscarf, as have been many European nations that continue to have some relationship to a national church such as Greece and the UK (Berghahn 11–18). Turkey and France, both with forms of government generally labeled more strictly secularist—practicing laïcité—have more consistent national bans of headscarves. Contestations over the figure of the Muslim woman in relationship to secularism, democracy, violence and public space play a crucial, albeit obscured, role in allowing Germany to position itself as the embodiment of the ideals of the EU, and of European democracy. The Muslim woman becomes the border between a violent East outside or before modernity, and an enlightened, modern West. Her veiled or covered body within the West marks the "limits of tolerance" as well as a fundamental challenge to a narrative that produces the racialized Other as lying outside modernity, secularism, and democracy, while producing violence as fundamentally lying outside Europe.

This process is dramatically revealed in the contrasting responses to Ludin and el-Sherbini, both of whom emerged into the public eye for wearing the headscarf; yet they are rarely discussed in relationship to each other. To some extent, the headscarf debates were so contentious because Ludin sought to participate in a special institution for forming the public sphere, the public school (Weber,

"Cloth"). Examining these two cases together allows us to better understand the power that the headscarf has in ordering the public sphere. Ludin and el-Sherbini's actions disturbed the narrative of Muslim women as victims of Islam, who were unable to participate in German democracy, and furthermore troubled the perceived connection between Islamic covering practices and violence. Their challenges reveal the need to retheorize the relationship between modernity, religious difference, secularism, and violence.

Susan B. Rottmann and Myra Marx Ferree have pointed out that race and racism have remained largely absent in the headscarf debates (Rottmann and Ferree). Not only is this focus absent in terms of its intersection with gender and other forms of difference, but it is also absent in terms of the importance of antiracism in European values, or in terms of EU policies. Court cases about whether public schoolteachers can wear headscarves to work dominate public discourse whereas debates about German compliance with EU antidiscrimination laws are largely avoided (Rottmann and Ferree 481–513). A new theorization of the relationship between secularism, religious difference, and violence must thus address the existence of racism in German democracy, construct new relationships between religious/communal attachment and notions of the public/private, and provide new understandings of secularism and its relationship to a nonviolent future. It must also consider the ways in which the discursive assumptions made about Islam, which lead to demands that women make choices between supporting human rights (by removing the headscarf) or visibly demonstrating their religious identity (by wearing the headscarf), may actually contribute to support for radical, politicized Islamism in Europe and prevent effective activism against violence against Muslim women.

The headscarf debates in Germany began in 1997 when Ludin, an Afghani born German citizen in the province of Baden-Württemberg, sought placement as a public schoolteacher while wearing hijab. The right-wing party *Republikaner* challenged her placement in a parliamentary debate. This provincial parliamentary move initiated a widely covered national debate, often referred to in German as the *Kopftuchstreit* (literally, headscarf argument). During this controversy the hijab was alternately seen and portrayed as a threat to German secularism, Christian culture, individual rights, feminist progress, the Enlightenment, and European values (Weber, "Cloth"). This ultimately led to the banning of the headscarf for public teachers in 8 of Germany's 16 provinces. Of these 8, only Berlin bans ALL religious symbols, whereas the others—explicitly or by interpretation—permit Christian and, to a lesser extent, Jewish symbols to be worn by schoolteachers in the classroom (Breger; Berghahn "Deutschlands" 45–50). The reactions to Ludin's case revealed extant fears as the immigrant woman became upwardly mobile and began to emerge as a German and European subject—one who would have access to economic, political, and cultural citizenship and who, as teacher, would play a key role in the reproduction of notions of citizenship.

Representations of the murder of el-Sherbini, alternatively, are revealing in terms of the potential for recognizing forms of discrimination against Muslim women in German society. When el-Sherbini was murdered in a German courtroom, she had just completed her testimony. Within the courtroom, Wiens continued his racist speech, declaring that Muslims and non-Europeans had no right to be in Europe. El-Sherbini's case challenges a dominant narrative in which Muslim women are the victims of Muslim patriarchy in several ways. El-Sherbini, as many hijab-wearing women in the public eye have been, was a self-assured woman claiming her rights under German law in the German court system—even though she was not a citizen or even a permanent resident. Her death was not at the hands of a family member—indeed, her husband was shot during el-Sherbini's attack by a policeman who entered the courtroom after the stabbing and assumed that the husband was the perpetrator. Yet the discourse at home and abroad transformed her from an active participant in the democratic process to a martyr for Islam.

Read together, the discussions surrounding the cases of Ludin and el-Sherbini reveal striking points about the position of Muslim residents in contemporary German society. While Ludin was Afghani born and el-Sherbini was an Egyptian citizen, both cases are used to assess the realities of the Turkish immigrant population and suggest the conflations of the diversity of Islamic traditions and Muslim subjectivities. Both Ludin and el-Sherbini interrupted a narrative of Muslim women as passive victims of Muslim violence by claiming their rights under German law and in doing so articulated experiences of discrimination and racism in public space. Ludin, a German citizen, sought to claim her rights to religious freedom under the German constitution to be allowed to teach while wearing the headscarf. El-Sherbini, an Egyptian citizen, claimed protection from hate speech under German law and the constitution by bringing charges and testifying against Alex Wiens for xenophobically motivated slander [Beleidigung aus Fremdenhass]. Public, political, and judicial responses portrayed the German state as the patronizing protector of the Muslim woman and thus served to legitimate the exclusion of women with immigrant heritage from successful work lives as well as from a special space of citizenship reproduction—the public school. El-Sherbini's murder more explicitly revealed the workings of racism and Islamophobia in discussions of the headscarf, even as her story was appropriated as "proof" that Germany is not racist.

In this way the debates around the headscarf demonstrate the complex constitution of the public sphere in Germany as a field of visuality. Alev Çınar argues that the public sphere is

> no longer a site of emancipation or liberation that comes through debate and dialogue but a field of visuality that subjugates through controlled silences, performative acts, speech acts, and visual displays. It is a visually constituted field of power relations where subjugation operates through the ongoing marking and categorization of diverse visibilities and subjectivities by the public gaze. (Çınar, "Subversion and Subjugation" 895–896)

In Western Europe the public gaze controls the public subjectivities of immigrant women in part through increasing legal regulation of women's covering practices—initially through regulation of appropriate attire in identification photos, then through the regulation of covering in public schools, and most recently through the proposed regulation of face veiling in public space. The constant presence of Muslim women in the public eye is accompanied by continued restrictions on their ability to participate in the public sphere. Like the situation that Çınar analyzes in Turkey, images quickly function as replacement for and repression of political citizenship. The representations of Ludin and el-Sherbini in public space also allow us to consider the visually constituted public sphere as a site not only of control and regulation but also as one of intervention. The headscarf itself—as a symbol of victimhood—is reconfigured through its association with familial violence in the 1990s as well as through an association with political, Islamic violence in the 2000s. Yet, representations of covering practices retain many affinities with those emerging from periods of European colonialism while simultaneously functioning to erase colonial violence. Emphasis on Muslim violence as domestic violence further obscures the experiences of other forms of symbolic, structural, and personal violence that continue to exclude immigrants from political participation. Nevertheless, contemporary responses to the Ludin and el-Sherbini cases in particular provide important moments of contestation during which experiences of racism and Islamophobia are made explicit and public, if for a brief period of time.

In the rest of this chapter I draw on a diverse archive to further consider these questions. To better understand the specificities of the function of the headscarf in the German public sphere, I briefly review the attachment of violence to Islam in representations of headscarves and veils in eighteenth- and nineteenth-century German thought, a tradition that provides a historical trajectory within which veiled or covered women have been deployed as markers of Europe's Other. Next I examine the place of headscarves and veils in academic and media representations since guestworker migration began, in particular to highlight the critical scholarship, often by women of immigrant heritage in Germany, which has often been ignored in academic engagements with questions of immigration and gender in Germany. I then turn to the relationship between violence and Islam in the representations of Ludin and el-Sherbini, drawing on court documents, legal scholarship, and print media. This analysis provides valuable opportunities for examining possibilities for a reconfigured public sphere that can allow for diversity while also allowing for the naming and critiquing of racism.

Trajectories of the Veiled Other: Covering Practices in German Thought

The representations of the headscarf in contemporary Germany exist in a long tradition of representing the "Oriental" Other. Although

Edward Said famously considered German Orientalisms largely "scholarly" (Said 19), given that there was little direct contact or specific colonial interests, this thought has been extensively challenged in recent years.[2] Furthermore, whereas Said largely talked about gender in the context of the feminization of Oriental men (Said 188), veils have been prominent tropes in travel writing, including that by women, in the eighteenth and nineteenth centuries. Philosophical writings and travel literature alike demonstrate a visual imagination of the veiled or covered Muslim woman who is embedded in a fantasy of a sensuous, sexual Orient, which is available to Western desires.

Within philosophy, the veil has often served as a symbol for something exterior to the self of the Western subject and the Other, which secures the place of the self (Yeğenoğlu 41). "Oriental" women were represented as doubly imprisoned, by the veil and by the harem, both of which become important symbols of Muslim sexuality for the West. The veil served as a screen for projections of new Western notions of a stable self, capable of moral agency, for many of the most famous German philosophers. For example, Immanuel Kant's 1764 essay "Observations on the Feeling of the Beautiful and Sublime" utilizes the harem as an example of the amorality of the Orient (Kant 109) over and against the Western subject: the harem demonstrates the "Oriental's" lack of aesthetic judgment that is necessary to also possess the capability of morality. A century later, the veil served Friedrich Nietzsche as a powerful misogynist trope for associating Oriental and feminine dissimulation and deception, as something that produces the illusion of a depth that does not exist (Yeğenoğlu 51–53), to challenge notions of the stable subject. As Christina von Braun and Bettina Mathes express in their comparative overview of the role of the veil in Western European culture, "If the veil did not exist, the West would have had to invent it, in order to find a place for its many fantasies of the Self in the mirror of the 'Orient'" (Von Braun and Mathes 19).

In nineteenth-century German philosophy and travel literature, representations of the veil emphasize the erotic nature of the Oriental or Muslim woman; seductive Oriental women elicited both European desire and Puritan condemnation for their sexual desirability and availability (Lutz, "Unsichtbare" 55). The harem functioned as an especially powerful fantasy that "filled the [Orientalists'] travel descriptions, although they generally never gained access to [the harem]" (Lutz, "Unsichtbare" 55), while the veil also played an important role as a deeply eroticized symbol of the unavailability and desirability of Muslim women. In many other Western European travel narratives, particularly British narratives, the erotic attraction of the veil in colonial writings is bound up both in the unavailability of the woman and in the fantasy of being able to "save" her; it is the immorality of Muslim men that makes veiling practices necessary (Ahmed 43–47). German women's travel narratives were less interested in "saving" the Oriental women than in an aesthetic aversion to the veil. Ida Pfeiffer, for example, in *Visit to the Holy Land*, presents the veil as a sign of the poor taste of Ottoman women, who appear in her text as either deeply impoverished or indolent and corpulent harem members (Pfeiffer). For other women with a protofeminist consciousness, such as Ida Hahn-Hahn, Ottoman slavery became a powerful metaphor for describing the need to emancipate Western women yet also served to demonstrate the impossibility for the Oriental consciousness to develop to a truly human level (O'Brien 39–41). Even as the gendering of the enlightened human subject took place, excluding women from participation in the public sphere, many women in turn produced the Muslim Other as unable to achieve the consciousness necessary for critical thought.

Post-World War II Migration and Representations of Covering

In the early twentieth century, the rise of biological constructs of race displaced the importance of veiling representations. Radical biological racisms began to emerge as early as 1850 in Western Europe, but they gained increasing currency in the early twentieth century as new forms of scientific racisms aligned with the anxieties, desires, and interests of culture to target the Jewish and Black Other (MacMaster 7; 13–14). Orientalist tropes have similarities with the representations of Black African and Jewish Others during this time, even though the power of harems and veils as visual metaphors lessened. Not until the advent of significant Turkish migration to Germany in the late 1960s did attention to veiling and headscarf practices resurface in scholarly and popular imaginations. In 1955, after World War II, official guestworker programs began to fill the massive labor shortage that, intensified after the building of the Berlin wall cut off supply of cheap labor from East Germany in 1961. During that year, Turkey also became the largest sending country of guestworkers. From the late 1960s until well into the 1980s, both scholarly and popular media attention in West Germany to veiling or headscarf practices was focused primarily on women *outside* Europe as a means of explaining the situation of women of North African and Turkish populations in Germany. However, since the fall of the wall and the subsequent reunification, there has been more specific attention to religious practices of Turkish Germans, who are now understood as German residents, if not necessarily as German citizens. This led to increased awareness of the place of veiling or headscarf practices within German society, often seen as practices "left over" from backward rural areas or as practices imposed on women by political Islamists. Although 9/11 does not mark a radical break in representations of practices of covering, contrary to what many assert, the 2000s do bring intensified fears that forms of covering, if allowed in public, will lead to the destruction of European democratic ideals.

Early attempts to challenge restrictive understandings of the headscarf were partly based on the same conflations of "Islamic culture" with archaic rural practices (e.g. Waltz 125; 127–129) that were present in scholarship on the honor-shame complex. Often, references to Turkish village life have been used as metonymical explanations for life in the Turkish diaspora, and even scholarly work seeking to challenge the negative associations of the headscarf relied on similar interpretations of the headscarf as connected to rural life (see, for example, Schönberger; Akkent and Franger 19–177). Yet the strict secularist tradition in Turkey, one which has led to Turkey's own debates about bans on headscarves in universities and public spaces after the 1989 headscarf ban (Çınar, "Subversion and Subjugation" 902–909; Göle, *Forbidden* 83–129; Göle, *Anverwandlungen* 104–130; Zaptçıoğlu 153–156) was often ignored. Academic work and work that targeted a more general audience paralleled each other, however, in slowly coming to see headcovering practices as intrusions from the outside rather than as a presence outside Europe.

Two anthologies edited by mainstream liberal feminist Alice Schwarzer, by far Germany's most famous feminist,[3] reflect the shift from discussing the veil as located "outside" to discussing headscarf practices as having invaded Germany. Her 1992 anthology, *Krieg: Was Männerwahn anrichtet und wie Frauen Widerstand leisten* [War: What Men's Insanity Starts and How Women Resist], primarily refers to the veil in the context of the patriarchy of the "Third World" (Schwarzer). Her 2002 and 2010 anthologies, *Die Gotteskrieger und die falsche Toleranz* [Warriors for God and False Tolerance] and *Die große Verschleierung: Für Integration, gegen Islamismus* [The Great Cover-Up: For Integration, against Islamism], turn attention to the dangerous arrival of Islam in Europe.

The cover for *Warriors for God and False Tolerance* demonstrates this "arrival" in Europe in oddly threatening ways. It depicts a woman whose face is covered by a heavy, thick black veil, which is topped by a crown of red barbed wire. The barbed wire evokes two immediate associations—a crown of thorns and the barbed wire of concentration camps. The reference to the Christian story of crucifixion via a crown of thorns marks the Muslim woman as a martyred victim. Rather than allying forms of gender inequities in Christianity and Islam, this image seems to strangely conflate the experience of the veiled Muslim woman with the martyrdom of Christ himself. Christianity thus serves as an unquestioned, powerful source of symbolic representation. Simultaneously, the use of barbed wire to imprison people also evokes imagery of concentration camps, which links the veiled woman to the victims of fascism. Thus the wearing of the veil becomes a form of imprisonment that is rhetorically produced as being equal to that of the concentration camps. Although such a link could possibly have suggested a (problematic) alliance between victims of anti-Semitism and Islamophobia, in this book the link is used to suggest that Islam appears in contemporary Europe as the new fascism. In the new focus on veiling practices in Europe, two metaphors for violence, which might often be considered specifically European through association with Christianity or with the Holocaust, are ironically used to produce Europe's outside. The ways in which this particular image of Muslim woman as victim of Muslim violence is shot through with Christian and European imagery reveal the importance of Christianity in the ordering of public space even in an increasingly secular Europe.

The feminist magazine, *EMMA*, for which Schwarzer was the longtime editor-in-chief, , also reflects this shift—articles that had focused on Islam before the 1990s address women primarily outside Germany; during the 1990s, the situations in countries such as Iran, Afghanistan, and Algeria were used to make extrapolations about the lives of Muslim women in Germany, whereas in the 2000s, articles demonstrate an increasing fear of the Islamization of Europe (see, for example, Schwarzer, "Kein Kopftuch in der Schule!").

Many of these articles have been reprinted in Schwarzer's 2010 edited volume, *Die große Verschleierung. Für Integration, Gegen Islamismus* [The Great Veiling: For Integration, Against Islamism]. Essays in this book include testimonials from converts from Islam, from women who stopped wearing the headscarf, as well as essays in support of bans on face veiling (often termed "burqa bans" although they apply to the niqab and other forms of face veiling as well). The shift from a focus on Islam "outside" versus Islam within Europe can be attributed to a growing awareness of Germany as a receiving country of migration and the desire to consolidate "German" identity in the wake of unification and in the face of migration. Yet a number of other factors have dovetailed with those events to contribute to the shift in focus. Especially since 1985, women belonging to minority populations that are primarily Muslim (although they may not identify as religious) have been struggling for recognition as active subjects in German society, a struggle which was, however, partially obscured in public perception by the events surrounding reunification. These activists have found renewed impetus in recent years bytaking advantage of the ease of online organizing to form new communties (I. M. Brown 446–450). The debates in France (beginning in 1989) around the place of headscarves in public schools served as an additional trigger for the German headscarf debates (see, for example Spies 637–640).[4] Furthermore, while 9/11 certainly contributed to the visibility of and the consolidation of anti-Muslim sentiments in Europe (Eley 160; 177), the coverage in the press suggests that the murder of Theo van Gogh and the Madrid bombings of 2004 intensified fears of the headscarf much more significantly than 9/11.

Nevertheless, there have also been attempts for decades to reduce the power of the headscarf as a marker of cultural difference. One strategy entailed comparisons to Western traditions of headcovering, a strategy that met with resistance. On the Left in particular, such comparisons generated fear that the economic issues impacting immigrant groups were being ignored. The history of a traveling exhibit on headscarves is illustrative. In 1985, a weekend seminar entitled "Rassismus und kulturelle Identität—Zur Entstehung und Wirkungsweise von Ausländerfeindlichkeit und Rassimus" [Racism and Cultural Identity—On the Emergence and Effects of Xenophobia and Racism] was held; this seminar eventually led to the collection of essays entitled *Die Schwierigkeit, nicht rassistisch zu sein* [The Difficulty of Not Being Racist] (Kalpaka and Räthzel). During the seminar, Meral Akkent presented on headscarf practices among rural German and Turkish women (Akkent 24) in an attempt to spur discussion of the headscarf that would go beyond simplified notions of "cultural difference" by showing that traditions of headcovering existed in German culture as well. Comments following the presentation reveal fears that the presenter, Meral Akkent, was essentializing cultures while ignoring class differences; and furthermore, that fighting racism by claiming that we are all "the same" could lead to a dangerous imposition of the dominant culture (Akkent 24–25): "I find it dangerous, when one argues against racism and xenophobia by saying that we are all quite similar and have much in common" (qtd. in Kalpaka and Räthzel 24).

Together with others Akkent developed a museum exhibit that was often updated and which then led to the publication of two exhibit catalogues: a 1987 catalogue published bilingually in Turkish and German, entitled *Das Kopftuch-Başörtü* [The Headscarf], and the 1999 *Kopftuchkulturen* [Headscarf Cultures]. While the 1987 catalogue contains images with very little critical contextualizing (Akkent and Franger), the 1999 catalogue shows a radical development (Akkent et al.) that seems to respond to many of the criticisms of the 1985 conference presentation. Beyond expanding the exhibit to include images from all over the world, it also includes critical articles by Gaby Franger, Yasemin Karakaşoğlu-Aydın, Helma Lutz, and Dilek Zaptçıoğlu that seek to frame these visual representations with a discussion of the implications of the Ludin case. This suggests that a history of critical approaches to headscarf discourses emerged as early as the mid 1990s. Because Ludin's case had entered the courts, it was at this point that the political implications of discussions around the headscarf had become particularly important for this exhibit's creators. Zaptçıoğlu's article in this anthology, for example, discusses the headscarf debates in Turkey, pointing out the difficulties many people face in believing that women take the headscarf of their own accord—and the questions raised by this conflict: rethinkings of democracy and modernity, the place of secularism, and the difficulties of thinking a public place for religion (Zaptçıoğlu 154). Unfortunately, this collection was rarely cited in larger discussions of the case.[5]

In the early 2000s, new ethnographic studies demonstrated that a new generation of German-speaking "Neo-Muslimas," primarily of Turkish and Moroccan heritage, had resulted from a "re-islamization" process in the second generation of migrants (Nökel, "Migration" 261). These women wear a hijab while vehemently rejecting full veiling (Nökel, "Migration" 265). Their approach to wearing the hijab is linked to a desire for class mobility (Nökel, "Migration" 264): with gains in education, in their minds, come the ability to better implement moral practices that they view as important to Islam. In turn, gender roles are redefined in more egalitarian ways based on rights that they see as guaranteed within Islam (Nökel, "Migration" 267–268). Furthermore, new Islamic feminist organizations in Germany have begun to provide an outlet for expressing a feminist Islamic positioning that challenges both the media discourse of the oppressed Muslim woman as well as conservative discourses within some Muslim groups, which would limit the public activity of Muslim women (Gamper 119–281).

From Cleaning Woman to Educated Threat:
Headscarves in Popular Print Media

The figure of the covered immigrant woman capturing the imagination of the German public and dominating discussions of immigration in Germany over the last four decades has evolved significantly. The cleaning woman, the *Kopftuchfrau* [headscarf woman], of the 1970s and the 1980s was a figure—less threatening and thus less present—that focused on national, class, and educational difference to locate immigrant culture in a rural, traditional, distant past. In 1980, for example, a *Spiegel* story addressed neo-Nazi attacks on Turkish immigrants. Images accompanying the story included those of a belly dancer, a woman in niqab, and women dressed in more rural clothing, with headscarves tied loosely ("Raus mit dem Volk"). This image reflects a larger tendency for dominant representations of the time to locate "cultural" difference in class and educational difference (Westphal 20–24), though religion exists side by side (Pinn and Wehner 39; Huth-Hildebrandt, *Das Bild* 46). The juxtaposition of the rural woman wearing a headscarf to the bared body of the belly dancer bears clear affinities with the longer trajectory of Orientalized representations of Muslim women. Nevertheless, these images portray the headscarf itself in a relatively normalized way—they do not explicitly portray threat or danger nor are the women necessarily represented as marginalized or poorly treated in any way. Indeed, the only sense of danger is presented by the words of a Neo-Nazi group (quoted in the article and in the caption of a street scene with women dressed in more rural clothing): "We will teach the rabble to fear us."

Gradually, however, and in particular after unification, media representations of immigrant women in Germany shifted to emphasize cultural difference, especially cultural difference located in Islam. The 1997 cover of *Der Spiegel* marks the contradictory aspects of this transition. The difference located in a nation remains at the forefront and is marked by a girl who appears to be angrily shouting and carrying the Turkish flag. The bulging veins in her neck suggest rage. However, her figure is contrasted with the quiet "Kopftuchmädchen" (headscarf girls) sitting in the background. These passive girls, indoctrinated into Islam, are actually becoming the dominant image at this point in time, though they recede into the background for this cover. They are accompanied by their dangerous, armed brothers, whose violence is manifested in the weapons they carry, their stance, and their facial expressions. The headline

"Germans and Foreigners: Dangerously Different: The Failure of Multicultural Society" suggests that the emerging cultural difference inherent in Islam also marks the failure of multiculturalism; an association that will often be repeated in the coming decade. This failure is in turn indirectly attributed here to the upcoming generations of passive girls and oppressive boys.

Hijab in the German Courts

Ludin's suit for placement as a public schoolteacher has dramatically increased the public attention to the position of Muslim women in Germany even as it has elicited longstanding stereotypes about Islam and women. Germany's incarnation of headscarf debates chronologically roughly parallels the emergence of France's second "affair of the veil" in the mid 1990s.[6] However, several relatively unknown cases preceded Ludin's in the German court system. A 1989 case granted an Iranian citizen German citizenship despite the fact that Iran refused to release him from citizenship. Though his wife had nothing to do with the court case, it was introduced in a legal journal with the heading, "German Law Does Not Entitle an Iranian Applicant for Citizenship to Have His Wife Photographed with a Chador against Her Will for the Iranian Authorities" (VG Berlin 108). However, in 2000 a Bavarian decision gave German police the right to force Iranian women to don a headscarf for Iranian passport photos, which was necessary to enable deportation (BayVGH; Janz and Rademacher). Here, the justification was that a headscarf is not a universally religious symbol and that the state was thus not enforcing a religious practice by forcing the women to wear headscarves. Whereas violence is represented as a part of Islam in the first case, in the second, where force issues from the German state, the topic is avoided.[7]

Fereshta Ludin and the Headscarf Debates

In a 1997 contribution to the Berlin daily the *taz*, Turkish German journalist, novelist, and children's book author Dilek Zaptçıoğlu was prompted by the parliamentary debates initiated by the *Republikaner* to comment on Ludin's case as an example of a growing fear of upwardly mobile Muslim women. Zaptçıoğlu points out that women wearing headscarves are often rejected in secretarial, sales, and other white-collar professions. In contrast, in the factories "nearly all women workers of Muslim faith wear a headscarf, the convoys of cleaning women generally have covered heads as well. Their employers not only accept this, but even welcome this for hygienic reasons" (Zaptçıoğlu "Kopftuchdebatte" 9). Zaptçıoğlu's comments may have been intended tongue in cheek, but they effectively reveal what the focus on cultural difference has obscured: the role of immigrant women in the German labor force and the fact that their labor in undesired occupations has often enabled upward mobility for ethnic German women (Rommelspacher 218).

In 1997 Ludin, who had worn a headscarf throughout her education, had completed the necessary coursework for a career as a teacher and was ready to be placed in a supervised probationary teaching position (*Referendariat*). The right-wing party *Republikaner*, which at that time had seats in the Baden-Württemberg parliament, initiated a parliamentary debate in which they argued that the Christian foundations of the Baden-Württemberg constitution must be honored. In particular, they called attention to the passage: "Youth are to be raised in the fear of God [...] Children will be raised on the basis of Christian and Western educational and cultural values" (Landtag von Baden-Württemberg 1632). The public had already been sensitized to this issue by the two waves of French debate widely covered in the German press.

Because the state has a monopoly on teacher training and education, Ludin was placed (Landtag von Baden-Württemberg, *Drucksache 12/1140* 2). Ludin successfully completed her time as a probationary teacher and received good grades and positive feedback. No parental complaints were lodged against her (Schmitz; Michael 258). However, after the completion of her probationary teaching period, Ludin was barred from placement as a public schoolteacher. Then Baden-Württemberg minister of culture, Annette Schavan, reasoned that the wearing of the headscarf was controversial even within Islam and was not clearly required by the Koran. Thus its wearing must be an inherently political symbol. Despite its designation as a political symbol, Schavan further considered that the headscarf could endanger students' freedom from religious participation (*Pressemitteilung Nr. 119/98*). Her decision evinces the overlapping, contradictory understandings of Islam, politics, and culture.

Ludin sued for the right to be placed as a public teacher, arguing that her headscarf was a personal decision, an article of clothing worn for religious reasons but without a desire to missionize for Islam. The lower courts finding against Ludin cited state neutrality, Ludin's inability to fulfill her duties as a civil servant, and the "visibility" and "demonstrative character" of the headscarf, regardless of her intentions (VGH Mannheim 2903; VG Stuttgart 960). The conflict between Ludin's freedom of religion and Baden-Württemberg's rootedness in Christian values, said the Baden Württemberg Administrative Court, must necessarily be resolved to Ludin's disadvantage to affirm Christianity's place in the provincial constitution, which is one of a relationship "only to cultural and educational influence, not to specific religious realities" (VGH Mannheim). In September 2003 the Federal Constitutional Court decided in favor of Ludin (5 to 3), but on the basis of a lack of existing laws in the individual Bundesländer that regulated the relationship between Church and State in the classroom (BVerfG, *2 BvR 1436/02 vom 3.6.2003*).

The Federal Constitutional Court decision explicitly states that a nondiscriminatory law that treats all religions equally and bans the headscarf could be constitutional. In the wake of this decision, eight provinces passed headscarf bans. Note, however, that many headscarf bans have explicitly banned Islamic symbols and permitted Christian symbols, whereas others are implicitly interpreted to permit Christian and Judaic symbols. Berlin is the only province to pass a law explicitly banning *all* religious symbols in the classroom. Ludin challenged the constitutionality of the Baden-Württemberg law but lost before the Federal Administrative Court in June 2004. At this point, Ludlin chose to end her battle in the courts rather than to pursue her case back to the Federal Constitutional Court. There was discussion about the European Commission reviewing the German laws for adherence to EU antidiscrimination guidelines, but this has not been pursued, possibly because of the assumption that because French, Turkish, and Swiss headscarf bans have been declared acceptable by the European Court of Human Rights (not an EU institution but a COE institution), the decision in this case would also support the German bans.

The Visual Constitution of European Secularism

The Ludin decision must be understood in the context of a particular manifestation of secularism in Germany that is understood as both specific to Germany and as a logical consequence of the European Enlightenment. Regardless of the position taken vis-a-vis a headscarf ban by legal scholars or court decisions, there is a general agreement that the form of secularism practiced in France, often designated laïcité, is not appropriate to Germany. Laïcité is understood as resulting in the radical expulsion of all religious symbols from the public sphere, particularly public space that is specifically designated as the space of the State. Laïcité is thought to be contrary both to the tradition of German secularism and to Article 4 of the German constitution (Debus 439; Michael 256; BVerfG, *2 BvR 1436/02 Vom 27.9.2003*; Böckenförde 726). Thus far, this perceived difference has prevented any bans against German *students* wearing the headscarf in the classroom. Nevertheless, although these differences are generally framed as *national* differences, the dominant discussions in the headscarf case are focused on the preservation of *European* culture and values.

Opinions diverge radically on the implications of this tradition for the headscarf ban for teachers. A number of scholars have suggested several bases for subjecting Islam to a more restricted role in public space than Christianity. Stefan Mückl argued that Islam is on the "offensive" whereas Christianity is on the "defensive," given decreasingly active participation in Christianity, which requires that the role of religion in the public sphere be rethought (Mückl 106). Mückl also saw secularism as fundamentally absent from the tradition of Islam, thus ignoring Turkey's secularist tradition (Mückl 119). Others argued that the Christian basis for Baden-Württemberg's constitution, or even for Germany's constitution, meant that Islam would necessarily be subjected to a more restricted role in German society (VG Stuttgart 961). Similarly, the *Republikaner* initiated the parliamentary debate on the basis of Baden-Württemberg's provincial constitution, which states, "Youth are to be raised in the fear of God [...] Children will be raised on the basis of Christian and Western educational and cultural values" (Landtag von Baden-Württemberg, *Plenarprotokoll 12/23 20.03.97*).

Often this more restricted position for Islam is legitimated with the assumption that Christianity can be understood as a secular cultural heritage rather than as a religion, whereas Islam never can be. In an odd shift from the Enlightenment trope of overcoming the irrationality of religion with rational reason, Christianity has now become the rational reason that can combat the irrationality of Islam. Islam is inherently radical and incapable of being part of democratic society for some (Hillgruber 538). Others stated the difference less strongly but also constructed Christianity as secular against an unavoidably religious Islam. This became obvious when courts and legal scholars sought to legitimate the existence of crucifixes in the schools while simultaneously denying Muslim symbols. The dissenting opinion in the Federal Constitutional Court decision, for example, stated:

> Children associate little with the mere everyday object on the wall, which demonstrates no immediate relationship to a concrete person or to life circumstances [Lebenssachverhalt]. The crucifix is so much—beyond its religious meaning—a general cultural symbol for a culture which is rooted firmly in values drawn from Jewish and Christian sources. (BVerfG, *2 BvR 1436/02 vom 3.6.2003* Para. 113)

In the dissenting opinion, then, the presumption is that the crucifix can stand for a wider culture because it belongs to the cultural representations of Christianity, whereas the headscarf, in its association with Islam, can only be read as a religious symbol.

This attitude is reflected in several headscarf bans that have explicitly banned Islamic symbols and permitted Christian symbols. The Baden-Württemberg law cited in the epigraph to this chapter codifies a particular definition of Christian and Western as by definition being unable to infringe on individual human rights or on the principles of liberal democracy. Through the headscarf, in contrast, Islam is assumed not only to be capable of infringing on basic human rights but also likely to do so. This position is supported by some legal scholars as well, who argue that the headscarf clearly demonstrates an inability to be neutral and to maintain a necessary distance from religion (Goerlich, "Distanz" 2930–2931), or an inability to fulfill the responsibility of enabling the fundamental rights of others (Halfmann 868).

This language of Christianity is supported on a federal level by the final decision in the Ludin case, the decision by the Federal Administrative Court in response to Ludin's challenge of the Baden-Württemberg headscarf law (again, to be clear, the case was never brought back before the Federal Constitutional Court). The decision states that the Baden-Württemberg ban's use of the term "Christianity" conflicts neither with the federal constitutional mandate for religious neutrality nor with the right to both positive and negative freedom of religion. The term "Christianity" in the headscarf ban

> refers to—regardless of its origins issuing from the realm of religion—a set of values [*Wertewelt*] separated from religious content that issues from the tradition of Christian—Western culture, a set of values that is the recognizable foundation of the Basic Law, and that is valid regardless of its religious foundations. The conception of the inalienable and inviolable right to human dignity (Article 1 of the Basic Law), of the general right of free action (Article 2), of the equality of all people and genders (Article 3), and of the freedom of religion including the negative freedom of religion (Article 4), all belong to this term [Christianity]. Furthermore, this term [Christianity] includes humane values such as the willingness to help, altruism for and general consideration of others, as well as solidarity with those who are weaker. The mandate to propagate Christian educational and cultural values thus confers upon the school neither the responsibility nor the right to disseminate particular theological beliefs but rather evokes values that every civil servant who stands on the foundation of the Basic Law can unreservedly agree to, independent of his or her religious convictions (BVerwG, "BVerwG 2 C 45.03").

It is worth noting that even the notion of a "Judeo-Christian" cultural world, which has often been opposed to Islam, has disappeared here. The language of the decision clearly constructs a specifically Christian tradition that unquestionably supports human rights, whereas other traditions are an implied threat to Christian humanism. Furthermore, the court decision implies that the language of humanism and human rights is adequately named by the descriptor "Christian." The covered Muslim body thus comes to stand in for a larger potential Muslim threat to human dignity, which is protected by Christianity.

The content of the relationship between the body of the Muslim woman and European secularism is thus deeply contradictory. Ludin's body is paradoxically produced at times as not Christian enough to support state neutrality, given the foundation of the nation on Judeo-Christian traditions. More frequently, however, the conflict is produced in terms of the religious Muslim body and the abstract/secular/cultural nature of Christianity. Throughout the Ludin case, the covering or revealing of her body became evidence of her ability to participate in a modern, enlightened German/European society as evidenced by its relationship to European secularism and tolerance. As is clear from the language of the Baden-Württemberg ban and the court decision that upholds it, many discussions around this case, particularly those in support of headscarf bans, have constructed Christian and Western cultures as being supportive per se of freedoms and the liberal democratic order. Their relationship to secularism, then, does not need to be examined as, by definition, they support secularism (and as I discuss below, European tolerance), whereas Islam is considered necessarily and inherently antagonistic to secularism.

The presumption that Islam necessarily occupies a more restricted place in German society elicited several dissenting arguments. The Federal Constitutional Court decision itself explicitly states that only a nondiscriminatory law that treats all religions equally can be considered constitutional. That same decision argues that neutrality partly lies in being open to other religions. A lower-court decision regarding a separate headscarf case in the province of Lower Saxony drew on the notion of European humanism to come to the conclusion that European tradition demands respect for Islam and Judaism, a respect that must also be demonstrated in mutual expressions of tolerance (VG Lüneburg). Consequently, according to this lower court, a teacher may not be prohibited from teaching merely because she is wearing a headscarf, though any form of missionizing may lead to her dismissal. This 2000 decision was overturned by an upper provincial court in 2001 (OVG Lüneburg).

Many legal scholars have also been quite critical of the headscarf bans and the presumption that Islam should be subject to greater restrictions than Christianity. Anne Debus, for example, suggested early on that notions of neutrality are actually being used to privilege Christianity (Debus 442), whereas others argued that there cannot be a hierarchy of religious freedoms—indeed, that the privileging of Christian symbols and language is incompatible with the constitution (Janz and Rademacher 444), and can only be explained by xenophobia (Rux 1542) or by a lack of understanding of the fundamental openness of the German state to other religions and worldviews (Treibel 626–627).

The Battle between Tolerance and Condemnation of Violence

Despite these opposing views, the current prevailing legal opinions have ultimately framed the discussions of secularism as a "conflict of cultures" that reveals the "true danger" of Islam in Europe (Bader 365; Bertrams 2254; BVerwG, "Die Einstellung als Lehrerin an Grund- und Hauptschulen im Beamtenverhältnis" 2254; Goerlich, "Distanz" 2032–2034; Morlok and Krüper 2021; Schöbener 186), and one that occurs because immigrants do not arrive from "secular countries" (Häußler 36)—Germany is suffering from the threat of "foreign religiosity" (Kerscher).

In the context of the headscarf debate, the notion of the clash of cultures became a debate about tolerance with two major questions: (1) What decision would demonstrate "European tolerance" vis-a-vis an intolerant Islam?; and (2) How much tolerance is too much? Both these questions posit tolerance in potential conflict with peace, partly because of the violence of Islam. Ludin embodies the cultural opposite of emancipation because the headscarf reveals Islam's tendency toward violence (Reimer 1; Henkel-Waidhofer; Behr), as well as cultural exclusion (Waidhofer). Consider, for example, the parliamentary debate that preceded the Baden-Württemberg headscarf ban. Members of the Center-Left SPD greeted the debate as a necessary corrective to the excessive tolerance of the past; "especially we [SPD members] must help those girl students who cannot resist indoctrination and influence by fundamentalists" (*Plenarprotokoll 13/62* 4395). The headscarf is linked to a host of problems that are viewed as endemic to Muslim families, particularly forced marriages (*Plenarprotokoll 13/62* 4395). Indeed, Ludin's own claim to tolerance toward those of other religions or toward Muslim women who do not wear hijab is considered irrelevant (VG Stuttgart 960–961); because she insists on the headscarf, she demonstrates the inability to be tolerant (Goerlich, "Distanz") toward the majority.

This tendency toward violence is juxtaposed with the inherent tolerance of Europe. The dissenting opinion in the Federal Constitutional Court decision argues:

> The crucifix is so much—beyond its religious meaning—a general cultural symbol for a culture which is rooted firmly in values drawn from Jewish and Christian sources, yet is open and has become tolerant through rich but also tragic [leidvoll] historical experience. (BVerfG, *2 BvR 1436/02*)

This passage illustrates a larger tendency to assume that Christianity (sometimes expressed as Judeo-Christian culture) is inherently more capable of tolerance than Islam. The latter phrase stands out from other such representations, however, in a curious way. The word used for tragic, *"leidvoll,"* literally means full of suffering. The evocation of "leidvoll" historical experience seems to suggest a reference to the history of fascism and the Holocaust. Yet the tenor of the sentence seems to almost position a shared national history of suffering without reference to the problematics of a heritage of antisemitism and racism. Thus, in a strange slippage, Europe itself has become the historical victim of violence, whereas European Jewish culture and experience can be contained under the symbol of the cross.

Tolerance, thus, is constructed as uniquely Christian: "Tolerance of those who think differently is a particular cultural marker of Christianity" (VGH Mannheim 2901). The converse position is often taken as well: permitting the headscarf would evidence

Christian tolerance: "Shouldn't this headscarf, the symbol of a supposedly repressive religion, be banned in the name of progress? Or wouldn't it be precisely an exemplary sign of Western tolerance to permit the headscarf?" (Bednarz 112).

Although the assumption of Muslim intolerance ultimately prevails in the courts, this position is also contested by legal scholars. Early in the headscarf debates, Debus argued that a mutual expectation of tolerance is fundamental to a "tolerance principle" that is a basic right, even in education (Debus 436–437). Indeed, the state, through public education, is responsible for the promotion of "friendly and tolerant living together" (Debus 437). The problem with a headscarf ban for Debus is that it would be a tolerance that no longer considers responsible behavior of the majority group vis-a-vis a minority group but, rather, a tolerance that expects the minority to "silently suffer" the majority group's free and unhindered self-fulfillment and development. The idea that it is in the first instance the minority group's responsibility to practice tolerance vis-a-vis a majority group is, ultimately, a fundamental destruction of the notion of tolerance (Debus, "Machen Kleider" 1357–1358). A lower court decision in Lower Saxony also demands respect for other religions as part of the mandate of tolerance and as a logical consequence of European Humanism (VG Lüneburg).

Tolerance, however, gives way to a notion of protecting "religious peace" by limiting visual representations of Islam. The wearing of the headscarf is seen to be a threat to the "peaceful coexistence of differing religious views and worldviews," one that will necessarily evoke protests and conflict with parents (VGH Mannheim 2904; further, see OVG Lüneburg; Mückl 127; BVerfG, *2 BvR 911/03 Vom 27.9.2003*—dissenting opinion). The Federal Constitutional Court, alternatively, clearly stated that it is unconstitutional to anticipate such conflicts, though certainly an abstract possibility for conflicts may exist (BVerfG, *2 BvR 1436/02*). As one legal scholar put it, given the lack of conflict during the probationary teaching period, it is clear that pluralism doesn't necessarily disturb the peace (Michael 258).

Feminist responses to the headscarf debates have been divided. In the case of Fereshta Ludin, responses were dominated by Alice

Schwarzer, who even today continues to be the public face of German feminism—to the frustration of many feminists. Furthermore, a few women of Turkish heritage who reject Islam and argue that it is fundamentally incompatible with women's rights also became visible in the headscarf discussions—several of them, including Kelek and Ateş, went on to write bestselling memoirs. The insistence on incompatibility with women's rights or a modern life belies research that suggests that many women who choose the headscarf also insist on women's autonomy in work, education, and relationships (Nökel, *Die Töchter*).

Public Sphere and Public Space: Visualities

The case provides us with a unique way of examining the public sphere as visually constituted. Ludin's fight in the courts constitutes an attempt to gain entry into a special space of citizenship production, namely that of the public schools. This is a double participation in a democratic public—by claiming rights through the courts and educating students into democratic citizenship. Ludin's action in the courts further propels her temporarily into the public sphere, that discursive space of social interaction through which politics can be formed. However, the discussions in the courts and the legal realm ultimately expel her from both spaces. That expulsion is linked to the visibility of the scarf, which is a "thorn in the eye...that can never be normalized" (Morlok and Krüper 1021). As argued before the Federal Constitutional Court, the headscarf is "provocative"[8] and capable of endangering the "religious peace in society" (BVerfG, *2 BvR 1436/02 vom 3.6.2003* Paragraph 99). Thus the headscarf became both the grounds on which Ludin could access the public sphere and, given the importance of visuality to the public sphere, also the grounds by which she is removed from it. As the embodiment of the threat of violence and the marker of the Muslim woman's endangerment, the scarf thus becomes both a visible threat to peaceful coexistence as well as a reminder of Christianity's inherent tendency toward peace. The headscarved woman occupies a significant place in the public imagination, even in public space, but is unable to emerge as a European subject in the public sphere. Instead, she serves as the marker of a threat to foundational notions of that subject, predicated on the freedom and inviolability of the body.

This outcome of the Ludin case is well represented in the November 2004 *Spiegel* cover, "Allah's Daughters without Rights: Muslim Women in Germany". The female figure, depicted on the cover, is in all black, including a long coat and headscarf; her face is hidden from the viewer, not by the veil, but because the head is bowed and turned slightly away from the camera. The title points to Muslim women as "in Germany," not as Germans. The white background is also suggestive. While the faded windows of the background may be intended to suggest the transparency and openness of democratic society, they stand in such stark contrast to the mysterious black figure that one is also reminded of the ways in which Muslims are racialized. The specificity of the black body is contrasted to the abstract white background. The title could be ambiguous—presumably such a title could also address how the lives of Muslim women are circumscribed by their Othering within German society. However, the fact that the title is in green, which is perceived as the color of Islam, already points to the tone of the cover stories inside: in them, the rights of Muslim women have been repressed by their families and by Islam itself, not in any way by German society or the German state (Schießl and C. Schmidt; Akyün and Smoltczyk).

Thus, with women wearing hijab being effectively removed from the public sphere, even as their image is circulated so widely in public space, the image of such women can again be unproblematically used to invoke the violence of Islam against women in the family. This location of violence within the Muslim family functions in a twofold way: (1) to limit the emergence of the Muslim subject to the public sphere via relocation to the private sphere of the family; and (2) to obscure the forms of racism that may be preventing the emergence of immigrant woman as political subject. Accusations of racism are merely dismissed by many, including Schwarzer, or returned with the response that it is racist to "tolerate" other cultures when they are misogynist and against human rights (Schießl and C. Schmidt). A typical dismissal occurs in response to an open letter published by 60 migration researchers, which called for a rethinking of the stereotypes that inform the politics of integration. Mark Terkessidis, a writer and antiracist activist, is dismissed by Schwarzer as "one of those postmodern, self-referential, pseudo-radical intellectuals, who have a lot to do with their own self-representation and little to do with comprehension of the world" (Schwarzer, "Eine Offene Antwort an '60 Migrationsforscher'" 160).

The Murder of Marwa el-Sherbini

In it is in this context, then, of a public increasingly hostile to visible symbols of Islam, that el-Sherbini's murder occurs in 2009. Indeed, just days before the murder, French prime minister Nicholas Sarkozy had given a major policy speech denouncing the wearing of face veils in public. El-Sherbini was murdered by Alex Wiens in a Dresden courtroom, where his appeal to a conviction for xenophobically motivated hate speech had just been heard. Because Wiens continued to make racist comments in the courtroom, arguing that Muslims had no right to be in Europe, el-Sherbini was told that her testimony was unnecessary. She nevertheless insisted on taking the stand. After her testimony, Wiens removed a knife from his bag and stabbed her repeatedly. When el-Sherbini's husband, Elvi Ali Okaz, struggled with Wiens, he was shot by a policeman who had just entered the courtroom and who had mistaken Okaz for the perpetrator.

Whereas the murder quickly gained attention in Egypt, and the German Central Council of Jews as well as the German Central Council of Muslims both gave public statements condemning the crime, federal and local officials were slow to react publicly to the murder. By the time German officials and media did respond, el-Sherbini was being referred to as a "hijab-martyr" in the Islamic world and her death acknowledged as the first Islamophobic murder in Germany.

While the headscarf was not specifically mentioned in the complaint against Wiens, the fact that el-Sherbini wore hijab was perceived to be provocation both for the verbal attack as well as for the murder. Her murder was seen internationally as indicative of a growing German and European Islamophobia; indeed, protests in Iran used the slogans "Down with Germany" and "Down with European Racists" ("Murder"; Connolly and Shenker; Windfuhr and

Zand; "Afghan Daily"; Cerha; "Egyptian Fury"; "Iranians Protest"; al-Aswany). Also widely reported were the contradictory reactions of el-Sherbini's family: the father calling for an end to all forms of hate, the brother swearing vengeance (Cerha). As this reaction widened to the US and UK press, increasing pressure was put on German media and government officials to respond to the crime; seven days after the murder stories began appearing.

Eventually, Wiens was convicted of murder. All the court officials as well as the police officer who shot Okaz were cleared of any wrongdoing. In 2010, media researcher Sabine Schiffer was charged with slander and fined €6000.00 or two months' imprisonment because she stated in an interview that the mistaken shooting of the victim's husband by a police officer must be examined for possible racist connections (upon appeal, these charges were dropped).

The press coverage and ongoing discussions about el-Sherbini's death reveal obvious ways in which integration debates in Germany have often been intensely gendered, often portraying the German state, supported by white German feminists, as the patronizing protector of the Muslim woman. (The debate among Turkish heritage communities has been much more complex, which has been additionally inflected by the complicated debates about Turkish secularism). This act of violence does not follow the typical pattern of media stories, films, and bestsellers in which a Muslim woman escapes the violence of her Muslim oppressor by rejecting her heritage and wholeheartedly embracing liberal German democracy. The danger that the Sherbini case reveals is one relocated outside Europe, to the anti-European sentiment of the so-called Muslim world. The reduction of her case to an example of martyrdom abroad, and to a woman insufficiently protected by the German state in German coverage, repress her participation in German democracy and limit the impact her story might have in the public sphere.

Racist Germany?

When the media and government officials began to respond, it was often to point out why this case does NOT indicate German racism. One Dresden official even claimed that, clearly, Dresden was not racist since he had a Korean wife (W. Schmidt 5). The charges brought against media researcher Schiffer in 2010 for suggesting that racism might have led to the shooting of el-Sherbini's husband show an aversion to recognizing institutionalized racism—racism as an individual motivation, alternatively, can be easily dismissed. When the crime is labeled xenophobic, racist, or Islamophobic in motivation, it is seen as a rare crime committed by a fanatic individual (Dernbach). Potential violence, on the other hand, threatens from without in the imagination of masses of Muslim protestors.

These stories drew connections from el-Sherbini's murder to the Muhammad cartoons that appeared in Denmark in 2006, and the ensuing international protests (Dernbach, "Marwa S"; "Der Zorn der Muslime"). Ludin's case, alternatively, rarely emerges. This suggests that a link was conceptually made to other forms of Muslim protest that were often seen as expressions of unreasonable and dangerous Muslim anger. In this way el-Sherbini's story could be appropriated for a context that emphasized the danger of Muslim violence. At the same time, by ignoring the connections to the larger representations of headscarves in Germany, considerations of forms of racism are effectively avoided. Affinities to the response to the cartoon affair, however, reveal another similarity. As Geoff Eley points out about a number of contemporary debates surrounding Islam in Europe, including the cartoon affair, "Few seem willing to acknowledge just how powerfully ideas about race are defining the ground from which Europeans are now able to respond to such events" (Eley 175).

This "trouble with race" marks the response to el-Sherbini's murder in troubling ways in the representations of Wiens's ethnic background. In many cases the media emphasized that Wiens was a so-called *Russlanddeutscher* (a Russian of German heritage). Under Germany's historical policy of privileging "blood" in immigration to Germany, Russians of German heritage were for some time welcomed as preferable immigrants. However, in response to el-Sherbini's murder, Wiens is excluded from the German national and ethnic community on the basis of his status as an immigrant. In the initial stories about el-Sherbini, there was an anticipation of a discovery that Wiens's Islamophobia had been "pre-programmed" during his time in Russia (Heine). Repeatedly, commenters asserted that Germany is not Islamophobic and that Wiens's emigration from Russia contradicts accusations of a German Islamophobia: "What does this uprooted man have to do with us Germans?" (Krause-Burger). Indeed, the murder supposedly tells us "as much about the dominant Islamophobia in Russia as about xenophobia in Germany" (Avenarius). One of the few stories to actually address the impacts of this murder for debates on multiculturalism in Germany, published in the *Süddeutsche Zeitung*, drew parallels to the L.A. riots and suggested that el-Sherbini's murder was the consequence of conflict between two "niche cultures" (Kreye). This desire to locate the roots of violence outside "German" culture is reinforced by an absence. The *Russlanddeutscher*, once understood as "German" enough to be a more desirable immigrant, is now conveniently "not German" and is unproblematically referred to as a *Russlanddeutscher* to emphasize his difference from Germanness. This can cover up the racialized understandings of Germanness that initially led to a notion of the *Russlanddeutscher*.[9] Only rarely did stories approach this from a critical perspective, such as a report in the Left daily *die taz* that was critical of the desire to simply move on and to attribute Wiens's act to his Russian upbringing as "Russians are always quick to turn to the knife" (W. Schmidt).

Certainly, in this case it is important to acknowledge where the German legal system was working against racist speech. This suggests that a German secularism *has* emerged in which a subject might be marked by difference and yet be able to claim some rights under German law. The proper functioning of the legal system, however, does not serve as evidence that racism or Islamophobia is absent. When one considers el-Sherbini's murder and the responses to it in comparison to the ongoing and extensive discussions about the headscarf debates, it becomes obvious that the focus on the headscarf can indeed function to obscure forces of discrimination in German society. Although el-Sherbini—in her death—emerged briefly into the public sphere, in the end, the politics most effectively debated and addressed by discussions of her death dealt with increasing security in the courtroom, not with how to combat forms of racialization and discrimination in Germany.

Furthermore, the media coverage of el-Sherbini's death reveals issues that would seem to call for a feminist response and to enable a conceptualization of antiracist feminism; yet, feminist responses have been largely absent. For example, most initial press coverage states that Wiens also called el-Sherbini an Islamist whore. According to Steffen Winter, who was a rare journalist to actually examine el-Sherbini's complaint and testimony, she denied this claim (S. Winter). She brought her complaint to reject her positioning within German society as a terrorist and Islamist. Although she may have attempted to depoliticize the headscarf and degender her claims to human rights, the repeated circulation of a notion of an "Islamist whore" suggests the power that the sexualization of the Muslim woman's body continues to have in German discussions of integration.

Whereas accusations of Islamophobia or racism are firmly rebuffed, many were willing to entertain the possibility that security may be lax in German courtrooms ("Bluttat"). An investigation was opened into the possibility that the presiding judge inadequately provided for el-Sherbini's security in the courtroom, though no charges were brought. Necla Kelek, an outspoken proponent for a headscarf ban, is also one of the few to mention Sherbini in the context of headscarf bans. Kelek argues that the headscarf is necessarily oppressive to women but sees el-Sherbini as the victim of the court's inability to protect (Kelek, "Ein Verstoß gegen die Menschenwürde!" 98–99). The discourse of security removes el-Sherbini from her active participation in German democracy through claiming antidiscrimination protection and testifying at the trial. Instead, el-Sherbini is located as the recipient of physical protection at the hands of the court, as paternalistic representative of the state.

Reconfiguring the Public Sphere?

One must, however, consider the ways in which discussions in the wake of el-Sherbini's murder may be functioning to reconfigure the public sphere, or at least to begin that reconfiguration. Although it was an argument rarely attended to in the press, Stephen Kramer, the general secretary of the Central Council of Jews, responded much earlier to the murder than did government officials or most media outlets. He argued that attacks based on race, religion, or nationality are fundamentally attacks on democracy itself (Kramer). Kramer's remarks evoke the potential for a secular democracy that does not regulate difference through a condescending tolerance. Instead, Kramer seeks to respond to the "largely unchecked hate propaganda against Muslims spread by everyone from marginal extremists right through to people at the centre of society" with the hard work of respect.

Journalist Hilal Sezgin also seeks to recognize and name racism as it emerges in discussions of el-Sherbini's death. She counters the claim that Egypt and Iran's accusations of Islamophobia or discrimination against Muslims are merely appropriations of el-Sherbini's death (Sezgin). Sezgin evades the reduction of racism to an individual act, reminding the public that it gains its significance in a specific context. She also criticizes the many voices arguing that if any country knows how to be self critical when it comes to racism and violence, it is Germany. Germany will demonstrate its maturity as a democracy, she argues, not by being insulted by claims of discrimination but by being disturbed and investigating whether such claims are true. She argues,

> The growth in Islamophobia in Germany means, for example, that a pattern has been established in our public speech that evokes specific images (veiled women, scenes of masses of raised behinds in prayer), ignores some questions ("Why doesn't Islam possess the same legal rights as the Churches?"), and privileges others ("Why have they still not learned any German?) This pattern classifies members of a population group through stereotypes, and allows the individuals to appear more as performing mouthpieces of their supposed "culture" than as individual actors with their own preferences and decisions. (Sezgin)

Sezgin's discussion suggests that Islamophobia functions specifically through the regulatory practices of secularism, which exclude Islam from the contracts that manage the relationship between Church and State, and represent the embodied practices of Islam as indicative of difference that can only exclude Islam from the community. Andreas Fanizadeh, in *Die Tageszeitung*, emphasizes that the reduction of this act to a question of Left versus Right also prevents everyday Germans from working to prevent racism (Fanizadeh). He further argues that whereas laws have improved for minorities living in Germany who are discovering more trust in German civil society, these improvements have come at the cost of increasing attempts to cut off further immigration. Fanizadeh thus imagines a civil society with active participation by those of immigrant heritage and suggests a politics using antiracism as a focal point rather than as an affiliation with a political party.

The Violence of the Headscarf

The delayed and brief attention to the el-Sherbini case indicates the effectiveness of the discourses around the headscarf debates. The headscarf can trigger an already existing set of discursive regimes that were solidified through the Ludin case, and which assume the totality of a successful tolerant secularism that has formed a nonviolent West. These regimes can build on a long history of Orientalist constructions that use the representation of the Muslim women's bodies to construct the enlightened West. However, in contrast to eighteenth- and nineteenth-century representations, the sexualized and erotic elements in the discourse of covering and revealing are greatly downplayed, whereas a discourse of danger and threat is amplified. Reference to the headscarf activates a tradition that has located the origins of violence—primarily as gendered violence—so firmly elsewhere, that Germany is successfully able to evade a discussion of forms of racialized violence within its own borders.

The ubiquitous presence of the headscarf thus does not entirely mean that the German public sphere is visually constituted. To the contrary, visuality itself becomes a way of marking a dangerous, threatening difference. Although the visual constitution of the subject constantly places the Muslim woman in public space, it also prevents her participation in a democratic public sphere. The subject of democracy remains abstracted and invisible but firmly "European." The field thus constituted can only partially represent the subject of democracy as wearing hijab; she is quickly appropriated both as victim and as threat of Muslim violence, or she disappears entirely from public view. She must be "enlightened" through European conquest, whereas critiques of Islamophobia themselves become associated with anti-Enlightenment ideals. In *Konkret*, a

Left magazine for politics and culture, this occurred in an October 2009 issue containing a discussion between two journalists. Kay Sokolowsky takes the position that although Islam, like any other religion, is certainly a valid object of critique, this critique has been appropriated by racists. Alex Feuerherdt argues that Islam should be understood per se as a reactionary, antimodern political ideology, not as a religion. Again, the veiled Muslim woman, who serves as the emblem for a debate about the relationship between Islam and modernity. She marks not only the limits of "tolerance" but also the limits of enlightened antiracism. The cover of the issue, published just months after el-Sherbini's death, draws on familiar tropes. While the most recent women in the press because of covering practices wore a headscarf, the image instead shows a woman wearing a niqab, a full body veil that covers the entire face except for the eyes. The article, featured above the other headlines in a more prominent font size, is entitled "Islamkritik: Zwischen Aufklärung und Rassismus" [Islam Criticism—Between Enlightenment and Racism].

The discursive exclusion of Muslim women from democratic participation is incomplete, however, and reveals ruptures that may have been precisely enabled by the desire to avoid a discourse of racism in the face of el-Sherbini's murder. Many women experience a new willingness to acknowledge experiences of discrimination due to headscarf since el-Sherbini's murder (Yücel). Sezgin and Fanizadeh's contributions to the discussion, while evoking little response, nevertheless emerge in a forum with a fairly wide readership. These voices point to a discourse of secularism that can function without the epistemic violence of constructing an Other. Such a discourse would seek not mere regulation of violence, but prohibition, and would see that prohibition to include the prohibition of racist violence. Such a discourse could also imagine the headscarved teacher participating in a democratic public space and the hijab martyr as an example of existing racist violence. Sezgin and Fanizadeh point to this possibility when they seek to consider an institutionalized racism that could exist outside individual intent and consciousness and to place Alex Wiens's actions firmly in that context. Chin and Heide Fehrenbach have recently pointed out that although discussions of European democracy have remained predicated on notions of ethnic homogeneity since 1945, difference and diversity have in reality been fundamental to the development of postwar democracy (Chin and Fehrenbach 135). A rethinking of secularism that allows for religious difference and names racism's presence in contemporary secular democracies may better allow that difference and diversity to become visible.

It seems appropriate to conclude with Ludin's response to el-Sherbini's murder, which remained absent from the press coverage. Her brief speech at a memorial in Berlin praised el-Sherbini for her fight against hate and for justice. She states, "Marwa, you, your children and your husband are and remain victims of hate, violence, xenophobia and Islamophobia. We ask all state institutions [...] to set a sign for tolerance and the recognition of Muslim men and women" (Ludin). Despite the recognition Ludin had gained through her court case and the fact that she rarely makes public statements, her comments were cited only at Islamic websites, and relatively conservative ones, at that.

The erasure of her words is significant. Yet the import of her actions might extend far beyond the content of the call for tolerance that her speech contains. An approach to European secularism that derives from the assumption of a European history that by definition promotes peace, juxtaposed with a Muslim tradition that promotes violence, not only obscures Europe's own history of colonial and racist violence but actually prevents Muslim women from participating in the public sphere. A vision of democratic modernity that is rooted in equal access to exchange of ideas in the public sphere will always be thwarted so long as these blind spots in European history obtain. However, the headscarf discussions, read together, also reveal potential for a new reconfiguration of the public sphere. The potential for these reconfigurations is also evident in the performance and art I explore in the following chapter. This reconfigured sphere activates the desire for a utopian Europe that prioritizes human rights in the context of a revised secularism. Such a revised secularism seeks to incorporate an understanding of difference into the public sphere, beyond notions of tolerance, to reveal the structures of xenophobia, racism, or Islamophobia at work. Only in this way could democratic structures be imagined that ban rather than regulate violence.

Chapter Three
Troubling Headscarves: Covering, Artistic Reconfigurations of Public Space, and the Muslim Woman's Body

In the ten photographs that make up Iranian artist Shadi Ghadirian's 2006 series *Ctrl+Alt+Del*, a black-clad woman's body disappears into the black background against which she is photographed, preventing any sense of depth or perspective within the image. Only her face, hands, and feet—those parts of the body traditionally considered "naturally" visible and therefore not subject to laws of covering—are visible, as pale white contrasts to the black of the photograph. The black on black, however, creates an illusion for the viewer that the woman may be either "covering" or wearing tight black clothing such as might befit a dancer. In each photograph, familiar computer icons have been digitally added; sometimes they follow the lines of the woman's body, sometimes she pushes them away.

Curator Nilüfer Göle included these images in the 2008 exhibit *Mahrem. Footnotes on Veiling*, presented at the Tanas exhibition space in Berlin's Wedding neighborhood. In the context of the exhibit, Ghadirian's photos layer veiling practices with the ubiquitous markers of contemporary technology, which become the means by which the viewer can voyeuristically "see" the hidden body. The photographs in this way make visible a form of visual violence enacted by a viewer, a voyeuristic "gaze," while locating the Muslim woman in interaction with, rather than excluded from, a space made "modern" via technology. In seeking to "know" the victimized veiled woman, the viewer is confronted with symbols of technological progress; only these icons can make that body visible. The viewers' interaction with notions of the Muslim woman's body and modernity are thus powerfully disturbed. Public space is also unsettled through the making-obvious of the two-dimensionality of representation of Muslim women. The Muslim-woman subject cannot be defined solely by veiling practices, which might be associated with the space of domesticity. Instead, she is always already inscribed by modernity, an inscription that flattens the image to the two dimensions. Through the making-obvious of the viewer's voyeuristic viewpoint, the photographs prevent the viewer from constructing a position of innocence vis-a-vis the Muslim Other.

I introduce this chapter with Ghadirian's work to illustrate the possibilities for expanding discussions of Islam, gender, violence, modernity, and secularism. The regime of violence at work in deliminating potential subjectivities for Muslim women in Germany, as I've explored in the previous two chapters, functions effectively through the trope of the veil, which configures the Muslim woman's body as simultaneously object of violence and margin between public and private. As is apparent in the representations of Fereshta Ludin and Marwa el-Sherbini, the headscarf and other forms of Muslim headcovering have remarkable power in Europe as a symbolic boundary between public and private, as demarcation of a European self from a racialized Muslim Other. The headscarf becomes a marker of access to or denial from public spaces. Artistic works engage with the exclusion of Muslim women from the public sphere through a complex thematization of veiling practices.

In the previous two chapters I focused on the construction of violence in public discourse. In this second section I seek to practice a politics of careful listening. This chapter and those that follow offer up readings that search for lesser-known "archives" of representation and hope to enter into dialogue with lesser-heard voices and repressed conversations. I hope, in other words, to listen carefully to the potential interventions into the public sphere via representations of Islamic covering practices in public space, and to the alternative discourses about veiling and violence provided in a range of artistic works, with particular attention to those by women of Muslim heritage or women of color. In this chapter I explore the ways in which three public performances respond to and reconfigure public space through representations of veiling. I desire here to move beyond a discussion of stereotypes or clichés and their undoing. Rather, I am concerned with the potential interventions that can be made in a public sphere that otherwise avails itself to Muslim women, primarily by offering up subject positions as victims of domestic or familial violence. In what ways do public, artistic representations of forms of covering open up space for democratic subjectivities? How do these artistic interventions function as political? These are openings to a discussion of secularism and the role of Islam in Europe that may move beyond confining Muslim women to a physical boundary between a European body politic and its Muslim outside.

Introducing the Archive

The three examples I take here as my archive—a dance performance, a comedy performance, and an art exhibition—may appear oddly incongruent at first glance. Yet, collectively, though not through explicit engagement with politics in a traditional sense, they offer up a range of overlapping interventions into popular discourses, as well as challenges to the exclusion of Muslim women from the public sphere. Serpil Pak first gained some measure of notoriety as a cofounder of the comedy duo Floor Cosmeticians [Bodenkosmetikerinnen]. An ironically self-described "rap-stand-up-artist," Pak went on a solo tour with "In Veil Prison—An Orient Valkyrie Lets Loose" ["In Schleier Haft—Eine Orientwalküre packt aus"] in 2008; her performances under this title have continued into 2010 and have won her positive press coverage, attention from national politicians, and notice from mainstream feminists. In May 2010 she also won the prize for best individual performance in Berlin's famed "Carnival of Cultures."

The art exhibit *Mahrem, Footnotes on Veiling* was curated by sociologist Nilüfer Göle for the project "Non-Western Modernities," which was first presented at the Istanbul gallery SantralIstanbul and then at the Berlin exhibit and project space, Tanas, in 2008. Tanas' explicit goal is to serve as a platform for presenting up-and-coming Turkish artists to Berlin, and the gallery works closely with artists in Turkey and receives Turkish federal funding. This particular exhibit showcased a number of artists from the so-called Muslim world, including Turkish and Iranian artists, several of whom now make

Berlin their home. The artists included in *Mahrem* provide interpretations of veiling practices that work outside the dominant binaries of public and private, instead revealing the supposedly private as intimately bound up in the public.

The theatrical, musical modern dance performance, *BurkaBondage,* premiered in Berlin in October 2009 and has since toured through Germany and internationally performing in India, Pakistan, Sri Lanka, and Afghanistan. Conceived of, directed, and choreographed by Helena Waldmann, the performance creates a provocative interplay between bondage practices and the wearing of the burqa. The complex performance links the contradictory experiences of freedom and confinement that are inherent in both practices and implies a similar contradictory experience of liberation and constriction in contemporary Western culture.

These are radically different forms of performance in the public space, not least because of their generic variety. This difference, however, provides an interesting range of possibilities for constructing alternative public subjectivities for Muslim women. All three serve as displacements, even deconstructions, of the regime of violence that structures Muslim and Turkish women's public subjectivities. Whereas some moments serve as radical openings, and others provide more explicit critiques, these displacements permit the emergence of a Muslim-woman subjectivity into a public sphere via a challenge to the spatial metaphors evoked by discourses on veiling and violence, thus seeking space in the political realm for women of Muslim or immigrant heritage.

In Veil Prison: An Orient Valkyrie Lets Loose

Serpil Pak's career as a comedian began in the 1990s, when the group Floor Cosmeticians was founded as a response to the rising xenophobic and racist violence of the early 1990s, immediately after German unification. Part of a wave of political and critical Turkish German *Kabarett,* the group was known for recreating and deconstructing clichés about Turkish German groups, in particular, of women—as suggested by the group's name, a playful euphemism for cleaning women (Boran 177–178). Pak continued with solo performances when the group disbanded, partially in response to the proliferation of depoliticized "ethno-comedy," particularly aired on television in the late 1990s (Boran 178; 182). She also participated when the group regrouped from 2004 to 2007.

Erol Boran has pointed to the fact that the Floor Cosmeticians emerged as part of a wave of ethnic comedy that drew on the specifically political tradition of German cabaret, or *Kabarett* (Boran). The metropolitan German cabaret scene emerged during the interwar period in Germany but was heavily censored during Nazi Germany. It reemerged after World War II with an intensified focus on political critique and was radicalized during the 1960s (Boran 173). The emergence of Turkish-German cabaret performances coincided with a rise in the production of Turkish-German film comedies. These film comedies were an important challenge to the earlier cinema of migration, which focused heavily on dramas portraying Turkish women as victims or Turkish men as criminals. Deniz Göktürk argues that these new comedies reverse the "ethnographic gaze," incorporating the parodied nonimmigrant viewers into the film:

> By watching these unexpected [humorous] interactions, the audience, too, is incorporated into the culture of performance. Immigrant [film] comedies at their best can train spectators in not taking themselves too seriously. Through strategies of ethnic roleplay, distancing and disguise, irreverence and reversal, stepping outside and back inside, mimicking and mocking social conventions, they have the power to destabilize discourses and iconographies of power. (Göktürk, "Strangers in Disguise" 121)

Like the film comedies to which Göktürk refers, Pak's performances parody the perceived prejudices of the nonimmigrant audience members to destabilize discourses of power. At the same time, Pak's performances function through a certain failure—the nonimmigrant audience members are largely unable to be fully reincorporated into the performance, remaining uncomfortably outside.

I attended a performance of Pak's *In Veil Prison: An Orient Valkyrie Lets Loose* at the Neukölln Saalbau on October 12, 2009. The Saalbau is a cultural center in Rixdorf, in the heart of the much-maligned Berlin district of Neukölln, the neighborhood Pak now calls home. Although the northern part of Neukölln (affectionately termed Kreuzkölln), which borders on Kreuzberg, has recently become the new destination for artists, students, and young bohemians, Rixdorf is the historic center of Neukölln and lies in the heart of an area that is dominated by working-class people of German, Turkish, and Arab heritage. The audience for this midweek performance was fairly small and largely devoid of local residents.

Ghettos and Veils
In German, the first portion of the title is a pun that divides the word *schleierhaft*, which means mysterious (literally, veil-like), into its two component parts, *Schleier* (veil) and *Haft* (prison). Pak's title intertwines the spatial discourse of an imprisoning "ghetto" with the spatialized understanding of "veil." When Pak took a quick poll about who was actually from the neighborhood (only three volunteered to say they were), she sarcastically congratulated the remaining audience for braving it all the way to scary Neukölln. Pak's comments make their meaning against the background of a decades-long portrayal of Neukölln as the truly troubled, dangerous, "ghetto" of Berlin. Ghetto constructions of Turkish German neighborhoods have often imagined a space that eludes the power of the state, marked by dangerous, violent, nonwhite masculinities that effectively function as Other to Europe (Stehle, "White Ghettos" 167–168; 177), thus producing a peaceful, enlightened, civilized Europe. The prison of Pak's title gains a special significance when performed in Neukölln, a neighborhood constructed alternatively as a place that the "immigrants" refuse to leave or one from which they cannot escape (Stehle, "Narrating the Ghetto, Narrating Europe" 48–55; Stehle, "White Ghettos" 170). Pak's performance interrupts—but uneasily—this narrative in several ways. Furthermore, in this performance in particular, that interruption causes the comedy to "fail" as an unsure audience struggles to locate themselves vis-a-vis the uncomfortable and shifting-tropes Pak cites.

Pak implicitly brings together two narratives of spatial difference—that of the veil and that of the ghetto—to challenge their constitution. The ghetto first of all is revealed as the object for the exoticization of those who travel to the heart of darkness, so to speak, to demonstrate their participation in liberal multiculturalism and urban hipness. The ghetto's violence and criminality are playfully recontextualized through her "confession" of her own participation in criminality—as a schoolkid who forged her parents' signatures to ease the hassle of constantly obtaining them for various permissions. In this way Pak downplays criminality as the defining feature of Neukölln life, instead striking an affinity with the audience through the normalization of childhood pranks.

As Pak's routine progresses, however, the veil, much more than the ghetto, becomes the discursive "prison" in which she has had to live, although both are constructed by the majority culture. Pak's performance implies that she is in "Veil Prison," not because she has been forced to wear the veil or headscarf, but because the dominant society has turned the veil into such a fundamental aspect of her identity as a woman of Muslim and Turkish heritage. This discursive prison has even had concrete effects on her own working life by potentially denying her access to certain careers. She points out that she was constantly told that she should seek work as a social worker, which would be appropriate work for a woman of her background and language skills. This, she says, is how she became a "Career Turk" [*Berufstürkin*], whose expertise is limited to knowledge of "her people." Pak's experience is echoed by those of other women of immigrant heritage who found their access to education and practica hindered by stereotypes about Muslim women (Farrokhzad, "Bildungs- und Berufschancen" 58). Pak's story opens lines of connection to many Afro-German women, who in literature often relate similar experiences of being told to "help their people" (Ayim 18; Hügel-Marshall 59) rather than pursuing careers of their own choosing.

Oppressive spatial constructions were often produced by popular films in the 1990s, such as *Yasemin* and *40m2 Germany*, which confine female characters of Turkish/Muslim heritage to small, claustrophobic domestic spaces in which women lived at the mercy of their violent male relatives. Pak replaces one trope, the prison of the domestic space policed by violent Muslim men, with another, the confinement of veil and ghetto. However, her experience of the veil and ghetto are not literal but are created by the tendency for popular culture and German society to locate her within them.

Pak challenges her location within these metaphorical spaces with a juxtaposition of tropes of female purity, violence, and honor, which are generally associated with the Muslim immigrant population, to forms of purity that are particularly associated with conservative German conceptions of white womanhood. The notion of purity, often attributed to the honor that is seen to serve as motivation for domestic violence in Turkish communities, is rethought through her name. Since few (or, rather, few ethnic Germans) can remember the name Serpil, she says, she offers them "Persil" as mnemonic device. Persil, a popular laundry detergent made by Unilever, often utilizes the slogan "Not only clean, but pure." Many in the audience might recall a 2006 Persil ad campaign in Germany that became controversial among antiracist groups for equating "purity" with white babies.[1] She then points out that her surname, Pak, also means "pure" in Turkish. She thus offers up an (impossible) method for remembering her name by remembering her as doubly "pure," which is unthinkable in two ways: (1) because of the racialized notions of whiteness that surround the Persil ads; and (2) because of the assumption of a Turkish or Muslim discourse of honor that can only render her impure, given her explicit claims to sexual freedom. In another performance on WDR's *Fun(k)haus*, she has discussed her naming and her relationship to honor as evidence of her status as an "integration victim" rather than as one of "successful integration" with which she is often labeled ("WDR-Fun(k)haus").

To be sure, Pak also points to moments when she has experienced harassment by Turkish German men. She does not hesitate to demonstrate indignity at Turkish youth who suddenly decide they have some responsibility for her "honor." However, she renders such instances strange rather than normalizing them. When she discusses victimhood, it is portrayed as at the hands of a migration victimhood, a regime that constructs her future, as she says in another part of the program, as necessarily located somewhere between "forced marriage and honor killing." Because her prison is revealed to be the discourse of Turkishness rather than the honor imposed by male Turkish violence, the audience has difficulty making sense of her, and the laughter is limited and uncomfortable. Pak thus disturbs the construction of a specifically Muslim violence that is enacted through enforcing feminine purity by considering a discursive violence, which is performed at the intersection of competing discourses of purity.

The reactions to her playful use of clothing are equally mixed. In a performance of her act for the Berlin Quatsch Comedy Club, for example, she initially appears onstage wearing a headscarf. At the end of the first segment, she asks the audience to clap in rhythm to a little tune, which she ends by rather unceremoniously and undramatically taking off the headscarf—the audience has no idea how to react until she relieves their silence by saying: "That was the headscarf striptease," which is greeted by much applause. At the heart of the discomfort lies her deliberate desexualization of the headscarf by performing a striptease that is not recognizable as such. Although Pak had earlier humorously demonstrated the usefulness of a headscarf as a flirtation device on the subway, her matter-of-fact removal of it couldn't be further from a striptease. An audience seeking a particular "liberal multicultural" reaction to Pak's performance is repeatedly challenged and confused. The removal of the headscarf is not a fundamental transformation in the roles that Pak plays throughout the performance, nor do her actions fulfill an Orientalist expectation of sexualization through the headscarf. The removal is neither funny nor dramatic, either of which would require a particular parody that could perhaps too easily be consumed by the audience without the necessary discomfort. She thus potentially unsettles the deeply entrenched discourse of Islam/headscarf as violence.

In the Neukölln performance, Pak appeared onstage wearing a modified dirndl over ripped jeans to demonstrate her "fashion integration." This outfit, also worn for the image used in a postcard marketing her performance, doubly parodies popular discussions of integration. On the one hand, it points to the desired visual transformation from "Turkish" (represented via the headscarf) to German. She has further parodied the reduction of integration to fashion, following the discussions about the headscarf to their "logical" conclusion: that the dirndl, worn by so few German women, signals Germanness for the Turkish immigrant. Her outfit also imitates a longstanding Berlin fashion of wearing dresses over jeans (one that significantly predates this fashion in the United States), a sort of ugly chic that places her locally as well as nationally. Pak acknowledges, however, that the dirndl isn't the form of bodily integration that is usually desired from a society that has highly sexualized Muslim women, often demanding sexual availability as a marker of societal integration. Pak plays with the competing expectations around sexuality by joking that she had her virginity "surgically removed" at a young age, but that of course one can have it surgically restored as well. Optimally, she decides, a zipper would be the best solution, allowing her to lose and restore her virginity at will.

These comments seemed particularly uncomfortable to members of her audience, who shifted uncomfortably in their chairs and laughed only awkwardly. Pak's comments disturb partly because, rather than suggesting sexual oppression solely at the hands of Muslim men, they reveal the violence inherent in a gaze that constructs integration as dependent on her (hetero)sexual activity. Her routine faces the audience with the fact that her sexual availability is represented as a form of participation in public space, but a form of participation in public space that makes the woman's body available for private consumption, not a participation that enables visiblity in a public sphere that is dependent on political debate and participation.

The "Orient Valkyrie" between Two Worlds
Serpil Pak noticeably refuses to engage with the rhetoric of being caught between two cultures, whereas she is simultaneously critical of the constantly changing terminology that has succeeded "two cultures" in the constant search for a politically correct terminology. She often introduces herself as a "passport German with migration heritage," in some settings adding "lesbian and migration heritage" (Haase), and as an atheist with a feminist mother and a "forced Muslim" [*Zwangsmuslimisch*] background. These identity namings serve as a strategy against the impositions of ethnic-based subjectivities. At the Neukölln performance she made reference to an (unnamed) conference that she had recently attended, concluding from the discussions during her attendance that "transcultural" and "cultural hybridity" are the latest rage. Not to be outdone in

participating in the latest hip research, she decides that as a psychologist living in Neukölln, she will engage in her own form of "intercultural research," namely, the various ways in which men of different cultures scratch their privates. This latter joke received a hearty laugh from the audience at the Quatsch, but was received with absolute silence on Fun(k)haus and uncomfortable laughter at the Saalbau Neukölln. Part of the discomfort certainly lies in some audience insecurity about unexpected vulgarity, but this also seems layered over with something else. Pak here has returned the gaze: by stepping into a position as a "Western" researcher who has the capability to "know" the subject of research and by reversing the presumed gaze as a woman vis-a-vis Turkish men. She thus becomes both possessor of her own body and creator of knowledge—even if this knowledge is parodied. She also occupies an "unthinkable" position as a Turkish German lesbian. Furthermore, an audience fear that Pak might be repeating cultural stereotypes is confounded by Pak's poking fun at "intercultural research," at the same time that she establishes a vulgar similarity, rather than a difference, between "German" men and "Turkish" men—both of whom scratch themselves, only differently. The audience is left unable to securely grasp both difference and universality and is faced with the violence of its own gaze.

When Pak juxtaposes descriptions of herself as an "intercultural success" and "cultural hybrid" with the designation as a "migration victim," she demonstrates how ongoing discussions on how to imagine the relevant notions of culture are inadequate for thinking a whole range of potential identities claimed by Germans of Muslim heritage—as lesbian or atheist, for example. She scoffs at the usual catalog of terms made available to her (such as Oriental, Turkish German, and German woman of Turkish heritage) by deciding at one point to become a "fundamentalist dominatrix" named the "Black Sultaness." Her new name, a genuine contrast to the doubly "pure" identity she claimed earlier, is equally uncomfortable. The doubly pure, doubly victimized Turkish German woman now claims an exaggeratedly powerful position, one that renders Orientalism and other forms of racialization powerless. Her inclusion of "blackness" via the name of the Black Sultaness further hints at the ways in which Turkish Germans have been racialized. Furthermore, her routine—often at the points where the humor "fails" most, points to the structural problems often covered up by the "culture talk" that takes place at academic conferences as well as in the media. At one point she states, "I would like to talk about politics, but as a Career-Turk [Berufstürkin] I am not permitted." She finds herself positioned publicly as an expert on "culture" but not on "politics."

Yet, talk about politics she does. She shifts abruptly from a discussion of terminologies of culture to the changes taking place in other important terminologies: for example, the "right to stay" [*Bleiberecht*], a designation used for asylum seekers who were not granted asylum but are temporarily allowed to stay, has been transformed into a "tolerance" [*Duldung*]—a terminological shift that illustrates the difficulties facing political refugees as access to asylum is increasingly restricted in Germany. Talk of culture can also inadequately account for or challenge the treatment of her bald friend, Murat Arslan, who was arrested, called a neo-Nazi, and nearly deported because another man by the same (extremely common) name stood on the deportation list, or for the fact that every time she moves and must register her move with the police, she is forced to provide more documentation of her legal status than Germans without a Turkish name. In both cases, names serve as a signifier of culture with deeply political effects that are rooted in state violence. In the first case, a double absurdity underlies Murat's near deportation. Because of his shaved head, he is assumed to be a neo-Nazi, a presumption made "possible" by the attribution of anti-Semitism to all Muslims; at the same time, an extremely common name marks him as deportable. He becomes a generic figure of the Turk whose very identity is policed by the state and yet is infinitely replicable. Pak's name further subjects her to extra regulations within the supposedly objective system of law—she has to "prove" her legal residency, whereas those with "German" names do not. The hierarchies produced by the embedding of "cultural" difference within institutions are more explicitly revealed by using a metaphor of the train system. "It's like the train system—the first class the West Germans, the second class the East Germans (who nevertheless arrive at about the same time), and the slow train—the passport Germans." The naturalized Germans are not only a different class but a different train—produced as outside differently than Germans from the former East. Although many of the tropes are similar to those deployed immediately after the fall of the wall—namely that East Germans were incapable of democracy, tended to violence, and were outside modernity—those characteristics are more deeply entrenched in representations of Islam.

Pak's uncomfortable political comedy will never achieve the wild success of somebody like Kaya Yanar, a television comedian whose parodies remain superficial enough that the audience can laugh comfortably without much challenge to their ways of thinking. Pak's positive reception is furthermore often marked by a reinscription of the usual clichés about Turkish German women as well as the depoliticization of her work. Positive comments in the press describe her as somebody who destroys clichés but focus on her use of "shopping as therapy" (Borowczyk) or her "forced schizophrenic existence" as the consequence of "being between two cultures" (Lehnhard); recognition of her reference to forms of European violence are generally absent. If her insistent inclusion of political and institutional aspects of the restrictions experienced by Turkish Germans emerges in the media, it is often disconcerting and marked by the disappearance of laughter. Indeed, during a recent night-long Berlin festival of Turkish German culture, she was considered extremely "uncomfortable" in comparison to all the other Turkish Germans trying to "build bridges" (Brozska). One exception, however, is the online feminist magazine *Aviva*, which considers Pak political in the best possible way (Fertig).

Her initial positive reception marked her as a possible positive "mediator" between Turkish and German culture. After all, as a feminist atheist who has never worn a headscarf, she is easily marked as a well integrated "good immigrant." However, Pak's challenge to the comfortable imagination of "bridge building," a phrase that serves as shorthand for a comfortable re-presentation of cultural difference, may come at the expense of more widespread success. Nevertheless, the disturbance she creates provides a possible way to make visible the boundaries created for Muslim women in the public sphere while challenging the heteronormativity of public space and to create space for thinking about women both as Muslim and as members of a political community.

BurkaBondage: Challenging the Ties that Bind

BurkaBondage had its worldwide premiere on October 9, 2009, at the Haus der Berliner Festspiele, a theater in the heart of the former West Berlin, which stages large, fairly traditional productions on its main stage but also has a small Black Box theater in which *BurkaBondage* premiered. Support from the Goethe Institut enabled ongoing international performances through 2010, including ones in Sri Lanka and India. Although Waldmann is credited with direction, concept, and choreography in the credits, the program notes state that she was assisted in direction by Afghani director Monireh Hashemi (Luzina), and developed the project collaboratively with the international group of performers, including dancers Yui Kawaguchi (Japan) and Vania Rovisco (Portugal), video artist Acci Baba (Japan), and musician Mohammad Reza Mortazavi (Iran).

The advertising for the avantgarde dance performance initially suggests a stereotypical portrayal of clichés of violence and sexuality. The short description circulated as a press release for the performance describes it by drawing connections between blown-up Buddha statues in Afghanistan, burqas in Afgahanistan, and Japanese bondage practices: "The burqa is a coat worn by Afghan women, completely covering them. Bondage is a technique which ties Japanese women submissively up [The Bamiyan Buddhas] were blown up because the body is deemed unbearable." This seems to unproblematically invoke a number of controversial tropes linking violent constraint of the body and shame to a generic Asian culture. A reading of this performance, however, suggests a very different set of approaches to violence at work. The performance troubles the constellations burqa-imprisonment and bondage-imprisonment by depicting both burqa and bondage as potentially enabling and destructive, as freeing and constricting. The performance further destabilizes the link between violence and Asian cultures by locating Europe itself as one potential source of violence. The introduction to this press description becomes a performance in itself, setting up citations of dominant discourses that will be undone in the stage performance.[2]

Press and program notes state that the production emerged from two points of contact between Japan and Afghanistan that were noticed by Waldmann while working on another production in Afghanistan. Her encounter with youth from both countries revealed an intense outrage over the destruction of Buddha statues by the Taliban in 2001. At the same time, youth from both countries depicted themselves as a generation of young people with little chance for control over their own future, and therefore as lost generations. Despite radically different contexts, the youth of both cultures were struggling with similar contradictory desires. They expressed longing for a radical freedom to determine their own identities and their path into the future, quests the youth viewed as circumscribed by their "culture." At the same time, they all desired grounding and connection, seeking to regain traditions they saw as stolen from them. In particular, the destruction of the Bamiyan Buddhas in 2001 by the Taliban sparked reflections for these youth on a simultaneous disappearance of the body in public and of cultural tradition. The body hidden by the burqa and the body bound by Shibari bondage practices both generated further questions about freedom. Ultimately, the youth began to question the "frame" within which the body is placed, imagining the body as beyond possession. The body, they suggest, belongs to nobody, not even to the subject itself; the body "searches for trance in its loneliness, in order to overcome its own narrow boundaries" ("BurkaBondage—No Ordinary Experience"). Unlike the representation produced by the advertising, then, the project seems to emerge not from a strange conflation of "Eastern" cultures and gender violence but, rather, from a moment of encounter between differing reflections on agency, freedom, liberation, and the body.

The performance took place on a set equipped with ropes, a cubic cage wrapped with slightly translucent strips of white cloth, and a huge, white parachute cloth. The first moments of the performance gesture toward elements the audience likely associates with "tradition." Kawaguchi danced in a white kimono with a red sash, singing traditional Japanese music. Rovisco appeared in a red burqa, prayed, and sang an Afghani lullaby. This became a visual and aural echo of the "traditional culture" performed by the initial paragraphs in the press description, which seemingly located the performance in traditional folk cultures. Those two cultures were drawn together by the red and white comprising the palette of each costume. The overly stylized nature of the costumes, exaggerated dancing, and singing already hinted at potential parody, and thus at an undoing of the European expectations of tradition.

The audience was quickly confronted with the inadequacy of its expectations when the dancers shed those clothes for simple, white, tight-fitting tops and leggings that appeared almost like rags, while the music shifted to original compositions by drummer Mortazavi, played from within the cage. This transformation immediately challenged the viewer in unique ways. The dancers changed their clothes from within the cage on stage. The shedding of confining traditional clothing did not appear to be freeing, quite the contrary, as the dancers convulsed against the cage walls. Eventually Kawaguchi exited the cage and was fiercely tossed about on the ropes attached to the cage as the violent rhythms of the music in the cage appeared to cause the shaking.[3] This initiated a meditation on notions of culture, agency, and subjectivity that would potentially contextualize sexualized forms of Orientalism as the show progressed.

BurkaBondage also implicitly questioned conceptualizations of freedom. Hashemi, a consultant on the production, who wears a headscarf, is not interested in Western feminists' desire to focus on the burqa to justify their desire to "save" Afghani women, emphasizing that although the burqa certainly is not freedom, it becomes a *form* of freedom in a particular context, freedom to move outside the home as well as freedom from a male gaze (Luzina). Waldmann repeats similar assertions in an interview ("Fessel"). By the same token, bondage itself became a form of freedom and connection in the performance. After Rovisco carefully bound Kawaguchi, Kawaguchi soared above the stage as Rovisco manipulated the cords, pulling the parachute cloth behind her to make it appear like a billowing burqa closely resembling a flying kite. Rovisco wrapped her own head with cords that Kawaguchi would later tenderly and lovingly unwind. When Kawaguchi bound Rovisco, Rovisco's gentle swinging above the stage seemed to release her from the pain and effort associated with seeking the ground, especially in the agonizingly slow series of *en pointe* steps taken before the ascent into the air. Each form of constriction or bond took on its meaning in conjunction with a context and shifted its meaning throughout the performance.

The dancers were playful and demonstrated a relationship of trust when tying each other or binding each other, but this trust was betrayed by lapses into violent degradation. At one point, for example, Kawaguchi reached her hand into Rovisco's mouth until the latter gagged and pantomimed vomiting. The complete offering up of each other's bodies in a relationship of love and trust transformed into a violent relationship which ceased to offer freedom via the literal ties of the ropes and metaphorical emotional ties. In this pantomime, intimate violence was located as a potentiality in the dancer's relationship. It existed outside of any notion of cultural specificity, which was noticeably irrelevant to the form of clothing worn.

In another section, fashion became a more explicit tool of violence. Dressed in black robes, which included a collar that obscured the lower half of his face, the video artist, Baba, played the traditional role of a *kuroko*. In traditional Japanese *kabuki* theater, the *kuroko* dresses from head to toe in black to remain "invisible" onstage while he helps the performers with costume and prop changes. Baba's visibility, however, suddenly increased when he aided Rovisco in donning a tight cloth corset-like garment over her torso, which was made of strips of cloth resembling mummy bandages. The playfulness of the bondage practices now evaporated as her breath was constricted by the garment, and she squeaked repeatedly. The squeals continue as she fell over while donning tall, tight, white plastic boots with heels that can only be described as Lady Gaga-like and then while she applied bright lipstick. Emergence as a subject of violence occurred here in a contradictory manner: as an agent who chose and donned painful footwear in the name of fashion even as she subjected herself to the corseting at the hands of a man. Baba, in contrast, became visible yet continued to be partially veiled via the covering of his lower face when he came to the forefront as an agent of violence. Thus, in the performance, restrictive clothing produces and defines the body. Like veiling practices and bondage practices, the corset has a history of multiple and conflicting meanings. Sometimes considered torture and associated with bad health, the corset is also associated with self-discipline and erotic allure and has even made a fashion comeback. This meditation on violence via the constriction of clothing cannot easily be resolved into tropes of victim and agent. Nor can the viewer equate the revelation of the body with freedom of any kind, and certainly not with freedom from violence.

As Kawaguchi retook complete control over her own body, ending in a twirl aided by ropes, she also began a playful dance, the initially movements of which were seemingly inspired by a belly dance, but then quickly transformed to forms of traditional South Asian dance. Kawaguchi then concluded the performance by slowly and jerkily wrapping herself from the waist down in the white parachute cloth, creating the image of a mechanized doll wrapped in a fluffy white wedding dress. Rovisco also moved mechanically, helping Kawaguchi arrange the cloth. A brief moment of play and seeming control of Kawaguchi's own body quickly morphed into recognizable symbols of Western heteronormativity. The shift from a more playful, free dance to the mechanized movements insist that "becoming Western" in this context is not necessarily a moment of liberation but a shift into other constellations of freedom and confinement. These latter moments challenged the "performance" of the advertising and the title. The affinities of violence between two non-Western cultures, once triangulated with similar moments of violence in European culture, can no longer be safely relegated outside European culture.

This performance thematized a positioning in public space rather than in a public sphere. However, the dance tore violence out of a context in which intimate violence is specifically linked to Islam. It laid out a more open terrain on which to imagine the construction of freedom, female subjectivity, and bodily discipline. The burqa appeared as one of a series of pieces of cloth or clothing (kimono, corset, ropes, a billowing parachute, boots) that may serve as a form of violence but may also enable forms of agency. The physical confinement through ropes, garments, and emotional connection or ties were portrayed as sometimes enabling and freeing, at other times violent and constraining. The radical contextualization required to apprehend agency also proved necessary to interpret any particular moment of dressing practices, or of freedom and unfreedom. The meditative nature of the performance resisted any sort of closure. Instead, the audience's thwarted longing for the voice of the subject demanded a radical listening to the self-imposed body practices.

Mahrem: Footnotes on Veiling

Given: (1) the narrative of European modernity as a narrative of non-violence; (2) the very real violence that is a crucial part of European modernity; (3) the exclusion of Islam from Europe, based on its relationship to violence; and (4) the role of the Muslim woman as both defining and troubling a boundary between public and private and between religious and secular, an exhibit on veiling could very well contribute to a discourse in which women's participation in public sphere excludes her political voice by reducing her to an object that is more or less revealed and more or less subject to the violence of Islam. *Mahrem. Footnotes on Veiling* was exhibited in August 2008 at Tanas, Berlin, in a small exhibit space devoted to Turkish art. The exhibit was developed in collaboration with Göle, whose book, *The Forbidden Modern: Civilization and Veiling*, provided groundbreaking analysis of the ways in which many contemporary young Turkish women who take the headscarf often do so specifically to participate in a Turkish modernity. Given Göle's own intellectual projects, which explore headscarves both as a marker of entrance to and as exclusion from public space in Turkey (introduced a in chapter 2), this is not surprising. Here I wish to consider, however, how such an exhibit functions in Berlin space. In particular I consider how these works both revealed and challenged the conditions under which contemporary notions of Muslim violence are created. This exhibit negotiated those pitfalls by revealing the limiting ways in which Muslim women are allowed to participate in public spheres, as well as challenging those limits, juxtaposing symbols of transnational power with local specificities and inflections. I'm particularly interested in how these images functioned when displayed in Berlin; How do the traveling symbols take on a particularly local inflection? What does this mean in turn for a relationship between Germany and Europe? How do they enable a listening for Muslim voices in the public sphere?

The exhibit was an attempt to present multiple engagements with the organization of public space and women's bodies in those spaces. What is particularly productive, I think, is that it did so in ways that are sometimes playful and are far beyond the popular discourses of violence. German visitors may well recognize one of the exhibited pieces, *Friday*, by the Iranian-born artist Parastou Forouhar, because the third panel served as the cover of Necla Kelek's bestselling book *Die fremde Braut*, which became controversial because of its total rejection of Islam as incompatible with a modern, democratic Germany. The hand emerging cautiously from the mass of black fabric highlights the importance of questions of concealment and revealing. Forouhar's work is particularly interested in critiquing the manifestations of Islamic fundamentalism in Iran, where her (secular) parents were victims of politically motivated murder. The inclusion of this image, loaded in its association with the book, is a caution not to ignore those concerns but rather to bring them into dialogue with the multiple forms of violence that are revealed by the exhibit.

Forouhar's series is entitled *Schilder* [Signs], two pieces of which further highlighted the gendered organization of public space. In these pictograms, she particularly calls attention to our construction of difference via the woman's body. The male pictogram has nothing to locate it culturally or to differentiate it significantly from any other symbol for the male. Referencing a particular gendered division of public space that occurs regardless of cultural background, restrooms, or while calling attention to the role of gender as rendering Islam Other, this set of restroom signs unsettles the assumptions of European viewers. Confronted with a difference that is obviously constructed through a woman's body but is minus the violence of the male body, the viewer cannot easily make assumptions about who has constructed that difference. Forouhar has reflected on how her displacement to Germany, which at some point changed her to become "Iranian," has also displaced the meanings of symbols: "Strangers are identified by markings which are paradoxically familliar [sic]. But the automatic recognition of the unfamilliar[sic] is an indication for the way in which "reality" is constructed—also by preassumptions [sic]" (Forouhar). In Germany again, but in different ways than in Iran, she has experienced societal restrictions on personal and individual expression. Hung as they were in the Tanas exhibit, the viewer who glanced up was disoriented both by the unfamiliar signs as well as by the fact that they both hung over a single doorway that was situated between rooms and thus failed to "properly" organize the public space by indicating some form of gender divided space.

The inclusion of the 1999 video installation, *Women Who Wear Wigs,* by Turkish video artist Kutluğ Ataman (who also directed the German language film *Lola + Bilidikid,* set in Berlin) raises particularly intriguing possibilities. The hypervisibility of the Muslim woman's body via the headscarf disappears, as the covering is displaced onto that which is covered, the hair. More importantly, however, each of the four women interviewed tells a story of why she wears a wig, which is connected to her participation in political activism. In the first, a woman reminisces about her life as a leftist activist in the 1970s, who concealed her identity with a long, blond wig whenever she needed to go underground. The second, a successful television journalist, tells the story of wearing wigs while undergoing chemotherapy for breast cancer—but also at points discovers openings for remembering her own long-forgotten past as a Left activist during the 1970s. The third woman is never shown for fear of disclosing her identity; faced with a black screen, the viewer hears and reads her story of wearing a wig to "cover" after Turkish universities begin to force women to either remove the headscarf while on campus or to face expulsion. Her activism has been in support of ending this headscarf ban and supporting young women's right to education. Ironically, the law forcing her to uncover has made her completely invisible. Finally, the fourth narrative tells of a male-to-female transgender woman for whom a wig was an important part of achieving her identity as a woman during transition. As an activist for transgender rights in Turkey, she has been arrested, sexually abused, and beaten as a consequence of her own activism.

This installation displaces narratives of "covering" to narratives of hair to reveal women's participation in a public sphere and a democratic modernity that goes beyond the mere exposure of their bodies. In each case, the wearing of the wig is part of a clearly identifiable intervention into the public sphere: as journalist, Left activist, student activist, and transgender activist. The bodily discipline enacted via the wig is shared, whereas the political content varies radically. In this way the meaning of the wig, like that of the burqa, bondage, or corset in *BurkaBondage,* are removed from a specific cultural context. Here the wig becomes a political symbol which is given meaning only through the narrative of public agency that is specific to each woman. Violence against those bodies occurs at the hands of a religious State in the context of Iran, but violence is also revealed as a violence committed not by Islam but by the construction of the Muslim Other, or even by the violence of a secular State. All these pieces unsettle the way in which the Muslim woman's body is used to reinforce a particular understanding of secularism. Ataman's piece also suggests a narrative of secularism that locates violence as displaced rather than as eliminated by modernity.

Reconfiguring Public Space

These three performances of veiling permit a form of resistance to the regime of violence that can reconfigure the relationship between Islam, violence, and the public sphere. Practices of covering have been used to symbolize and define Muslim violence as a violence emerging from spatial confinement and control over the woman's body, which is matched in its discursive power only by the largely masculinized violence of terrorism. Scripts of female victimhood, Muslim masculine perpetratorship, and European salvation are key to this discourse.

An interruption of the symbolic violence that is performed by a regime of violence, which often constructs Muslim women as victim of the veil, occurs in a number of ways in the art I've addressed here. Often this occurs as reconfiguration of space itself. In Pak's performance, for example, the assumed prison of the veil is paralleled to the power of the discursive prison constructed by a society that makes assumptions about veils. In *BurkaBondage* the burka became a part of a global history of restriction performed and autonomy claimed through items of clothing, all of which might restrict or enable freedom—or do both at different moments. The veil can no longer serve as any kind of boundary between public and private, constructed as it is of the same cloth that also forms billowing kite and wedding dress, finding its repetition in kimono, boots, and corset. *Mahrem* addressed forms of covering as potentially restrictive, particularly in pieces emerging from the Iranian context that emphasize the veil as a tool of enforced uniformity. Yet *Mahrem* also revealed the role of covering in making women hypervisible, not merely invisible, in Western contexts. Particularly in pieces where a political subjectivity as democratic agent is claimed, the veil itself disappeared entirely.

In all these cases, however, a key factor in rethinking Muslim women in public space is to move the discussion beyond dress practices to reveal interventions into the public sphere, even into institutional structures of oppression. *BurkaBondage* performed a radical opening that demands thinking violence and the subjectivities it produces as deeply contextual and constantly in flux. Such a dramatic displacement, even a deconstruction of the regime of violence, is necessary to enable new ways of thinking that can address experiences of economic inequality and racist violence. *Women Who Wear Wigs* displaces covering to wigs and in doing so outlines a range of positionings for women as political actors, a range which converges, however, in self-understanding as a participant in struggles for social justice. Viewed in Berlin, it made impossible a regime of violence that traces a history of headscarves to a Turkey that exists both contemporaneous to and out of time with contemporary Europe. Instead, the genealogy of a Turkish German heritage, written with this installation in mind, would include the context of women political activists. Pak's comedy enabled a reflection on the power of the headscarf regimes to determine understandings of Turkish and Muslim subjectivities so thoroughly that women's already limited educational opportunities are restricted further by assumptions of what they can and should study.

These are openings to a discussion of secularism and the role of Islam in Europe that may move beyond confining Muslim women to a physical boundary between a European body politic and its Muslim outside. When the Muslim woman ceases to function as such a boundary, and her body loses its hypervisibility as victim of violence and prisoner of headcovering, more productive ways of imagining Muslim women's participation in democratic modernity become possible—imagining women as activists, as politicians, as workers, without making the rejection of faith a prerequisite for democratic participation nor precluding a possible rejection of faith that may still draw on a cultural background.

Chapter Four
Freedom to Imagine the World: Violence and the Writing of Self

In 2012, Necla Kelek, a German feminist of Turkish heritage, who has become notorious for her positions on Islam and Turkish integration into German society, gave a talk that elicited the following response on the satirical blog AggroMigrant. The blog entry laments the rudeness of somebody who arrives late but preaches German punctuality, and then asks:

> So are you Muslim, or not? What is really your take on Sarrazin's statements about biological intelligence? And why do you preach things that you yourself don't adhere to, like German punctuality? In [your] dissertation you still wrote how important Islam is for integration, but in your presentation you speak of how it is a hindrance. You explained this contradiction by insisting that you changed the conclusions of your dissertation to please your doctoral adviser [...] I almost can't help but think of the bad word: Opportunist.

Amusing as the insistence on "German punctuality" may be, the frustration underlying the post expresses a common irritation with Kelek's public persona. At times she rejects Islam, at others she identifies herself as Muslim; despite this set of contradictions she consistently associates violence with Islam.

This position was an important factor in Kelek's role as one of the most visible members of the first group of the German Islam conference (Deutsche Islam Konferenz; hereafter DIK). The DIK is a working group formed in 2006 by the German federal government, on the initiative of the Christian democrat minister of the interior, Wolfgang Schäuble. The DIK was formed with the goal of stimulating dialogue between "Muslims" and "Germans" and comprised representatives of the "Muslim community" and of the German state. The DIK has sought to chart out the problems preventing the "integration" of Muslims into German society and to formulate possible policy solutions. Kelek was chosen after she gained enormous attention for her bestselling memoir entitled *The Foreign Bride* [*Die fremde Braut*, 2005]. Kelek was a controversial choice to represent the Muslim community—in part because of her explicit rejection of Islam in the very book that led to her status as an expert on Islam in the eyes of the German state. *The Foreign Bride* reinterprets her dissertation research by weaving in stories from her family's history. As a consequence, whereas her dissertation argued for the importance of Islam in integration, her bestselling book attributes the lack of integration of Turkish immigrants to the "backwardness" of Muslim culture and the violence inherent in Muslim masculinity. Kelek finds an acceptable action against violence largely in the repudiation of active participation in Islam.

Kelek's eligibility for participation in the DIK has been predicated on the notion that she has been able to cast off the naïveté of liberal multiculturalists to bravely face the problem of violence against immigrant women. Despite numerous criticisms of her positions in the press (see, for example, Am Orde; Seidel)[1] and in scholarship (see, for example Rommelspacher, "Islamkritik") Kelek's narrative of the relationship between Islam and gender violence retains particular resonance in the public sphere, as evidenced by her invitation to join the DIK and her extensive presence in the media. As Birgit Rommelspacher points out, Kelek's work has led to a reduction of the complex issues around immigrant participation in German society—to a question of privileging either women's rights or "cultural" rights (Rommelspacher, "Islamkritik" 434). As Rommelspacher argues, this constructs a false relationship of causality that understands the experience of domestic violence as a sole consequence of Turkish or Muslim heritage, obscuring the roles played by a lack of access to financial independence or access to education (Rommelspacher, "Islamkritik" 436). I further argue that her books, together with other similar autobiographies, are powerful participants in two key narratives that prohibit effective activism against violence. In the first, secularism is constructed as a paradoxical, Christian-influenced, turn away from religion that is necessary to prevent gender violence. In the accompanying public narrative, attention to Islamophobia and racism is discredited as naïve and itself a contributor to gender violence—in other words, not only Islam but antiracist and anti-Islamophobic intentions are attributed responsibility for the existence of gender violence today. Muslim women in Germany today must create their sense of self in dialogue with these two narratives, even though their own understandings of self contradict those narratives. These popular memoirs play an important role, then, in structuring the possibilities for imagining Turkish German women as political subjects who are not only subjects *to* but subjects *of* the making of a German public, who have not only freedom from violence but the freedom to create a world in which they fight against violence. Kelek's popularity certainly contributed to a new recognition of Turkish German women's voices at several important moments. During the headscarf debate, she was recognized as a crucial figure in response to a new desire to hear immigrant voices. After the publication of Thilo Sarrazin's *Germany Does Away with Itself,* she became an important ally and advocate of Sarrazin's ideas. Yet her work demonstrates some of the major restrictions on how women of immigrant heritage can be imagined in the public sphere.

The Foreign Bride was part of a resurgence of bestselling autobiographical books that tell similar stories; a second, Seyran Ateş's *Große Reise ins Feuer. Die Geschichte einer deutschen Türkin* [The Great Journey into the Fire: The Story of a German Turkish Woman, 2003] has earned Ateş a similar expert status, including eventual participation in the DIK. Ateş's and Kelek's dominance in media representations of Muslim women has even extended internationally. In the United States, for example, the mainstream press has often cited or interviewed Kelek and Ateş, with occasional reference to writers of similar autobiographies.[2] Ateş, Kelek, and their contemporaries claim the right to "represent" immigrant women's concerns, yet their prominence obscures attempts to construct critiques of violence that also challenge cultural racism. In this chapter, I wish to consider the specific ways in which violence is conceptualized in popular memoirs in relationship to Islam. The victim narratives, which were particularly popular mid-decade, stand in stark contrast to a more recent body of autobiographical works that were recently dubbed "chick-lit alla turca" (Yeşilada 121), a body of literature in which Turkish German women in their mid-30s engage and negotiate their multiple heritages matter-of-factly and humorously. Given the rather specific context of "chick lit" in the United States and UK, however, I will term these narratives Turkish German women's pop autobiographies. The protagonists of these books are not "caught between two worlds," nor do they tell their life stories as successful journeys from a violent Muslim culture into enlightened European culture. Instead, they complexly situate themselves among multiple contexts that allow a more fluid conceptualization of relationship to multiple communities. Furthermore, many open up possibilities for conceptualizing relationships between gender and racialized violence.

Many of these books are written by journalists who published the pieces as weekly columns before they were gathered as a book. The authors of these books often lightheartedly play the "nice Turkish women from next door" in amusing vignettes; their humor disarms the audience rather than sparking a fear of the Muslim woman (Yeşilada 135). Because they do not focus on violence against women, they are sometimes accused of inauthenticity (Giordano) and have never attained Ateş and Kelek's bestselling author status. Whereas Hatice Akyün's *Einmal Hans mit scharfer Soße* [An Order of Hans with Hot Sauce] became the most well known of these, there have been a number of similar books, including Akyün's follow-up, *Ali zum Dessert* [Ali for Dessert]; Dilek Güngör's *Unter uns* [Among us], *Ganz schön deutsch* [Really Quite German] and *Das Geheimnis meiner türkischen Großmutter* [The Secret of My Turkish Grandmother]; Asli Sevendim's *Candlelight Döner*; and Iris Alanyali's *Die Blaue Reise* [The Blue Journey]. Hilal Sezgin and Dilek Zaptcıoğlu, alternatively, have responded to both autobiographical trends with books that are based on a series of interviews (though Sezgin's book has oddly been marketed, at least visually, as one of the pop autobiographies).

The gender work performed by victim narratives has been seen as crucial to a shift toward constructing difference in Europe in terms of transnational, religious difference rather than ethnonational difference (Yıldız 466). In this chapter, I wish to highlight a different kind of gender work performed by those same narratives, one best revealed with the juxtaposition of victim narratives with the pop narratives of successful integration. The techniques of self that are employed by the wildly popular victim narratives are potent factors in how Islam and violence are understood in German society. They predicate entrance into German society on adherence to a nonreligious identity (or one sympathetic to Christianity) rather than on participation in the public sphere. Potential identification with German society, generally defined through "European" values, is seen as possible only through an individualist identity. Alternatively, the pop narratives reveal a complicated writing of self both against the victim narratives and into the public sphere. Although they only rarely specifically address violence, this avoidance itself becomes a strategy for undoing the power of victim narratives. The possibilities for fighting for rights and for functioning in the public sphere are deeply imbricated in the ways in which stories of self are narrated and powerfully impacted by the function of violence in the narrative of self.

In what follows, I first situate these competing autobiographical trends in a larger discourse within which the German state asserts a national (German) and transnational (European) identity over and against a national (Turkish) and transnational (Muslim) heritage to claim a position as the proper guardian of (immigrant) women's rights, which are primarily framed as Muslim women's rights. The victim narratives, in which violence against women plays a fundamental role in the understanding of self, and in which women undergo a journey in which they ultimately reject Islam and arrive as emancipated "European women," gain popularity because they dovetail so neatly both with popular and with state discourses. The Turkish German women's pop narratives, alternatively, write a subject position in which gender *and* racialized violence overdetermines self together with family, education, relationships, etcetera. A space for the writing of self in relationship to multiple, complex communities is created, which then permits a conceptualization of violence that includes racist violence. My concern here is less with what the imagined Muslim woman tells us about the European who imagines, and more with how the popularity of victim narratives continues to inhabit the public imagination and to inhibit a public presence of Muslim activists against violence, while the pop narratives open space for a more complex relationship to violence.

In the next section, I examine the victim memoirs. My point is not to deny that violence against women is a real and painful part of some immigrant women's lives nor to discredit these particular personal narratives of experiences of violence. Rather, I am interested in how the discourse of Muslim violence circumscribes the writing of self in autobiographical works by Muslim women and how the writing of self in turn creates new possibilities for a public subject. My concern is that an assumption that violence against women is necessarily and intrinsically a part of Islam prevents the writing of a subject who might enter into productive alliances with members of many groups seeking to end a *range* of violence. An invitation to consider and critique violence against women cannot reject potential feminist activism by religious women who both affiliate themselves with a religious heritage or community and reject violence; an assumption that Islam is singular, unchanging, and immutable can only continue to reinforce essentialized positions and can hardly contribute to an effective integration of Germany's Turkish Germans.

In the third section of this chapter, I turn to the body of Turkish German pop integration narratives. Autobiographical writing serves as one possible terrain for constructing an active public self, though the authors I analyze are publicly active in additional ways as well. My analysis of these lighthearted works focuses particularly on forms of affiliation with Muslim heritage, notions of secularism, and education. These themes are deployed by the authors to recontextualize violence, which is removed from a sole location in specifically Muslim or Turkish contexts. As a consequence, these pop pieces are able to negotiate much more complex and fluid relationships to forms of community. They allow the imaginations of Turkish German women, who are educated and active in the workforce, without the outright rejection of Islam and Turkish culture that so often exists in the victim narratives. They furthermore challenge the symbolic function of the Muslim woman and imagine forms of Turkish German female subjecthood that might claim agency in the public sphere.

The competing forms of autobiographies on the European markets by Muslim women demonstrate the deeply conflicted and fraught relationship both to the heritage of the European Enlightenment and to contemporary public spheres. The emergence of a constellation of genres—autobiography, fictional memoirs, and epistolary fiction during European romanticism points to the close link between the foundations of modern conceptualizations of self in response to the enlightenment and their reflection in literary genres (Stelzig 1–2). The *Bildungsroman*, a genre in which the main character journeys outside his or her community in a process of self-education and emergence into reason, has much in common with the structure of the victim narratives I discuss here. Many victim narratives also often follow a structure that is similar to much testimonial literature in which an individual speaks directly to an interlocutor (as opposed to an author speaking *for* the oppressed) to create a joint authorial voice that can bear witness. Whereas testimonial literature has generally served as resistance to an oppressive state, however, this set of victim narratives leads to a recognition of the European state as the proper guardian of human rights rather than as resistance to an oppressive state, as has often been part of the heritage of testimonial literature.

Kelek and Ateş, have written their own texts, claiming to speak not only from their own experiences but also on behalf of Turkish German women. They replicate a discourse of victimhood that greatly limits the terrain on which Turkish German or Muslim women are able to negotiate a presence in the public sphere. Novelist Hatice Akyün has lamented,

> I am not from an Istanbul family of intellectuals. My parents came from an Anatolian village. [...] We are a classic guestworker family! The lawyer Seyran Ateş, whom I truly admire, criticized me for my first book [*An Order of Hans with Hot Sauce*]. But she takes the perspective of the problem cases, the women who come to her office to get help. It is important to bring public attention to these cases. But one cannot only speak of these problem cases! Women such as Seyran Ateş und Necla Kelek have made my German-Turkish life difficult. [...] Simply because they have managed to make their view the dominant one. They are the reason I must justify myself every day. The view that there are forced marriages, honor killings and an abusive father in every family has become predominant. (Am Orde)

Public discussions about Islam and women's rights in Germany continue to be largely shaped by two assumptions: (1) that Islam and women's rights to bodily integrity are mutually exclusive; and (2) that Muslim women are unable to contribute to activism for gender equality and women's rights, particularly if they retain their religious affiliation. The most visible participation in the public debates by immigrant women and women of immigrant heritage is currently largely limited to women who reinforce these assumptions; the bestselling victim autobiographies I discuss here are one manifestation.

Autobiographical narratives have been an important strategy for writing self into history and the nation for many postwar minority groups in Germany, particularly Afro-Germans (Wright 299). For Afro-Germans, writing self into the nation, however, required acquiring a sense of diasporic identity that emerged through contacts to communities outside Germany (Wright 301). Early Turkish German literary works, on the other hand, have been seen as contributing to the formation of a diasporic communal memory that sparked aesthetic and formal experimentation (Seyhan 13). The authors of the victim narratives reject strategies of diaspora building. Instead they seek to write self into a German nation via a dismissal of communities that are non-German. Furthermore, they participate in the shift of writing the Other as a civilizational and transnational Other rather than as an ethnonational other (Yıldız 455–456), while simultaneously seeking a German national identification against identification with Islam. The writers of the pop autobiographies have begun a different kind of political collective work in the broadest sense of the political, as an intervention into relationships of power. Lighthearted as these books are, they gesture toward other imaginations of violence, and in doing so, imagine self as a full participant in German society with connections to Turkish or Muslim communities, which are fraught and tense, as those connections may sometimes be.

Arrival into Modernity as Victim of Violence

The large number of autobiographical narratives in Germany that have been published by Muslim women (or written in collaboration with Muslim women) since 2003 reflects a Europe-wide trend. Widely read, sometimes even attaining bestseller status, they tell of violence at the hands of Muslim men, usually ending with an achievement of freedom from domestic violence by moving to Germany or by escaping their "Turkish" or "Muslim" community. The most popular of these in Germany include Ateş's *Große Reise ins Feuer*, which was published by Rowohlt, and Kelek's *Die fremde Braut* [The Foreign Bride], published by Kiepenheuer and Witsch.[3] Somali Dutch writer Ayaan Hirsi Ali's memoirs *De Maagdenkooi* [The Caged Virgin] and *Mijn Vrijheid* [Infidel] gained massive international attention, and French Algerian Samira Bellil's *Dans l'enfer des tournantes* [To Hell and Back] was also translated into English and attracted significant attention.

One might have expected that the popularity of memoirs by Muslim women, in and of itself, would have created tremendous potential for undoing the assumption that Muslim women are silent. Ironically, the opposite has largely been the case: the authors of these memoirs acknowledge their Muslim heritage but either state or are understood to state an outright rejection of Islam to claim entrance into German society. The autobiographical "I" can establish a claim to authenticity through her status as a victim of violence at the hands of Muslim men, which is seen as legitimized in some way through Islam. This authenticity is further established through a period of isolation; in a twist on the traditional bildungsroman (novel of education) the characters are first isolated from their families and communities and then achieve a successful adulthood—not through reintegration into the community from which they started but, rather, through integration into an ethnic German community, often a community of feminists. When the authors are activists, they work together with their "German sisters" but not with other immigrant women. The narrative structures and strategies of these books echo a similar string of works published in the early 1990s, which were exemplified by a wildly popular translation of American Betty Mahmoody's *Not without My Daughter* as well as by Saliha Scheinhardt's *Frauen die sterben, ohne gelebt zu haben* [Women Who Die without Having Lived, 1983], which gained notoriety through its film adaptation, Tevfik Başer's *Abschied vom falschen Paradies*

[Farewell to a False Paradise, 1989]. Despite this earlier wave of popular victim memoirs, the recent memoirs share as their premise outrage that the plight of Muslim immigrant women has been silenced in German society. Given the hyper-visibility of Muslim women in Germany in discussions about immigrant culture at least since the late 1980s (Göktürk, "Kennzeichen"; Lutz, "Unsichtbare"; Terkessidis, "Globale Kultur"; Weber, "Cloth"; Weber, "Beyond the Culture Trap"), this claim is odd. However, the construction of a continually new crisis, accompanied by the trope of an always blind German society, is crucial to the framing of these books as well as to their popularity. Such framing allows the reader to easily occupy a position on the side of gender justice without questioning how gender disadvantage is racialized. These autobiographies also position their narrators in a world that is clearly composed of "us" and "them;" the narrators' development within the texts consists primarily of moving from the "Turkish world" to the "German" world rather than constructing a new position that can take the narrators' own life experiences as a place from which to reformulate understandings of Turkishness and Germanness, a new position that might be related to what Randall Halle, in his discussion of contemporary German film, terms the possibility of "transnational habitation" (Halle 164–168).

These autobiographical stories function by drawing on personal experiences, not only to establish claims of authenticity about their analysis of a Muslim culture of violence but also to "explain" why immigrant and Muslim women are incapable of making such an analysis themselves if they remain strongly linked to or embedded in an immigrant or Muslim community. A crucial part of the women's survival is developing an independent, individual, "Western" identity that can combat the backwardness of communal identities (beyond, of course, a potential identification with the German state). The books do not function merely as autobiographies; they have effectively served as interventions in the public spheres by launching numerous discussions and debates in the pages of Germany's newspapers and on German airwaves; from Fox News to CNN to National Public Radio, Kelek and Ateş have also been interviewed for many US stories on Muslim women in Europe.

Seyran Ateş, *Grosse Reise ins Feuer*

Ateş moved to Germany at a young age with her Turkish parents. In her book, she details ongoing physical abuse at the hands of her parents and brother, with whom she continues to have a complicated relationship. She intersperses her descriptions of her own experiences while growing up with comments about "das türkische Volk" (The Turkish People; Ateş 30) and their traditions. Her narrative echoes many other narratives that circulate in popular newspapers and television stories: she was treated as her brother's personal slave (53), was repeatedly hit by her brother, father, and mother, and was rarely allowed to leave the house except for school. In 1986 she was seriously wounded in a shooting (she believes by a Kurdish man motivated by his association with the Grey Wolves, a Right-wing group in Turkey) while working for an organization that aids immigrant women; a colleague died in the shooting and she barely survived (Sokolowsky 127). Though this episode is not contained within the book, in 2006 Ateş was forced to briefly give up her practice as a lawyer because of an intensification of the ongoing threats and attacks to which she has been exposed throughout her career ("Ates Wieder").

In her narrative Ateş often attributes her experiences of violence to a "backwards" culture that she defines sometimes as actually more "traditional" than "Muslim" (70), or sometimes as traditional, religious, and feeling threatened by Germans (71). "Our" culture is marked by a willingness to commit violence that serves as the very definition of Kurdish and Turkish culture. Hope for change is rooted in contact with German culture:

> The willingness to commit violence in the Turkish and Kurdish culture will always be a mystery to me. It is beginning to lose its hold in places where Turks and Kurds nurture contact with Germans. But otherwise it is, at the moment, the central difference between our cultures. My story could have befallen every person of every nationality everywhere in the world. It is only the violence and lack of freedom that I experienced as a woman that is, in our time, specifically Turkish or Kurdish, perhaps more attributable to the Islamic culture. [...] Overall, the willingness to kill somebody appears to be more widespread among the Turks and Kurds than among other European people. (239)

As Ateş continues her discussion, she complicates her position. She suggests that the problem is not as simple as she has just described; for example, one ought to recognize that societies develop unevenly (240). Yet, her continued opposition of a modern Germany to a past that is either Muslim or Turkish is indicative of her inability to imagine an Islam of the present, or an Islam capable of change. In this way she adheres to a Western historicist narrative—the distance of Muslim people from enlightened German or European realities becomes one of time, and progress is measured in a teleology that progresses from a Turkish past to a European present.

Interestingly, Ateş's opposition between an enlightened Germany and a backward Turkey immediately precedes a reflection of what it has been like to work in organizations made up almost entirely of German women of nonimmigrant heritage. She suggests that the immigrant women at work in such organizations are often treated as the "little sisters" of the better qualified German women, who do not bother to engage seriously with immigrant women to discuss the latter's needs. The German feminists consider feminism to be German and view the rest of the women in the organizations through an "ethnic lens" (243). Indeed, she suggests that this ethnic lens is the origin for many German feminists' viewpoints of "tolerating the headscarf" (246). Her description of German feminist paternalism indirectly challenges discriminatory feminisms, which often exclude the voices of immigrant women. Yet, for her, it is the willingness to allow a public presence for Islam that is based on ethnic reductionism.

Ateş's work reveals a fundamental contradiction that drives the body of work I've called victim narratives here. Writing self becomes "impossible" at the intersection of several narratives at work: although Ateş reifies the narrative in which Turkish and Kurdish cultures promote a willingness to commit violence, whereas Western Europeans are considered less violent; she also finds herself continually located by German feminists as the "little sister" who must be (and yet can never fully be) educated into Europeanness.

Necla Kelek, *Die fremde Braut*

Kelek's book also draws on her own experiences and those of her mother to validate her account of "Muslim culture." She further solidifies her voice of authority as native informant via her PhD and her interviews with several women who experienced arranged marriages. Kelek has been criticized by academics for reinterpreting the interviews she analyzed in her dissertation for this book, coming to altogether different conclusions than she did in her dissertation (Sokolowsky 121). She has responded by claiming that her advisor placed her under too much pressure while she was a student, preventing her from calling attitudes among Muslim women "neo-Nazi like" (Kelek, "Glück gibt es").

In her book, Kelek juxtaposes her personal experiences and her description of her "community," section by section. In the first half, she tells of her grandparents' marriage, her parents' marriage and divorce, and her childhood. She follows her familial history with a short chapter that tells the history of Islam and women. This juxtaposition reveals the larger tendency to insist that her own story is both synecdoche for and exception to a larger story of the relationship between Islam and gender—typical because of her experiences of violence, exceptional because she has been educated into Europeanness.

Kelek views marriage practices as an important indication that Muslims are unable to adequately participate in German society. One autobiographical chapter ends abruptly with two anecdotes about Muslim men who take advantage of the German welfare system to finance multiple marriages; these anecdotes serve as a transition to a discussion of her interviews with women about their arranged marriages. In these discussions Kelek implies a fundamental incompatibility of Muslim masculinity with subjection to the German nation-state, an incompatibility that is manifested in the oppression of women. Kelek further indirectly conflates polygamy, forced marriage, and arranged marriage, further arguing that forced marriage and arranged marriage are the same (222). She suggests that the practice of arranged marriage is widespread and that those marriages nearly always take place within families, predicting that this will lead to countless genetic problems (231–232). She diagnoses the larger problem as Muslim tradition. For Kelek, Islam is clearly linked to the past and is incapable of dynamically participating in modernist discourses such as feminist discourses: "How little Islam is capable of being reformed at the moment can best be seen from its relationship to women" (Kelek, *Die Fremde Braut* 164); she then lists several Koran verses, and states: "This—in no way complete—list of Qu'ran verses should show that one can hardly speak of a principle of equality in Islam" (166).

Her contradictory arguments reveal her inability to imagine Muslim or Turkish cultures as changing or progressive change as possible. For example, she refers to the headscarf as the flag of the Islamists and criticizes it as the simplification of Islam (246). Yet she herself performs a reduction of Islam to Islamism when she says, "In Muslim communities a dividing line between men and women has been constructed. The man is in the public, the woman in the private, she is the house and the 'honor of the man.' According to Islamic teachings, [she possesses] no reason-, but [is] rather, a sexual being, she lacks the biological preconditions for reason" (242).[4] Though she states explicitly that religion must be understood as responding to historical change (247), she is unable to recognize that many women who identify as Muslim are independent, successful women working to effect change. Instead, Kelek positions herself outside a community with immigrant heritage while using the term migrant to refer to immigrants and those of immigrant heritage: "Can't the migrants open their own mouths? Can't the migrants do something for their own integration?" (255).

Kelek repeats a common move by locating the problem in "tolerance." She argues that tolerance is destroying German culture because "particularly the well-meaning German tends to see in every asylum seeking foreigner the return of a Jew who needs to be saved from the Holocaust" (256). One should note that this is a different rhetoric about the notion of tolerance than the one introduced by Ateş, who critiques a tolerance that reinforces ethnic differences and leads to a paternalistic attitude of ethnic German vis-à-vis Turkish German feminists. Whereas Ateş's point is rooted in an implicit rejection of essentialist understandings of ethnicity, Kelek's rejection of tolerance insists that the history of the Holocaust has made Germans overly sensitive to difference. This "guilt complex" (254–258), Kelek suggests, makes German society overly concerned with identifying racism, indeed, more concerned with protecting immigrants than with protecting the constitution. This position, which denies the ongoing forms of racist and xenophobic violence present in Germany, whether physical attacks or structural forms of racism, is not an uncommon one. Despite the perceived excess of guilt in German society, Kelek wholeheartedly champions German tradition as enabling of women's rights and sets up a dichotomy within which immigrant women must choose—between the German constitution and a misled tolerance that promotes violence. The decades-old tensions that have existed between feminist women of color and immigrant women in Germany and their white German counterparts remain unnoticed.[5] This reductionist rhetoric enables her to be accepted by Germans as a spokesperson for Muslim communities.

Chick Lit alla Turca as Challenge to the Regime of Violence?

Karin Yeşilada's analysis of the new wave of Turkish German women's pop literature locates it in two recent developments. The first is a body of literature that for a time came to be known, somewhat perjoratively, as the *Fräuleinwunder*. Considered evidence of the dominance of postfeminist sensibility, these were successful first-time authors whom media portrayed as young, writing freely about sexuality, and capable of rejuvenating a stagnant German literature; in reality the authors were a range of ages and had little in common (Graves 197–198). Chick lit, which provides the second important context, first became a phenomenon in North American and British culture in the late 1990s, with the immense popularity of *Bridget Jones's Diary*. Also considered proof of the arrival of a postfeminist age, this literature stresses relationships (though not only romantic relationships) and at least superficially independent women who stage new forms of femininity. Common to the Turkish German body of pop literature that Yeşilada has subsumed under *Chick lit alla turca* (at the same time that she problematizes this designation) is the theme of success at negotiating "two cultures." Unlike contemporary US chick lit, which is generally fiction and is often marketed with cartoonlike covers sporting pastels, much Turkish German women's pop lit is largely autobiographical and uses the author's photograph on the cover to further evoke a sense of realism. The use of photographs in promotional material and on the covers highlights the importance of a claim to authenticity for the Turkish German manifestation of this genre. The authors often write autobiographical pieces that invite the reader to observe the "real" Turkish German life in which they are successful career women (often journalists or writers), who ably negotiate "two cultures" partly by strategically incorporating the exoticization of the Turkish German woman into an autonomous sexuality. Such portrayals of Turkish German women undermine both the stereotypes of religious-patriarchal Turkish culture as well as the hypermasculinity constructed as an alternative via the Kanak movement (Yeşilada 136). Can this literature offer alternatives to the victim narratives I discuss above, alternatives that enable a more productive engagement with the public sphere? This is best achieved in the rare moments when these works move away from the emphasis on a revelation of a private, familial, or romantic space to the public eye, perhaps especially when they are haunted by moments of violence. I've chosen three books to focus on here: (1) *Einmal Hans mit scharfer Soße,* because of its popularity (though not approaching the popularity of the victim narratives); (2) *Die blaue Reise,* because it tells a different story—that of a girl growing up with a German mother and a Turkish father; and (3) *Typisch Türkin,* which deliberately moves away from the genre of autobiography in a move to undo perceptions of a "typical Turkish woman."

Hatice Akyün, *Einmal Hans mit scharfer Soße*

Like North American chick lit, Hatice Akyün's *Einmal Hans mit scharfer Soße* (and its sequel, *Ali zum Dessert*) is a lighthearted look at her own everyday life that ranges from her relationship with her parents, her lovers, and, most importantly, even encompasses her clothing and footwear. The subtitle, "Life in Two Worlds," immediately reveals itself as misleading. In the opening pages she describes herself as "A Turkish woman with a German passport, for politicians the best example of successful integration" (Akyün 7). She is also "a journalist [....] I don't wear a headscarf and haven't been forcibly married, which is why I still don't have a husband" (7). Unfortunately, this means that every time she visits Turkey, she is asked, "Have you found your Hans yet?" (8). While the initial pages suggest that the writer does not conceptualize her life as lived between two separate worlds, she also sometimes draws on a rhetoric of living in two worlds that simply don't come together. Yet the sort of trauma of "two worlds" that is often perpetuated in public discourse is humorously downplayed by Akyün—instead, her struggle is an attempt to unite the fortune foretold her (by reading her mokka cup in Turkey) with her reality in Germany.

The nimble negotiation of the complexities of life as a Turkish German extends into the author's engagement with religious life. Despite the book's lighthearted tone Islam is present throughout, but its association with violence is undermined. Like Kelek, Akyün invokes memories of religion through reference to Koranic verses. Hatice can still recite by heart verses her father taught her as being the "most important" verses of the Koran. Unlike the oft-cited verses in victim memoirs, which are linked to punishment for adultery, beating of women, headscarves, and gender segregation, the verses Hatice remembers and cites are those of a benevolent Allah (46). Muslim piety is linked to living in Germany; the author's father did not become religious until he came to Germany (66). Hatice's memories of her father and her childhood experiences of Islam appear nostalgic—inflected by the usual generational conflict, but without significant tension. Out of respect for her father, she wears knee-length skirts and 3/4-length sleeves when she goes to visit but doesn't feel oppressed as a woman by that choice (75). Indeed, any form of conflict is imagined as a fleeting consequence of youthful rebellion.

Akyün's mother's relationship to Islam is also relatively uncomplicated and is primarily expressed through the wearing of a hijab. In contrast to the constantly repeated mantra present in victim narratives of girls who are forced to wear headscarves from a young age, Akyün's mother emphasized that wearing a hijab was something that was only acceptable as a choice made, at the earliest, in late adolescence. For her, the hijab was more a question of Islamic tradition than of piety. For Akyün's sister, in contrast, taking a hijab marks both religiosity and personal fashion sense (70). Akyün herself does not wear a hijab; in fact, she insists tongue in cheek that her only "religious experience" involves shoes.

This isn't to say that her father wouldn't have liked to see her married to a Turkish Muslim. However, a forced marriage was never a threat, and when the question is posed to her about whether she wasn't to be married off, she answers in jest: "Yes, for four camels and a tractor, but there weren't any camels at the time in Central Anatolia, and the family wouldn't give up the tractor, because it was to be invested in the bride of the elder son" (105). Even an arranged marriage is barely of interest to the family. The one time Akyün's parents asked her to consider marriage with a man who had expressed his interest, she agrees to a meeting. The meeting goes comically awry when Akyün's father is so insecure and uncomfortable with his role that he suggests she take over the interview.

For much of the book, then, the forms of gender violence attributed to the everyday existence of German Turkish women are invoked only to point out the absence of gender violence in the author's life. There are only two moments in the book in which the author describes violence as actually occurring. The sudden shift in tone surrounding these two short passages highlight their importance: the tone of the writing becomes suddenly serious in this otherwise lighthearted book. The first is when Akyün remembers the victims of the xenophobic attack at Solingen in 1993. One of the girls who died was also named Hatice; consequently, she experiences the attack as directed at her as well. The second mention of violence is an abstracted violence that takes the form of an imagined bodily discipline: "Without a doubt, there are Muslim girls and women who are forced to wear the headscarf. But there are many more women like my older sister, for whom the headscarf is symbol of her religious belonging, worn by her own choice and with pride" (182). Her sister also has two daughters, who wear no headscarf, who "also are familiar with different parallel worlds, but dance effortlessly between them" (183). Whereas violence is thus imagined as possible within Islam, the threat of racist violence poses a more immediate threat.

Einmal Hans is certainly not a particularly complex engagement with the discourses of gender violence so prominent in Germany nor an explicit writing into the public sphere. As Yeşilada implies, it has the potential to become dangerous in its very harmlessness and avoidance of confrontation, even as it is subversive (Yeşilada

134–135). Its offering to the reader of a glimpse of an unknown, but "real" space potentially allows an easy appropriation by discourses of authenticity, of a desire to "know" the native informant. Yet, at these moments when the book goes beyond a mere invitation into the private life of its narrator, important strategies emerge. Although the stylization of self as a sexy vamp serves as the counter discourse to many representations of Turkish German women as victims of male violence, the haunting of the text by Solingen's racist violence opens the smallest space for rethinking violence as constituted not, or not only, by Turkish patriarchy but also by German society and racism. In a society where the position of the Turkish German woman is so often marked by a gender violence and danger that not only marks Muslim women as victims of gender violence but also produces the Muslim woman herself as a threat, the "harmlessness" of the non-threatening Muslim woman provides an intervention that enables a normalization of the woman of Turkish heritage as German subject. Although the narrative is personal, Akyün normalizes both the professional woman and the religious woman of Turkish heritage. Nevertheless, this normalization also entails a lack of critical engagement with the public sphere despite the author's own professional life as a journalist, which is dependent on an active public presence.

Iris Alanyali, *Die blaue Reise*

Iris Alanyali's *Die blaue Reise* [The Blue Journey], is marketed more similarly to US chick lit novels, with a cartoon cover that provides an obviously "Oriental" take on the popular chick lit shoe motif. However, fashion and romance play only marginal roles in the book. Alanyali is also a journalist, but as the daughter of a German woman and a Turkish man, the invitation to view the private familial life is an invitation to an already multicultural family. Indeed, for the autobiographical narrator, the title's Blue Journey is partly a journey to learn more about her Turkish heritage, though necessarily, as she says, from the perspective of a German.

The book's opening is telling in terms of reader expectations that the author hopes to undermine. She says she has a few things she had better immediately clarify to prevent disappointment: "I'm not sitting between all chairs [zwischen allen Stühlen] or swaying between two worlds [...] Apparently I am an unusual Turkish German woman. I can't stand platform shoes, and I don't have five brothers consumed by helpless rage [...] My father beats neither us nor our mother and can even form German relative clauses" (Alanyali 16). In an interview for her alumni magazine, Alanyali points to the importance of undermining assumptions about violence as well: "I wanted to provide an alternative to the forced marriage and kidnapping biographies" (I. Winter).

As counterpoint to the expectation of a narrative as victim of familial violence, Alanyali considers what it has come to mean to be constructed as Turkish in German society: "And so we were made Turks: by our Turkish relatives, who showed us the nice sides of their lives and, shaking their heads, filled us with familial dedication [Familiensinn] and love for home [Heimatliebe]. By the Germans, who happily praise us as ideal Turks, because we are so German. And by ourselves—because we have begun to search for our roots" (Alanyali 12). Unlike so many narratives, whether in the pop lit/chick lit style, or the victim memoirs I described earlier, Alanyali's book is not the story of a journey away from Turkishness to arrive into German modernity. She desires instead to find a connection to Turkish culture while avoiding the pitfalls of "searching for roots." Her writing of the book also takes place with full awareness of the discomfort she feels when her verbal portraits of her family in Turkey become dubbed tokens of "the true Turkey" and her personal and familial experiences are used to mark her as expert in all things Turkish (249). Her journey cannot take place without engaging the conflicting understandings of Turkish modernity that emerge in contemporary Germany, understandings that further reveal the divide between urban and rural Turkey as well as those between educational and economic groups in Turkey. In other words, in her "Blue Journey," Alanyali herself has to recognize her own positioning in these divides and eventually comes to a point where "At some point I began to look at Turk with big noses and headscarves as more than mere foreigners" (17).

Like many of the contemporary pop narratives, *Die blaue Reise* emphasizes that Alanyali has not been the victim of familial violence or forced marriages. Indeed, the only family in the book that sends a brother to protect the virtue of a woman is a Christian German family. One of Alanyali's father's early girlfriends, Hildegard, has a pastor father and comes from a conservative German Christian family. The narrative reconfigures the traditional kidnapping narrative that is often told in Turkish German victim narratives. Because Alanyali's father has been dating Hildegard, Hildegard's father accuses him of kidnapping. Hildegard's brother is sent to "rescue" her, and although Hildegard dismisses her brother, the intercultural relationship dissolves soon thereafter. Shocked by the behavior of Hildegard's brother, who seems to be echoing the behavior of an "Anatolian brother" (52), Alanyali's father breaks a wine bottle and threatens the brother with the broken glass.

This version of "Anatolian violence," sparked by "Swabian macho," (52) is paralleled only by one other incidence of violence on her father's part. In this case, he defends a Yugoslavian man who is being insulted and attacked, presumably by a Neo-Nazi gang. While the Yugoslavian man runs away, Alanyali's father is then assaulted and ends up in a hospital. Musing to herself, the author considers: "The Turk is fighting on the street, and the German [Alanyali's mother] complains about it to her eight year old. That's exactly what people want to hear" (53). Violence reveals itself, in this case located in a racialized Christian context, while Alanyali's adult voice exposes her concern that this story can easily be told as proof of "Turkish violence" rather than as an example of resistance to racist violence.

Islam itself is viewed by the author as a benevolent presence in her life, though religion is rejected by both her mother (also the daughter of a Protestant pastor) and her father. Her exposure to Islam occurs primarily through her grandmother and great aunt, who move to be near Alanyali's father. The grandmother presents an "Allah" as a sort of Santa Claus on permanent duty (93), while the great aunt simply sees Allah as the source of all good, in opposition to Germany as the source of all evil (97). The author speculates that Ramadan should have made Islam particularly appealing to the teenage Alanyali, consumed as she was by various diets. The idea of covering up in loose clothing and fasting for the month might have been a good solution, says Alanyali, but the problem was, Ramadan was about eating, not fasting (95).

Alanyali also wryly writes of her younger selves to dismantle the constructions of a division between "West-Turks" and Anatolians, one that many urban educated Turks deploy to position themselves as Western. She parodies the West-Turks as the fairly well paid, laicist Turks, generally from the well-educated middle class, for whom everything Western is better—from tea bags to American education. They love Atatürk and hate Islamists, but their deepest hatred is reserved for the behavior of the rural Turks (101), whom her own family calls the "Turks with moustaches and headscarves" or "Ali-Babas" (101). From the perspective of the West-Turks, the Anatolians are visible because of their moustaches and headscarves but are equally importantly marked by their tendency to honor murder and the imprisonment of their daughters. West-Turks are embarrassed by the visibility of the East-Turks, and irritated that countries are "dumb enough" to allow them entry (100).

Even though the two supposedly distinct groups manage to maintain their distance from each other in Germany, in airports they cannot avoid each other and are revealed as remarkably similar. Humorously, Alanyali displaces the difference between the two groups from dress codes and experiences of violence to groceries:

> And regardless of whether their members [the Anatolians] are deeply veiled, or the sons run around in pink polo shirts and the daughters in cropped tops – the bags of groceries they all schlep along are fundamentally the same. And not only back to Germany, but also back home. The German border officials grin with laughter, German tourists shake their heads in wonder – but the West-Turks crammed between their fellow countrymen cannot relax a bit. (102)

Alanyali and her sister replicate the division between West-Turks and Anatolians as children. They strike up a friendship with girls from an Anatolian family, which for the Alanyali sisters means using their superior position to order their friends around. They also see themselves as tasked with educating the girls but are certain that any books about modern Turkish girls will be incomprehensible to their friends. Alanyali thus suggests a division among Turkish Germans that rests upon the class and educational differences present in Turkey, but which nevertheless further replicates the differences constructed by many indigenous Germans. The West-Turks, including two generations of her own family, are able to occupy a position of "European" superiority vis-a-vis their Others, who are perceived as religious, rural, and uneducated. At the same time, by presenting this division Alanyali evokes a discrimination that has taken place in Turkey in conjunction with the turn to Europe and toward a European modernization process—a project of nationhood that excluded the rural east from the resources necessary for modernization—and that included the repression of Kurdish culture. The nationalist modernization reforms are invoked specifically only briefly, when Alanyali recalls that the Arabic script was banned by Atatürk, but then reveals that reform as incomplete (110). This history is remembered once more in the book, when Alanyali undergoes an interview for admission to journalism school. She is floored when she is asked what she thinks about the "Kurdish problem." Although her only personal connection to the "Kurdish problem" is "her aunt in Istanbul, who always shopped at Kurdish vendors at the market, because they had the best produce" (247), she frames her response in terms of violence and rights: "Well, the PKK is a terrorist organization that is justifiably banned. But the fact that the Kurds must repress their own culture is wrong. Of course they should be allowed to speak their language and dance their folk dances" (248). The interview committee is less than pleased with this response. At their attempt to interpellate her into their view of Turkishness by inserting her into a narrative of violence, she instead responds (though vaguely) with a condemnation of violence but also an insistence on the right to cultural expression.

The engagement with forms of discrimination in the text is, however, marginal—and deeply ambivalent. When asking her parents about their own experiences, Alanyali uses the metaphor of an eraser that leaves crumbs. Both parents claim that experiences of marginalization have been largely irrelevant to their lives; to Alanyali this seems as if many of their experiences have been erased, while Alanyali makes a point of discovering the "crumbs" left behind by the eraser. In a way this applies to Alanyali herself, who insists that being half Turkish lent her a special exotic flair rather than exposing her to any forms of discrimination (133). Yet other contradictory moments emerge in the text, from a Neo-Nazi demonstration in Sindelfingen to the expectations placed on her by her boyfriend and friends in Berlin. In these situations Alanyali becomes both the embodiment of an accessible Turkishness [eine Türkin zum Anfassen] and the completely different, exoticized Turkish woman (205).[6] The descriptions of witnissing domestic and familial violence contribute to this ambivalent relationship to a Turkish community. While in school, for example, Alanyali was asked to translate and mediate between a Turkish family who refused to allow their daughter to receive extra tutoring (133), whereas her father's project to "create" an educated Turk out of a distant cousin fails when the cousin marries a Turkish woman and beats her, then repeats the beatings in two subsequent marriages.

Die blaue Reise describes a repeatedly and in part deliberately thwarted journey into Turkishness. Because Alanyali can point to examples of familial violence, but cannot herself fulfill the expected mediatory role of the Muslim woman who would provide access to lived experience of Muslim violence, she becomes doubly Other. Based on her family's experiences, she must write both with and against the dominant narrative of Muslim gender violence. In doing so she finds herself written into other narratives—of East-West difference within Turkey and of Turkish-Kurdish violence.

Her uneasy relationship to her Muslim heritage is reflected by an equally uneasy response to violence. Whereas her friends may react to racist violence by participating in demonstrations, she views this sort of activism with a healthy "Turkish" skepticism (133). The experience of gender violence is so foreign to her, yet such an expected part of a Turkish German experience, that she finds herself unable to participate in action against it. Alanyali's reliance on education as the most important aspect of "integration," and her desire to consider the "Anatolian Other" more carefully, further removes her from involvement in a political community: West-oriented Turks hate her for her typical "multiculti" sympathy for rural Turks, Anatolians consider her a traitor for her dedication to secularism, and Germans are disappointed, depending on their political orientation—either because she thinks Turkey could join the EU or because she complains about Turkey's backwardness in some areas of politics (253–254).

The unresolved ambivalence vis-à-vis forms of community as well as the awkward negotiations of the positions constructed for her by German society disturb the easy tone of the narratives and the self-deprecating humor. Although Alanyali's narrative often rejects organized politics, *The Blue Journey* makes a potential political intervention precisely in its ambivalence. This uncertainty is not born of a rejection of Turkish heritage, but rather of a desire to seek that heritage while carefully attending to the layers of constraining narratives of "being Turkish" or "being Muslim," and while simultaneously rejecting a notion of authenticity. Whereas many Turkish German women's pop narratives use a claim to authenticity to counteract the dominant victim narrative, Alanyali has rejected this strategy in favor of consistent destabilization of narratives of ethnicitiy and, for that matter, of any narrative of self. Alanyali concludes the book with a brief epilogue:

> Whether the stories are all true? Well, I certainly may have confused many names, places and times. And I left many things out, and exaggerated much as well. But I can't remember everything exactly, and have also downplayed some things. So given all that, I would say the stories are very true. (254)

In this way Alanyali continues her strategy of narrative instability by destabilizing even her own relationship to memory.

Hilal Sezgin, *Typisch Türkin*

Among the recent Turkish German pop narratives, *Typisch Türkin* by Hilal Sezgin provides a particularly interesting alternative to the popular victim narrative. At first glance it may seem odd to include this book in a section on largely autobiographical narratives. A journalist, like many other Turkish German pop writers, Sezgin uses her position to enable several second-generation Turkish German women to participate in the construction of a collective autobiography. Rather than tell her own life story, Sezgin interviews 19 women to write a story of learning about the lives of Turkish German women. Through Sezgin's reflection on their discussions, her portrait of the nonexistent "typical Turkish woman" also confronts her with her own problematic assumptions about Islam. Thus even though the book is not an autobiography, it does contain the thread of an autobiographical story: the journey within the book, for her, as a relatively nonreligious Muslim, is partly a journey to acceptance of the range of possible Muslim Turkish and German identities.

In *Typisch Türkin*, the interviews Sezgin conducts serve as starting points for 13 essays, thematically organized, each of which reflects on the range of positions occupied by Turkish German women vis-à-vis the theme at hand. The book's structure alone serves to challenge the notion of a "typical Turkish woman." Sezgin seeks out a range of ages and occupations, finding the most important commonality in the desire to take advantage of the strengths of all cultures in which they participate (Sezgin, *Typisch Türkin?* 11). This book is marketed in ways that are similar to pop literature, but *Typisch Türkin* is less a participant in the Turkish German pop phenomenon than a response to it, a revelation of the problematic notion of the "typical Turkish woman." Whereas Alanyali destabilizes the narrative of "Turkish woman," Sezgin pluralizes it.

Sezgin's book addresses Islam much more overtly than the body of Turkish German pop literature. In fact, religion is a fundamental part of the various worlds negotiated by the women she interviews. Sezgin wishes to remedy the fact that "only the noticeable Islam makes headlines, only the violent Muslims are mentioned as Muslims" (150). She is further motivated by the inadequacy of the traditional explanation for increasing religiosity in Germany, namely, that isolation and ghettoization in Germany, together with an increasing distance to the "homeland," promote a search for identity that fossilize antiquated beliefs about Islam (110–111). Sezgin sees a fundamental misunderstanding regarding Muslims, Christians, and their relationship to rationality and violence. Rather than juxtaposing Christian or secular rationality to Muslim irrationality that leads to violence, she argues that Muslims understand their religion as compatible with rationality—the beliefs within Islam are neither contractor, nor in conflict with the knowledge provided by the life sciences (114). Her interviews also counteract accusations of self-isolation or segregation that are often leveled at Muslims in the victim narratives I discussed in the first part of this chapter. For example, one interviewee, Zeynep, has parents who insisted on Christian religious education as a means of understanding the world in which they live (112). As a result, her reflections on Muslim traditions are contextualized by her experiences with Christianity. Zeynep is prohibited from fasting until she reaches the age of 14; simultaneously she finds herself increasingly interested in the Christian culture, despite the shock she experienced on hearing that communion involves the consumption of the body of Christ. Zeynep finds participation in any German religious community, however, to be impossible. She is frustrated by the strict gender separation and conservatism of German mosques and thus enters mosques only in Turkey (116–117). Elif, alternatively, engages with Islam only after reading German author Herman Hesse's *Siddhartha*. She develops an eclectic understanding of religion through which she also feels a deep affinity to Christianity and Judaism, all developed as a consequence of her encounter with a fictional text written in German. For both Elif and Zeynep, the experience of Muslim culture occurs *through* German culture, rather than in isolation from it.

In the chapter "The Deal with the Headscarf" [Die Sache mit dem Kopftuch] the narrator sketches a range of positions within the Turkish German community regarding the headscarf ban for German public schoolteachers, a range that reflects the one held by women of ethnic German heritage (131). Several women are frustrated by the conflation of the headscarf with Islam and with terrorism (132; 134); as one social worker points out, "Everything is confused: headscarf and forced marriage, Islam and circumcision. In such a context the headscarf can only mean one thing: oppression. That isn't true, however" (133). Many find themselves equally frustrated with believers who have also equated the headscarf with Islam and have listened uncritically to the clerics, creating an unnecessary division between believers and nonbelievers (132). Others are irritated by the hypocrisy prompted by the fraught meanings attached to the headscarf. These include a young lawyer, who describes religious women in her practice who only wear the headscarf when their husbands are around (132). Yet others cite the fact that many girls wear the headscarf while living independent lives or point out the tension between a notion of neutrality and the fact that in practice, the children cannot be treated neutrally if the headscarf is banned (133; 136).

The discussions with the interviewees lead Sezgin to conclude that the headscarf functions to create a perceived boundary between "tradition and modernity, emancipation or not, democracy or religious withdrawal" (136), a revelation that in turn confronts her with her own assumptions about Islam. In approaching the book, Sezgin found herself in full agreement with the interviewee, Elif, who argues that a woman lawyer wearing a headscarf immediately signals an inability to be neutral (136). Then Sezgin meets Neslihan, a lawyer who wears the hijab. Although Neslihan considers the headscarf a religious obligation, she is nevertheless critical of its instrumentalization by some Muslims:

> First of all, what is a religious commandment or not, that is decided between God and each individual. It is not the role of any men, hocas, or whomever to declare that a woman should behave in this way or that. Furthermore it is a travesty [eine Schweinerei], when the headscarf is instrumentalized for their interest. When I hear that young girls are forcibly married, and then they say, "That is the way it is with us in Islam [...] I fight against it, that something like that would be justified religiously, also among Muslims. (139)

Sezgin is surprised by Neslihan's views—particularly by the fact that Neslihan insists on women educating themselves and working outside the home—and then disappointed in her own surprise, recognizing that she herself has incorporated the dominant representations of Muslim women into her own imaginations of Islam and gender. She is particularly impressed, however, by Neslihan's views on the scarf in relationship to a form of "protection" from the male gaze. Neslihan considers herself a feminist and has actively challenged a coworker who sexually harassed all the women coworkers, except Neslihan. Upon questioning him, he admitted that he viewed the headscarf as a prohibitive signal:

> Mr. Soandso, I said, you also cannot treat other women in that way! The fact that they don't wear a headscarf does not mean that they are free game! [...] Many Turkish men also think in this way, and even women! Once there was a rape trial, and the old women let loose comments like: "No wonder that happened, she was wearing a miniskirt after all." Then I said, 'EXCUSE ME? And what about the man? *He* is the one who raped her. (147)

Neslihan's words expose and challenge the heteronormative logic that assumes the rapability of the exposed body, and the problem with basing the right to wear the headscarf on such logic. The legitimization of covering to manage male desires is "a dangerous thing" (147). Neslihan thus provides an explicit contestation of gender violence from the position of a Muslim woman, one that challenges the logic of violence itself.

Certainly, this book is not a deliberate and extended engagement with the notion of Muslim violence. On the contrary, although *Typisch Türkin* quite explicitly engages with Islam and with women's experiences as Turkish Muslims, it only skims the surface of a number of successful negotiations performed by Turkish German women in radically different ways: negotiations of notions of rationality, religion, and science; of a range of potential religious positionings; and even of the imagination of various ways of resisting or speaking against violence. The necessity of a strategy of writing against the trope of the "typical Turkish woman" would make it difficult, on the other hand, to imagine organization against violence. The stories further remain the stories of individuals rather than those of individuals who participate in organization against violence. Yet the introduction of figures such as Neslihan opens the possibility for the imagination of the Muslim women as *present* and even *active* in the public sphere, both as Muslim and as standing against gender violence. These possibilities are further enacted by Akgün's later work, *Aufstand der Kopftuchmädchen* [Uprising of the Headscarf Girls], in which she documents Muslim girls' resistance to Islamist discourses. Sezgin also edited *Manifest der Vielen* as a response to Sarrazin's *Deutschland schafft sich ab*; the contributions to this book insist on the ways that Muslims are productive participants in German democracy and in determining a better future for Germany.

Pop Lit as Corrective to Victim Narrative?

The figures represented in these three books are able to negotiate much more complex and fluid relationships to forms of community than the victim memoirs discussed above. Like other pieces that have been considered as part of this genre, Akyün's negotiations often resort to the rhetoric of "two cultures," with repeated designation of "Turkish" and "German" characteristics and values, but they reveal women who are completely comfortable negotiating the cultures they view as so different. They move beyond a narrative of backward community, which is juxtaposed with enlightened Germany, to allow imaginations of Turkish German women who are educated and active in the workforce while claiming a connection to Islam and an affiliation with a Turkish or Turkish German community. Yet, for many authors writing Turkish German pop autobiographies, including Akyün, Alanyali, and Güngör, the narrative remains almost claustrophobically confined to the immediate family, with some exception for the romantic relationships developed by the narrators. We know that these women are working writers, but we see only the most fleeting allusions to that work in the literature. Although the space of home and family is no longer one that is marked by gender violence in the way that earlier fiction often portrayed Turkish German women, in a sense this simply redefines the limited space of home as playground rather than as prison. In taking away their freedom to imagine their world, their world seems to shrink surprisingly. This tendency seems particularly unexpected, given the authors' careers as journalists, and often takes critical stances on deeply political issues.

Sezgin, alternatively, permits a challenge to the symbolic function of the Muslim woman. *Typisch Türkin* imagines forms of Turkish German female subjectivity that claim agency in the public sphere. Sezgin's work, while also humorous and lucid, performs a much different intervention than that of the Turkish German pop autobiographies. Whereas the aspects of life associated with the private sphere, including gendered division of labor in the household, imaginations of ideal partnerships, and notions of fulfillment and happiness all are part of the book, the figures present in the book are also imagined as part of public life. Neslihan, for example, participates in the secular, democratic state every day by the nature of her job and also makes everyday interventions into gender relations that are informed by her identity as a feminist.

While in Akyün's work, violence is merely made harmless, as a threat that can be disarmed with humor, Alanyali seems occasionally to depict herself as so thoroughly different from other Turkish German women that her experiences of nonviolence become largely irrelevant. Sezgin takes on the complications of acknowledging the existence of gender violence while still considering challenges to the regime of violence. Sezgin's normalization of a Turkish German woman in German society does not rely on a simplified representation of the home as marked by the harmonious resolution of juvenile conflicts. Instead, conflicts are brought to the fore as forms of debate that take place, though not literally, between women in a range of positions. These conflicts also serve as impetus for Sezgin to reflect on the long history of working Turkish women in Germany.

Notably absent from the entire body of pop Turkish German autobiography, however, is a desire to turn to the State as protector from violence. Instead, the characters in these works claim a "freedom to make the world," (Sunder) which is predicated on a "freedom from violence" that exists, not because they have been freed by the German state or by German culture, from the violence of a Turkish Muslim heritage. Rather, their "freedom" has been negotiated from a complex engagement with multiple heritages, which are often contradictory and ambivalent but nevertheless successful and public. Their freedom to make the world by participating in the public sphere is haunted by the existence of violence—gendered and racialized—even as they articulate a world in which they refuse to allow violence to occupy significant space. Particularly when the pop lit texts are able to move outside a depiction of a family's private life, they represent immigrant women characters who successfully condemn violence without the need to reject affiliation with family and community. Indeed, even when the narratives are confined to a focus on the family, they nevertheless serve as another rejection of victim narratives—precisely by inviting the reader's voyeuristic gaze into the family home, the Turkish family is rendered as a space fraught with generational conflict, but as capable of nonviolence as that of the indigenous German family.

The claim to authenticity—in terms of writing self in the case of most of the writers and highlighting a range of voices in the case of Sezgin—becomes another strategy by which the victim narratives, so popular in Germany today, can be countered. In a context where the politics of "speaking for" has been claimed by a small number of Turkish German women and their ghostwriters who tell autobiographical stories of gender violence, the lighthearted narratives of the so-called chick lit can only be written as nonfictional narratives. Yet, despite their authors' successful careers as journalists, the books are confined to only moderate success by the very regime of violence they seek to challenge. As women whose very existence as public German subjects is predicated on a relationship to Muslim violence, they must write in relationship to that perception of violence, even if they reject it. This, then, becomes the founding violation of the subject, who is not only founded *in* violence but *as* violence. The representations of violence in the pop narratives echo those created by organizations of immigrant heritage women against violence. Take, for example, the group Göçmen Kadınlar Birliği, Bundesverband der Migrantinnen in Deutschland e.V. (National Federation of Immigrant Women in Germany; henceforth, BdMD), based in Frankfurt. This umbrella organization represents some 23 local organizations, claiming 500 active members and some 6000 sympathizers; they were the first migrant group to become members of the largest German feminist organization, the Deutscher Frauenrat (German Women's Association), another umbrella organization (Göçmen Kadınlar Birliği—Bundesverband der Migrantinnen in Deutschland e.V, "Verband"). The BdMD has been critical of recent changes to laws on forced marriage, which in the name of protecting the rights of immigrant women actually further restricted access to residency in Germany and made immigrant women more dependent on their spouses (Göçmen Kadınlar Birliği—Bundesverband der Migrantinnen in Deutschland e.V, "Presserklärung zum jüngst beschlossenen Gesetzespaket"). The group identifies its primary goal as the "integration" of immigrant women and further points to worker's rights as equally important to questions of domestic violence and forced marriage in this endeavor.

BdMD has also been outspokenly critical of Kelek and Ateş's claims that they speak for Muslims, and in particular for immigrant Muslim women. For example, after a series of brutal murders in Berlin, Göçmen Kadınlar Birliği articulated the following critique:

> We, the National Association for Immigrant Women, are concerned and angered about the way in which the current discussion about forced marriage and violence against women is being held. The results of years of immigration research are suddenly degraded as

unscientific and distant from reality. Instead, the representatives from politics and media rely on 2–3 women of immigrant heritage. Yet, there is precisely the huge contradiction: Those who are actually the subject of the contemporary debate are not allowed to speak. Certain women, such as Seyran Ateş and Necla Kelek, step into the limelight and "enjoy" their attention as self-designated representatives of immigrant women. They speak in the name of immigrant women—yet they AREN'T immigrant women! (Göçmen Kadınlar Birliği—Bundesverband der Migrantinnen in Deutschland e.V, "Menschenrechtsverletzungen")

These women are carefully considering the multiple politics of representation, both in terms of *Darstellung* (depiction) and *Vertretung* (political representation). The BdMD seeks active participation in the public sphere without rejecting a connection to Turkish heritage. At the same time, its membership is also open to women of other immigrant groups, while it avoids association with Islam.

I do not wish to paint an overly idealistic picture of this group, which could also be critiqued on several grounds. Religion and religious questions, as well as racism, are noticeably absent from their agenda, which nevertheless points out structural problems (access to work) and anti-immigrant sentiment (reflected in the latest "forced marriage laws") as major priorities for change (Göçmen Kadınlar Birliği—Bundesverband der Migrantinnen in Deutschland e.V, "Presserklärung zum jüngst beschlossenen Gesetzespaket"). My point is rather that the narrative which identifies immigrant women as unable to organize as a group—one that identifies *as immigrants* around gender issues—is so powerful that this long-standing umbrella organization remains virtually absent from press coverage, whereas Kelek and Ateş are considered well-known experts on immigrant women's issues.

A related point was made in a recent exchange between two journalists, Hilal Sezgin and Mely Kiyak, in response to a discussion about "the new feminism." In this discussion, much had been made of the difficulty German women have in balancing working lives and children. Kiyak published an article in July in *Die Zeit*, in which she expresses dismay that in this debate, immigrant women are conspicuously absent—as women who have *always* been working and maintaining families, and, furthermore, as women who are discriminated against in their access to employment. Their concerns are always subjugated to the "integration" debate (but rarely as concerns about employment access) and are never part of feminism debates (Kiyak).

Sezgin responds with an interesting rejoinder in the pages of *Die Tageszeitung*, arguing that immigrant women have been *too* visible for German feminists (Sezgin, "Das Schlagloch: Feminismus Ist Unteilbar"). Indeed, given the feminist industry trading in stories of oppressed Turkish women, Sezgin proposes that it may be more useful to think of an "indivisible" feminism that is relevant to all women, given that both violence and employment inequalities impact all women. Sezgin points to and values the important challenges made to feminism in the past by feminists of color and lesbians, but points out that once again, a German discussion of feminism has been focused on the heterosexual white woman. Yet she suggests that a new conception of unity might be necessary to combat the hyper-visibility of the Muslim woman in these discussions (and, she implies, to point out ways in which white heterosexual feminists profit by participating in this hyper-visibility). Recognizing difference, in other words, is not always a progressive move.

Groups such as Göçmen Kadınlar Birliği are almost never cited in the German press, nor did the discussion between Sezgin and Kiyak arouse the same kind of attention that had been received by Kelek and Ateş. Nevertheless, Kiyak's article did earn her some respect; as a consequence, she has earned a presence on the national stage as an expert on feminism, and this 2008 article is often cited as a reason for her invitation to panels. Her positions reduced her visibility in the DIK, where she also served during the first phase, which ended in 2009. While Kelek and Ateş were members of the highly visible "core" of the DIK, called the plenary [*Plenum*], Kiyak served as a member of a working group on media representation during the DIK's first phase. This working group seems to have had minimal impact. The goals articulated for the DIK's second phase are: to work on structural integration of Muslims, which is defined primarily as integration into state structures through the normalization of Islam as a religion under German law; and the achievement of integration, which is seen as achievable through a focus on gender equality and prevention of extremism and polarization ("Struktur der DIK"). This continued limitation of structural integration to incorporation of Islam into state structures that regulate religion, and of societal integration to the achievement of gender equality, continues to reinforce the sense that active participation for Muslims in German society can only be attained via the paternal protection of the state and the correction of perceived tendency to separation and violence. An addressing of Islamophobia and employment disparities remains noticeably absent from these goals. The complex relationship between Islam, immigrant women, and feminism in the fight against gendered violence further remains largely unrecognized.

The extensive attention to familial violence runs the danger of obscuring the economic and employment discrimination faced by women of immigrant heritage. In the rush to "women's rights as human rights," an admirable shift, perhaps, the concerns that are most relevant to immigrant women and women of immigrant heritage today may have disappeared. For feminist as well as European-studies scholars, attention must be paid not only to challenging the intersectional nature of the category of "woman" but also to how the concerns of minority women are "listened to." When Spivak reflects on the "inadvisable" remark she once made in her (in)famous essay, that "the subaltern cannot speak," she explains that although the subaltern had spoken, she was silenced by her "more emancipated" granddaughters. This silencing occured as a misreading of the very body itself, which is used as a form of text. The question has become not "Can the subaltern speak?" but, rather, "What is at stake when we insist that the subaltern speaks?" (Spivak, *A Critique* 309). Let us put aside again the question of whether we can use the term "subaltern"—it is as inapplicable here as it is for Spivak's examples.[7] The scholar's insistence on the speaking of a subject from below is dependent on whether and how one listens. At stake here is the breadth of the field of rights that are conceptualized as relevant to the needs of minority women in Germany. At stake as well is the reliance on an easy proof of "authenticity"—a Muslim woman writes an autobiography! We've read it! We've listened to the voice from below!—to substitute for the effort of listening to a wider range of voices, voices that might pose difficult questions that "we" (especially those of us who are white feminist scholars) are hesitant to grapple with. It continues to be necessary to recognize not only the complicated transnational developments informing the German context but also the particular and local inflections of debates about violence against women. This includes, however, attentiveness to a history of European rights discourse and of secularism, which recognizes their imbrication in structures of colonial and racialized violences. Writing a history of Europe as a history of violence would enable a more complex consideration of Sezgin's admonition to recognize the range of people who are impacted by violence. Those of us researching in feminist German cultural studies, particularly outside the discipline of anthropology, must also face the continued intellectual discomfort with addressing religious and spiritual aspects of women's lives—in particular, the discomfort with women who use Islam as a basis for legitimating a struggle against violence in multiple forms.

Chapter Five
Violent Authenticities: The Work of Emine Sevgi Özdamar and Feridun Zaimoglu

> *During the military coup in Turkey I was imprisoned for three weeks, because I had written news articles.... At that time words meant murder in Turkey. One could get shot, tortured, or hung due to words.*
> —Emine Sevgi Özdamar, Der Hof im Spiegel [The Courtyard in the Mirror], 127–128

> *I always played the mother or grandmother, the woman with the headscarf.*
> —Emine Sevgi Özdamar as character in *Die Deutschlandtür geht auf und gleich wieder zu* [The Germany-Door Opens and Closes Immediately]

In 2002 I attended a play based on the life of Emine Sevgi Özdamar, *Die Deutschlandtür geht auf und gleich wieder zu* [The Germany-Door Opens and Closes Immediately] at the Prater, a small experimental stage associated with the Volksbühne on Rosa-Luxemburg-Platz in Berlin. *The Germany-Door* humorously highlights the paradoxical nature of the characters that Özdamar has conceived of and played. Promotional materials repeat a line from the play: "I always had these mother roles. I am the mother of all filmic Turkish Germans. Perhaps even the grandmother" ("Die Deutschlandtür"). Two actors played Özdamar: Claudia Contreras, who formerly had a career in revolutionary Nicaraguan theater, and Mesut Özdemir, at the time known in Berlin as a transperformer at "Salon Oriental" (R. Müller). At the kitchen table, the two "Emines" exchanged stories in which both actors became the character of Özdamar (while the "real" Özdamar sat in the audience), interweaving their biographies to represent Özdamar both as a revolutionary theater mother and a flirtatious gender-bending performer. During much of the play, clips from Özdamar's film and television work appeared as backdrop to the performance, roles in which she often played "the mother wearing the headscarf." In Hark Böhm's film *Yasemin*, for example, she plays the protagonist's mother, embodying a Turkish culture of violence from which the protagonist will be saved by her German boyfriend.

This little-known performance demonstrates a rare moment during which Özdamar is recognized publicly and explicitly both as participant and as object of a discourse of Muslim Turkish female victimhood. *The Germany-Door* locates Özdamar in a tradition of revolutionary art and camp performance that simultaneously cites and undermines prevailing presumptions about Turkish and Turkish German women. I start with this performance to consider a set of questions that has been opened up by *The Germany-Door* around the regime of gender violence and its relationship to Turkish German authors, the reception of their works, and their presence as public intellectuals. To what extent does their success depend on their participation in discourses of Muslim violence? What openings to their works provide for challenging those same discourses? What possibilities do their works open up for considering violence in Turkish and German modernities?

Emine Sevgi Özdamar and Feridun Zaimoglu have played important roles in the public imagination as representatives of the first- and second generation of Turkish German literature. Popular guests on talk shows and at cultural events highlighting Turkish German culture, their writings continue to be the most well known of the large body of German literature by Turkish-heritage authors. Their careers have been sustained by a contradictory construction and deconstruction of the authentic Turkish German self via relationships to violence, especially in the marketing and reception of their work, and in the occasional controversies that issue from their writings. The persistent search by a literary critical apparatus for the authentic voice of Turkish Germany has resulted in a series of (mis)readings of their texts, in which the search for the markers of cultural difference and cultural hybridities obscures their characters' participation in the violence of the modern nation. Whereas Zaimoglu has gained critical acclaim for writing of violence and its victims, particularly when the violence can be attributed to "Muslim" culture. However, his attention to Turkish German women and their location in racist discourses and events received little attention. Özdamar, in contrast, is often read for her relationship to hybrid forms of culture with a particular emphasis on her unique use of language, but her attention to the violence played out in the name of the modern nation remains largely absent in discussions of her work. I examine depictions of the violence of modernity, moments of violence clearly located in European history, regardless of their relationship to Islam. In particular, the works I read by Özdamar (*Seltsame Sterne*) and Zaimoglu (*Leyla*) point to the experience of violence performed in the name of the modern nation and of secularism and experiences of racism.

Violence, Terror, and the Modern State: Emine Sevgi Özdamar's *Seltsame Sterne*

Özdamar has been an active participant in the production of German culture in many roles: as playwright, fiction and essay writer, theater director, and actress onstage and on screen, both for television and for film. She first came to Germany as a guestworker from 1965 to 1967, when she worked in a Berlin electronics factory. Upon her return to Turkey, she attended acting school in Istanbul; many of her first roles were in works by German authors—an experience that appears in many of her fictional works. After the military coup in 1971 (Özdamar was a member of the Turkish Workers Party) she returned to Berlin and began work at a (then East-) Berlin theater, the *Volksbühne*, with renowned directors such as Benno Besson and Matthias Langhoff (Ackermann). She eventually worked in West Germany with Claus Peymann and in Paris with Benno Besson; in Paris Özdamar also received a "Maîtrise de Théâtre." She directed her own play, *Karagöz in Alamania* [Blackeye in Germany] in Frankfurt in 1986 and has acted in television and film in West and united Germany.

Özdamar's literary production began with writing plays (the first from 1982); one of these was published as a narrative in the

1990 collection of narratives entitled *Mutterzunge* [Mother Tongue]. Her award of the prestigious Ingeborg Bachmann prize in 1991 for her novel *Das Leben ist eine Karawanserei* [Life is a Caravanserai; hereafter Caravanserai, published in 1992] amid much Orientalizing praise and criticism (Jankowsky) coincided with a new interest in immigrant literature among North American and UK German-studies scholars; a considerable body of Özdamar criticism has arisen on both sides of the Atlantic over the last decades. She has also been awarded numerous additional prizes and fellowships in Germany and abroad.

Özdamar criticism has paralleled the overall trends in the reception of Turkish German literature. There has been extensive attention to the use of language and Turkish cultural references. Early criticism praised and criticized her in Orientalizing ways, particularly after she won the Ingeborg Bachmann Prize. She was lauded for her works' creative "hybridization" of the Turkish and German languages; other critics derided her for the same reasons (Jankowsky). More nuanced critiques of Özdamar as self-Orientalizing soon followed, including Deniz Göktürk's analysis of Turkish structures to construct an exotic Other that nevertheless comments ironically on exoticizing clichés (Göktürk, "Kennzeichen" 526–532). Zafer Şenocak, a novelist, poet, and cultural critic, who tirelessly criticizes the trope of "between two cultures," wrote a parodic poem condemning her exoticizing prose (Senocak, *War Hitler Araber?* 55–59). Iris Alanyali's *Die blaue Reise* also expresses irritation at Özdamar's work, by depicting her as an outdated representative of an earlier generation that wrote novels solely about feeling "foreign and alone," spoke in broken German, and received prizes for a "new, but naïve" look at Germany (Alanyali 213). When asked about the constant attention to her ability to "translate" Turkish culture into German, Özdamar responded, "I find that to be shameless impudence. [...] That makes it sound like we Turks are not capable of writing" ("Manche denken").

Claudia Breger, Katrin Sieg, and Kader Konuk, alternatively, have considered Özdamar's unique prose as a sophisticated form of subversive citation; Özdamar writes moments, "in which the narrator creates an entry into the web of power and discourse while at the same time undermining it" (Konuk 64). Monika Shafi has studied Özdamar's fiction as an example of an alternative form of identity politics, while Margaret Littler sees Özdamar's work as performing diasporic identity. Both Seyhan and Kader Konuk are interested in transculturality and the linguistic aspects of Caravanserai; whereas Konuk employs metaphors of archaeology to discuss identity as created through language, Seyhan specifically focuses on Özdamar's linguistic magic realism as a form of transnational memory.

Despite these complex approaches to questions of language and performativity, however, it is relatively rare either for reviewers or for scholars to address the representation of work and politics and the protagonists' active participation in these realms (Weber, "Work, Sex, and Socialism"). Certainly, Özdamar's representations of violence do not exist independently of her strategies of citation or mimicry, nor of her characters' performance of diaspora. They are often disturbingly beautiful passages that echo Heinrich Heine's critical representations of German nationalism, substituting a naïve tone for a satiric one. However, without a recognition of the role of political activism and political theater in her texts, one cannot attend to the ways in which violence functions in her work. The critical works that come closest to addressing this violence examine forms of memory work that are performed by the texts. Adelson draws on Özdamar's early work to call for a move away from analyses of identity and culture, proposing the notion of "touching tales" as an analytical tool that can drive literary analysis beyond the cultural myth of "two worlds." Adelson's "touching tales" refer to points of cultural contact, including histories, that exist as points of orientation between German and Turkish culture in German literature of Turkish migration (Adelson 20). Her discussion of the narrative "Grandfather Tongue" from Özdamar's 1991 *Mutterzunge* suggests that it performs the imaginative labor of a touching tale of cold-war histories (Adelson 4–5, 26–7, 157), whereas "The Courtyard" invites the reader both to locate herself and to imagine new, nonethnic, forms of community (Adelson 54–59). *Seltsame Sterne* reveals a constellation of state and nonstate violence, struggles for progressive change, and shifting senses of modernity as one such touching Turkish German tale.

Özdamar's critical reception continues to demonstrate the ongoing limitations of literary criticism of "minority" authors, particularly of women writers, which often seeks an authentic subject/object of patriarchal subjugation or a native informant that writes self and can serve as the source of reliable truth. Alternatively, the authors are accused of self-exoticization and self-promotion because of their reiteration of stereotypes (Mani 95; 97). Özdamar's paradoxical relationship to the trope of the victimized woman is particularly evident in a juxtaposition of the roles she played in film with the characters she portrays in her fiction. Although critics may seek an "authentic" Turkish German voice, Özdamar's writing evades such notions of authenticity. Like B. Venkat Mani, I am interested in the ways in which Özdamar's "histories" constantly challenge the dominant narratives of history, only to immediately undermine themselves. Mani differs from Seyhan, who identifies a kind of transnational memory recovery work performed in *Mutterzunge*, in questioning the role of authenticity in those pasts. The kind of memory work performed by Özdamar's texts provides fragmented pieces of what we might call "subaltern" pasts, "without ordaining these pasts with authenticity" (Mani 117).

Monika Shafi's brief discussion of *Die Brücke vom goldenen Horn* exposes a particular "touching tale" that is also relevant, namely the transnational manifestations of generational conflict as the defining aspect of the 1968 generation in the texts of Özdamar and Uwe Timm (Shafi 201–216). Shafi's reoriented perspective on German culture reconsiders the memory of the Left movements. Her analysis also suggests to us that Turkish-German touching tales are not merely *effects* of Turkish migration, a rhetoric into which Adelson occasionally slips. Turkish leftist intellectuals played an integral part in migration history, and an integral part in transnational leftist developments that had their roots in transnational contact other than that of guestworker migration. Similarly, Patricia Simpson's exploration of the importance of Brecht for the narrators of *Brücke* and *Seltsame Sterne* concludes that "Özdamar's creative reception of Brecht holds up a beacon of leftist culture that would effect political change [and that] affirms at least the transferability of European cultural practices to transnational contexts" (Simpson 389). However,

I argue that in *Seltsame Sterne*, representations of violence show not only a "transferability of European cultural practice," but that Turkey and Germany's histories of violence are mutually bound up in uneven European modernities. *The Bridge of the Golden Horn* performs important memory work by revealing the participation of migrant women in Germany's economy and postwar recovery, in transnational political movements, such as the student movements of the 1960s and 70s, the contribution of Left movements in Turkey to the political understandings of migrant workers, and the intellectual contributions of migrants to the definition of Germanness in modernity and postmodernity (Weber, "Work, Sex, and Socialism"). *Seltsame Sterne* draws connections between the consequences of terrorist and state violence in Germany and Turkey. In this way, Özdamar's work does perform a kind of reparative memory work, similar to that Seyhan briefly describes in *Mutterzunge*, in which "Image, metaphor, and metonomy [sic] re-member bodies of language, culture, and their inhabitants dismembered by imperialism, war, conquest, colonization, poverty, and violence" (Seyhan 120). These acts of remembrance, however, further serve to recall violence in ways that reveal shifting reconfigurations of the relationship between violence and secularism. Özdamar's works imagine the "Red Decade" as a transnational phenomenon in which immigrant women take active, though marginalized, public roles. Her memory work also challenges the notion of "revolutionary" violence, whose effects in her work render revolutionary violence untenable in the forms it has taken in the 1970s.

Unlike Özdamar's earlier book-length works, which were fictionalized, *Strange Stars* is presented as nonfiction. Headlines from "newspapers of the last weeks and months" date the work by pointing to the (November 22, 1975) crowning of Juan Carlos as King of Spain after Franco's death (Özdamar 14). The first half is written in the form of memoir. In this section Özdamar describes her arrival in Berlin (both West and East—she arrives in the West merely to deposit her belongings in a locker and to travel to the East to seek out work in a theater) and remembers the traumatic events in Turkey that led to her return to Berlin. Özdamar's trauma causes her to distance herself from explicitly political activity at the time of the writing, however, she continually incorporates political events into the book, often via reference to various newspaper headlines, and understands her work as participating in a revolutionary theater tradition. This first section also details her new work as an intern under Benno Besson at the Volksbühne theater in East Berlin. In this section she lives in the West and works in the East while awaiting a resident visa from the German Democratic Republic (GDR).

The second section of *Strange Stars* excerpts Özdamar's journal from April 1, 1976, to January 13, 1978—including the infamous *deutscher Herbst* [German autumn] of 1977, the first peak in violence in the history of the West German radical Left (particularly the *Rote Armee Fraktion* [Red Army Faction], RAF), which was matched only by another wave in the mid-1980s. Here, Özdamar also relates some of her experiences in her West Berlin *Wohngemeinschaft*, one of the many small-scale, shared housing cooperatives, which, though formed in response to limited housing, were, often formed around an explicitly politicized Left identity. Moving back and forth between the two parts of Berlin also allows the narrator to gain insights into the political crisis of late 1970s in East Berlin. There, protest against the East German state is particularly remembered in connection with Wolf Biermann and Rudi Bahro. The popular and politically critical singer and songwriter, Biermann, was expatriated by the East German government in November 1976 while on a concert tour in West Germany. Biermann's expatriation sparked a wave of critique in East Germany, which was brutally silenced by the government andin turn resulted in a wave of emigration of East German artists and intellectuals. The terrorist events of 1977 in the West are paralleled by State violence in the East, which include the arrest of the critical political scientist, Bahro, who wrote *Kritik des realexistierenden Sozialismus* [A Critique of Real-Existing Socialism]. When Besson leaves East Berlin for Paris in late 1977, as part of the exodus of intellectuals and artists in the wake of the Biermann expatriation, he asks Özdamar to follow to "save herself from Germany" (236). The book concludes with her departure for France to write a dissertation on theater aesthetics.

The motif of observed violence repeats in multiple forms throughout Özdamar's work; violence against women is part of a landscape of violence that includes violence imposed by nation-states as well as that enacted by anarchist groups. The violence ensuing upon the military coup of 1971 in Turkey, particularly the persecution of the Turkish Worker's party, other Left groups, and the closing of Left youth organizations, haunts *Strange Stars*. Many of the personal aspects of the narrative and the journal entries are focused on the ability—and the inability—to experience pleasure; often the political forces of the time intervene. She particularly refers to political prisoners. Remembering her ex-husband, she reflects:

> When we made love, I always thought of the people in the prisons. They can't kiss anybody, they have nobody to spoon in bed. Every bit of meat we fried, every apple into which I bit, felt like a betrayal of those sitting in prison. A blind lawyer was forced to stand in a narrow cell in a prison on the Marmara See for a month. He couldn't kneel, lie down; around him lay the dried shit of former prisoners. He could only pee and shit while standing, and when the wind came up over the sea, the water rose through a crack in the wall to the knees of the blind lawyer. (25)

Images that she associates with the murdered political prisoners become an obsession. The wind is "a letter of the murdered," at night, she avoids stepping on shadows for fear they are alive, and she constantly views the things around her as parts of a prison cell and herself as a prisoner (26). She becomes obsessed with photography, trying desperately to capture everyone's faces before they are killed. Once in Germany, through her friends and family she hears the news of continued violence, including deaths at the May 1 demonstration of 1976: "The news from my country are a single word: Murder" (101).[1]

The violence that causes Özdamar to leave Turkey permanently is, in many ways, the founding violence throughout her prose. The trauma of the murder of student-movement leaders repeats in many of her works—alienating the protagonist of "Mother Tongue" from the Turkish language, causing the return to Germany of *The Bridge of the Golden Horn*'s protagonist, and, here, haunting Özdamar's homelessness in *Strange Stars*. This motif evokes the ongoing struggle over the meaning of Turkish participation in European modernity and the meaning of the Turkish nation.

Whereas the violence of the early 1970s is gendered in Özdamar's other texts, particularly *The Bridge of the Golden Horn* (Weber, "Work, Sex, and Socialism" 49–50), in *Strange Stars* gender violence is spoken of only in entirely different contexts. For a time, she lives with Gundula Bahro, who is still living with her famous dissident husband, Rudolf Bahro, because of the lack of available housing in East Berlin. The kitchen table conversations with Gundula Bahro and her friends challenge the narrator's simplistic appreciation for the GDR. For example, Gundula argues that socialist women would do well to heed lessons in solidarity from the West, especially the ways in which feminists organize without the State. "In the socialist system, equality of women is written into the law, but violence against women exists nevertheless. [...] here they are also sexual objects" (91). The brief mentions of Kurdish and Turkish men making sexual advances (41) take place in a context where she is equally objectified by the flirtations of the German men at the theater.

Throughout the book, Germany's Nazi history is increasingly taken on as part of Özdamar's context. Initially it appears distanced—German friends who want nothing to do with their Nazi fathers (13), friends who seek to gain conscientious objector status to avoid compulsory military service (15). Later in the book, however, the violence of fascism becomes something that she physically experiences as a link between Germany and Turkey. After a period of depression, missing her ex-husband, she escapes to a spot in the woods to cry and then realizes that a friend had just told her that the death march from Sachsenhausen concentration camp had passed by this very spot. Using the metaphor of wind, employed earlier, to think of Turkish political prisoners, she reflects: "At that time it must have looked like another planet, people like skeletons under moonlight. Huge eyes. Clothing, ripped clothing, that flies over the landscape with the wind" (114). Shortly thereafter she begins an affair with Graham, the English son of Jewish refugees from Berlin (117). This association with Nazi history could potentially be a manifestation of a popular, and deeply problematic, tendency in the 1970s to call "Turks the Jews of today" (Adelson 85). Adelson suggests, "When figural Turks and Jews make contact in German narratives alluding to stories of victimization and genocide [...] they evoke a culturally residual, referentially nonspecific sense of guilt, blame, shame, and danger" (86). What does it mean, as Adelson asks, when the Holocaust becomes a language through which something in the present is rendered intelligible (86)?

In *Strange Stars,* it isn't really an association of the plight of Turkish Germans with that of German Jews. Instead, it is a nod to a common European experience of nationalist violence that is manifested differently in Turkey and in Germany. *Strange Stars* reveals, for example, an additional shared experience of Turkey and Germany: the challenge to the legitimacy of a fragile democracy by terrorism. Turkey and Germany both experience a New Left movement that seeks a more democratic society. Özdamar was in Berlin when Benno Ohnesorg was killed by a police officer (125). His death both galvanized the student movement and contributed to the radicalization of a small group of activists, who eventually formed the RAF. In Germany, the radical Left became the first real challenge to post-World War II democracy in West Germany and was eventually met by such measures as the passing of emergency laws and the radical decree (Jarausch 150–151), whereas Turkey was shocked by the hanging of three leftist student leaders after the military intervention of 1971. Certainly, Turkey was experiencing significantly more violence on the part of both the extreme Left and the extreme Right, especially by 1976. Although the New Left movements largely understood themselves as international and in solidarity with peoples of the Third World and existing in tandem with antiwar movements in the United States and western Europe, the larger narratives of these movements exclude the transnational participation by immigrants in their midst: for example, Left intellectuals such as Aras Ören and Özdamar, who clearly situate themselves in relationship to other Left movements. Recent work pointing to the importance of transnational alliances in the student movement (Klimke 106) and among Left terrorist groups (Klimke and Mausbach 620–643) has yet to address their Turkish German connections. The Turkish worker organizations that appear in *The Bridge of the Golden Horn,* for example, rarely make their ways into traditional histories of the New Left in Germany.

This is partly a consequence of a long existing inability to imagine the immigrant worker as a speaking subject. Günter Wallraff's work stands as an excellent example of this: although his bestselling work *Ganz unten* functioned to expose the conditions of immigrant workers in Germany, his German narrator and the presumed "German" audience function together to foreclose immigrant subjectivity, reducing the Turkish worker to a trope standing in for all victims of capitalism (Teraoka 145–151; 60). As has often been noted, Homi K. Bhabha performed a similar move when he pointed to the silent German Turk as an example of the "radical incommensurability of translation."(Bhabha 238–239). Arlene Teraoka points out that representations of the "Third World" reveal the contested narratives of European humanism—in Left literature, the Third World sometimes functions to reaffirm the perceived superiority of the heritage of the European enlightenment. In other works, however, the "Third World" confronts the German intellectual with the limits of enlightenment narratives, throwing them into crisis and contributing to a potential decentering of the European subject. The immigrant worker, who is included in Teraoka's discussion of representations of "the Third World," is consistently represented in the sense of being spoken for without being represented as a speaking subject.

The RAF exists on the margins of *Strange Stars* in several ways. By coincidence, the apartment in which Özdamar lives when she is in West Berlin was once a meeting point for RAF members Horst Mahler and Ulrike Meinhof (68). Andreas Baader, Gudrun Ensslin, and Jan-Carl Raspe, members of the organization, appear in headlines of newspapers that are stacked in the bathroom of her West Berlin apartment; this would have been during the two-year trial of these three members, at the end of which they will be found guilty for four murders and twenty-seven attempted murders.[2] Although the narrative voice rarely comments extensively on political events, the distancing from this particular story is especially striking; only the names are actually mentioned (54); no further details are given until later, when it is briefly mentioned that the judge in the trial was changed at the last minute (206). Ulrike Meinhof's death in prison in May 1976 is learned of via a telephone conversation (106). Özdamar also notes the escape of four RAF women from prison (159), the murder of Dresdner Bank president Jürgen Pronto by RAF members in July 1977 (226); the kidnapping of Hanns Martin Schleyer in September 1977;[3] the related hijacking by Palestinian allies of an airplane filled with passengers bound for Frankfurt, which ultimately lands up in Mogadishu, Somalia; the storming of that airplane on October 17/18, 1977; the mysterious suicides of Baader, Ensslin, and Raspe, who are found dead in their prison cells the next morning; and the killing of Schleyer on that same day (233–234). All these mentions, together with the mention of Benno Ohnesorg (101), are noted with little additional elaboration or emotional response.

Özdamar experiences the news of the increasing RAF violence almost exclusively from East Berlin. Özdamar does enter West Berlin on the day that Pronto was killed, but is frightened by the extensive police presence in the streets and in the trains and immediately returns to the East. The atmosphere of anxiety recalls the violent repression of peaceful student demonstrations in Berlin in the late 1960s. The narrator's naïve view of the East as a Communist safehaven from repressive state activity also proves illusory. It is the end of this feeling of safety and at-homeness in the East (where she is often without a literal home) that ultimately provokes a more engaged response.

Censorship marks an initial experience of East German state violence. Fear that after the events of the German autumn in West Germany, East Germans would instigate a similar movement against the State led the GDR government to censor all newspaper mention of anarchist violence and kidnappings, even though it eventually provided a safe haven for some of the terrorists. Özdamar and her East Berlin friends primarily learn of the events during Özdamar's telephone conversations with her friends in the West Berlin apartment, which is constantly searched on the suspicion that there might still be a connection to the RAF. These events continue a period of relative repression in East Germany that ensued upon Biermann's expatriation. This manifests in the monitoring of the telephone when she is living with Gabi Gysi, Gregor Gysi's sister, who is a committed Communist but is somewhat critical of the GDR state (218). The Stasi also follows her at one point when she meets a Turkish labor organizer, a friend of her brother's, on the same day as the death of Meinhof (106). The artistic community is dismayed by the expatriation of folk singer Wolf Biermann (178); shortly thereafter Bahro is imprisoned (230).[4]

The linking of these events by proximity in her journal provides an implicit rejection of violence, which becomes explicit at only one place in the book. Özdamar reflects on a newly articulated desire to establish more regular contact with her friends in Turkey. This reestablishment of a transnational connection proves productive, both artistically and politically (133). Here a criticism of violence is made explicit, and furthermore, through a reflection on the naïveté for which Özdamar's writing is so well known. In fact she seems to propose art as an alternative to the violence that is often seen as necessary to effect change: "We must force each other to think, inspire. Changing, sharing experiences with others, is very important. But [we must] not want to change anybody with violence. [We must] relieve people of their fears. Remain naïve for art" (133). This "remaining naïve" becomes a political act as well as an artistic one. Her "naïve" writing reveals, rewrites, and further maintains a perspective from which the author can hope for positive and progressive change both in Turkey and in Germany.

While *Seltsame Sterne* refers to ongoing secular violence, Islam itself is nearly nonexistent here and is mentioned only when the grandmother is thrilled when Özdamar's friend, Joseph, claims to convert to Islam, as she is certain that she has now secured her place in heaven (Özdamar 22). Nor is racism alluded to, except for when she is accosted on the street by a German, who yells, "Off to the gas chamber" (166). And in Özdamar's case, this absence is partly the point: In a context where Turkish women are thought of in relationship to Muslim culture, Özdamar writes the memoirs of a woman who is insistent on her history in Left politics and her current participation in Lef theater.

Nevertheless, Özdamar's conception of art in this text has much in common with Margaret Littler's description of the place of Islam in Özdamar's work—not as a religious framework, but as cultural tradition. Littler points out that in *Bridge of the Golden Horn*, the narrative espouses secular values even as it points to an Islamic cultural tradition in "which sacred and profane are shifting and overlapping categories" (Littler, "Intimacies Both Sacred and Profane" 232). Littler sees in Özdamar's work a specifically Turkish reception of Ottoman poetics that imagines original artistic work as that which can bring not yet existing material relationships into existence (227). This conception of poetics is remarkably similar to Özdamar's imagination of art in *Strange Stars*, as having the potential to inspire progressive change, yet as reliant on naïveté. Given the love of *Brücke's* protagonist and Özdamar in *Strange Stars* for Brechtian theater aesthetics, Özdamar's comments on naïveté and art place her conceptualization of violence not only as part of an Islamic cultural tradition but also as a part of contemporary struggles for the meaning of nation, democracy, and modernity.

The search for an "authentic" Turkish-German voice obscures a key aspect of Özdamar's, namely, the depictions of secular violence enacted in the name of the nation-state, in the battle over national narratives. Out of their experiences of trauma, the narrators show how the violence from a range of political perspectives, regardless of how it is legitimated, evokes a paralyzing fear that also prohibits progressive change. Özdamar turns to the theater and to literature as the place of revolutionary action, but does so without claims to an authentic story or vision of the future: she is continually concerned with imagining yet another "reality behind the reality" (Özdamar 118). She looks to art, particularly revolutionary art in the form of Brechtian revolution of theater, as the necessary catalyst for change. Her immersion in archival work—examining theater notes—is her work to "destroy idealist thinking," for "now is the time to become softer, richer through knowledge" (105).

These are forms of memory that cannot be confined to the battle between secularism and tradition, which is often considered to inform the politics of Turkish-German writing. As Seyhan has suggested in relationship to Özdamar's earlier work, her rewriting of national memories insists on the use of story to tell histories (Seyhan, "Lost in Translation" 421). Following Benjamin, Seyhan argues that for histories to become emancipatory they must be reconfigured to "release their emancipatory potential" (Seyhan, *Writing Outside the Nation* 34). Citing Benjamin's oft-repeated idea that articulating the past means seizing a "memory as it flashes in the moment of danger," Seyhan implies the importance of understanding Özdamar's writings of the past in the context of the present. Adelson points out that Özdamar's writing participates in *German* memory work, not only in the memory work of Turkey. Implicitly answering "yes," Adelson poses the question, "Can one say that the split Turkish memory that Özdamar articulates becomes an integral part of a German memory, one that is fractured and remembered in more than simply dichotomous ways?" (Adelson 328). Özdamar connects German and Turkish pasts at an important "present" moment: during and following a decade of xenophobia after the unification and the erasure of immigrant female agency in the discourses of oppression by Muslim culture. She speaks to the present with the secular violence of the past: the RAF, the repression of the Turkish Left, and the censorship and imprisonment of East German dissidents. Her work thus exists at a complex nexus of resistance—not only to the tendencies to write immigrant, especially Turkish women, as victims of cultural oppression but also to write a national history that enables this reduction by imagining Turkish history as "outside of Europe"; or to write a supranational history that does the same through the writing of "Western" civilization.

Thus, as Özdamar insists on "remaining naïve," her works create a network of allusions that reveal deeply modern relationships rooted in processes of struggle for democratization and justice as well as in processes of globalization. Women workers and intellectuals are those who rewrite the narratives of modernity, in which a new contestation of European modernity occurs, namely, one that produces a history of modernity as a history of violence. The figure of the migrant no longer exists solely as symptom of Turkish or Muslim violence, but as a participant in the writing of history through a writing of the history of European violence.

Feridun Zaimoglu and the Gendered Public Sphere

Zaimoglu has come to stand in as representative for a second (and sometimes both second and third) generation of Turkish-German literature. His career has been marked by contradictory impulses to construct an "authentic" Turkish Germanness, often through a violent sort of street language; and to de-essentialize understandings of the German Turk. In the continual desire by the public to find an authentic mediator of Turkish-German culture, and more recently, of "Muslim" culture, Zaimoglu has come both to fulfill and to disrupt these desires—especially through his role as an author of two books—the early (1995) *Kanak Sprak* and the more recent (2006) *Leyla*. These works were published in the context of two primary roles assumed by Zaimoglu as public intellectual. *Kanak Sprak* led to a loosely defined movement often called the "Kanaksta" movement; as a result, Zaimoglu became a figurehead for the antiracist cultural activist group *Kanak Attack*, which was founded in 1998 (Cheesman 23). On the other hand, the reception of *Leyla*, much of which relied on certain misreadings of it, led to Zaimoglu's participation in the DIK. The shifting reception of Zaimoglu's work is part of a parallel shifting emphasis, from the "authentic voice of German Turks" to the "authentic voice of Islam," aided by Zaimoglu's own increasing acknowledgment of an identity as Muslim (Cheesman). A new search for the authentic mediator has emerged in the mid-to-late 2000s, one that focuses on an authentic voice of Islam that adequately demonstrates its authenticity by criticizing the violence, in particular the gender violence, of Islam. Whereas the changing readings and representations of Zaimoglu's work reveal the shifting constellations of racialized conceptualizations of Turkishness and Islam, Zaimoglu's own role as public intellectual and the reception of his work expose the gendered and racialized constitution of a public sphere from which Turkish and Muslim women are excluded. Yet a careful reading of the women figures in Zaimoglu's text reveals an insistent challenge to the processes that would exclude Muslim women from public life.

Zaimoglu's early *Kanak Sprak* was often understood as affording access to the "real" life of the German Turk on the streets or as constructing a viable "hybrid" language and identity. The early Zaimoglu contributed to this reception in his self-marketing, constantly making claims to authenticity that rested "on a definition of authentic as original, genuine, unadulterated, unmixed" (Mani 132). He simultaneously relegates earlier Turkish-German authors to "mere folkloric antiquity, declaring the superiority of his literary work and his work as a public intellectual" (Mani 132). Indeed, in a curious mix of marking himself as ethnic Other and inventing himself as hybrid, he constructs a hybridity that "essentializes itself" (Mani 126). The ensuing "Kanak chic" that was used to market *Kanak Sprak* has been widely criticized by antiracist activists and scholars alike (Cheesman, *Novels* 23). Despite the immense attention paid to *Kanak Sprak*, however, the later book *Koppstoff: Kanaka Sprak vom Rande der Gesellschaft*, which provided the voices of women, went largely unnoticed. This book may have remained a footnote to *Kanak Sprak* because it provides characters that clearly challenge the public understanding of Turkish- German women in Germany (Weber, "Beyond the Culture Trap"). In effect it could not be made sense of within a discourse that so heavily emphasized Turkish German women as victims of violence. Zaimoglu's participation in the film *Kanak Attack*, based on his book *Abschaum*, draws on obvious stereotypes of violent masculinity; his use of the name, for the title of the film, led to his break with *Kanak Attak* (Cheesman, "Akçam" 192). Yet, Tom Cheesman also shows that Zaimoglu's work, by providing material to the public that revealed the contradictory politics of authenticity, sparked a movement that transcended the essentialism of Zaimoglu's own work (Cheesman, *Novels* 22) and enabled a publicity machine, which served as a platform for numerous other Turkish German writers (Cheesman, *Novels* 27). If Zaimoglu's approach and political demands are unoriginal, his contribution in part can be seen as a "literary language [that] enacts this struggle as a creative process within German culture" (Cheesman, *Novels* 28).

Zaimoglu's popularity was tremendously heightened by the novel *Leyla*, the story of a young woman whose youth is marred by her abusive father. Though *Leyla* is quite traditional in structure and language in comparison to Zaimoglu's earlier, experimental works, it is *Leyla* that gained him acclaim as a mature author who was capable of authentic representations of the Turkish-German woman. As Ipek Celik has pointed out, "The critics immediately appropriated the text to point out the borders between the liberal democratic European family structure and what is perceived as the typical traditional Muslim family—a union of abusive husbands and sons with oppressed wives and daughters" (Celik 208). Celik shows the importance of Zaimoglu's work in constructing a new realism, in which violence predominates; the valorization of this realism figures prominently in processes that exclude those of immigrant heritage from positions as liberal subjects in Germany (Celik 117–189). I would like to approach *Leyla* from the perspective of a focus on familial violence to: (1) be attentive to the ways in which, contrary to much popular reception, Zaimoglu's female characters actually claim an ambivalent position in the public sphere that challenges these exclusionary processes; and (2) consider how this leads to a rewriting of European modernity as itself a narrative of violence.

Leyla became immensely popular because of the misreadings that link the book to Muslim violence, even though Islam is largely absent from the book, and which also describe it as deeply relevant to contemporary Turkish-German women, even though it tells the story of a woman in Turkey in the 1950s. The potential for Zaimoglu's women figures to intervene in the public sphere both within and outside the text is best understood, however, by taking into consideration Zaimoglu's own positioning as a public intellectual. I thus conclude this section with an examination of Zaimoglu's participation in the DIK. During his participation Zaimoglu has used his status to vocally challenge the gendered regime of violence and the lack of participation of Muslim women in the DIK.

From *Provacateur* of *Kanak* to Mature Critic of Gender Violence: Zaimoglu and *Leyla*

Since *Kanak Sprak* and *Koppstoff*, Zaimoglu has published a number of novels and short narrative collections. Many were stylistically unconventional narrations of frustrated sexualities in one form or another; many demonstrated in style and tone a sort of stylized gangster talk not entirely alien to the language developed in *Kanak Sprak*. In 2006 Feridun Zaimoglu published his novel *Leyla*. Weighing in at over 500 pages, this novel is a radical departure in tone, style, and genre from Zaimoglu's early work. It is highly conventional—a long, linear family saga narrated in the first person, using a spare, realistic language stripped of the sense of play that characterized Zaimoglu's earlier work. Set in the 1950s and the early 60s, it is the story of Leyla's coming of age—first in Malatya, then in the Kurdish regions of Turkey, and finally, in Istanbul. In the concluding pages, we find Leyla on her way to Germany with her husband and her mother, Emine. In part, Leyla's life story is also structured as a narrative of escape from her father, Halid. Halid physically and verbally abuses the family, rapes his daughter Yasmin, and forces his son to kill the child conceived as a result of the rapes. Halid insists on Leyla's absolute silence (10) and denigrates Emine as an ungrateful Armenian whore (11).

The family narrative takes place against the backdrop of the events in Eastern Turkey in the first half of the twentieth century, including the Armenian genocide of 1915, Turkish participation in the Korean war, and Kurdish insurgency after decades of cultural and political repression. These events are absent from the reception of *Leyla*, whereas the reception's focus on the domestic scene played a large role in Zaimoglu's transformation from the *provocateur* of Kanak both to participant in "high culture" (Schröder) and to critic of the representations of Islam in Germany. This image makeover is relevant more in the context of popular media; in the academic and scholarly context he was already taken seriously as an author and had also received a number of "serious" literary prizes. Zaimoglu describes the writing of the novel as a "new beginning" (Hammelehle), now that the time of "Kanak" is over, and reviewers seem to agree, seeing this novel as a sign that he has matured into a serious author (Cizmecioglu; Spiegel).

While the only description of life in Germany that is represented in *Leyla* is the arrival to the Munich train station in the last two pages of the book, the move to Germany figures prominently in the book's reception. For example, one reviewer states that "Leyla suffered much in the Turkey of the late 1950s and 60s, before she came to the country that was, for her, both new/strange (fremd) and wealthy: Germany. She stands representatively for a generation of women between cultures, who lost a home and never really found a new one" ("Von der Kunst der Einfühlung"). Leyla's struggles are also representative for some reviewers of the lives of Turkish German women today: "We don't know, how past this past really is, and slide against our will into the present" (Spiegel), an attitude potentially reinforced by *Leyla's* opening line, "This is a story from old times. It is not, however, an old story" (7). Critics laud the novel for providing a much more important provocation to Turks in Germany than *Kanak Sprak* ever did (Spiegel), implying that the provocation is a coming-to-terms with violence against women today; the relevance of the book for today was emphasized when Zaimoglu was awarded the Grimmelshausen Literary Prize. The prize announcement called the book one of the most important current books for understanding entire "generations of guest workers" ("Grimmelshausen-Preis"). Zaimoglu's "arrival," then, as a legitimate author is closely linked to the authenticity found in his supposed representation of the familial violence of Turkey and of Islam. The unchanging violence from the 1950s is seen to be of constant relevance, without change, to the situation of women today.

While in the novel itself the father's abuse is not linked to Islam, the reception makes this link, at times by using the familiar trope of the veil: "This tone, this apparently authentic narration from the life of a woman, a secret girl, deeply veiled and hidden in provincial Anatolia" (Minkmar and Weidermann 21; further see Bahners, "Feridun Zaimoglu" 40). Equally familiar tropes of honor are used, including one by, Hubert Spiegel, who, while giving the speech awarding the Grimmelshausen prize, stressed that there is no higher call for Leyla than to preserve her honor (Spiegel). Although an emphasis on violence and honor predominated, there are other voices, for example that of Ulrich Rüdenauer, whose characterization of the novel as a grand family saga goes beyond ideology, religion, and politics to tell the story of the dream that brought guest workers to Germany; he also recognizes that Leyla is aided along the way in her escape from her tyrannical father by her emancipated aunt (Rüdenauer). Iris Alanyali argues that the novel is being read against the backdrop of discourses surrounding Hatun Sürücu's death; and that the novel actually shows precisely that Islam has very little to do with domestic violence (Alanyali, "Ihr seid nichts").

However, Zaimoglu's work is largely considered authentic precisely because it finds an authentic voice that can articulate violence within a Muslim family, particularly violence directed at the women of the family. Even in a review that pointed to the fact that religion played a relatively small role, one that was only briefly used by the father to legitimate his violence and was revealed as deeply hypocritical, the critic argues that the revelation of Islam as an instrument of power that was wielded by Leyla's father is a "form of secularization" that was performed by the novel itself (Bahners, "Feridun Zaimoglu: Kritiker der Islamkritikerinnen"). Precisely because *Leyla* is seen to point out a link between Islam and violence, the reviewer seems to suggest, it may serve as a step toward secularizing the Turkish German community. This reception is particularly peculiar given the interviews Zaimoglu gave at the time. The novel was published shortly after the 2005 Danish cartoon controversy, so he was asked to comment on that as well during interviews. He considers his novel as paying attention to details as a strategy against grand narratives, which for him can only be a lie. As example, he opposes the detail-oriented novel to the grand narrative of the supposed "Christian-Muslim culture wars," which for him was nothing but a misdiagnosis: "What I don't see in the German media is: What about the silent majority of Muslims? They are peaceful – and find the caricatures terrible nevertheless [...] The vast majority of Muslims here consider themselves part of German society, and are nevertheless not amused" (Hammelehle).

Whereas familial violence is ever present in the popular reception of *Leyla*, the political aspects that are represented in the text, which include the Armenian genocide (Celik 120–121), the Korean War, the Cold War, and Kurdish rebellion, remain largely absent. The Armenian genocide haunts the novel at the edges, a presence made explicit only upon Halid's death, when the novel reveals the Armenian genocide as the founding violence of the relationship between Leyla's parents. Halid witnesses Emine's rape, which takes place during the days of massacres against the Armenians and before they are married, a marriage which, it is implied, played a role in rescuing her from the killings (Zaimoglu 195–196; 517–519). This moment of gender violence takes place in the name of the foundation of a nation that seeks to exclude its religious and ethnic minorities to achieve a mythical homogeneity, which is thought to be essential to nascent modernization efforts.

The distintegration of the multiethnic Ottoman Empire and the accompanying ethnocultural nationalism closely followed the patterns of German nationalism (Dirlik, "Race Talk, Race, and Contemporary Racism" 1368), which marked a transition from a Muslim empire to a secular state (Dadrian 43–44). The Armenian genocide of 1915 followed decades of more isolated incidents; the Armenian resistance was rooted in engagement with Western European notions of rights and independence (Weitz 3). The Committee for Unity and Progress both planned the initial stages of the genocide and played a key role in founding the Turkish Republic in 1922. It has often been acknowledged that the removal of Armenian claims to self-determination and nationhood were considered "necessary" for the successful establishment of the Turkish republic (Akçam 10–11). Even as a doctrine of homogenous nationhood was followed in Turkey, the language of democracy and human rights eventually became associated with colonialism, as it had been used to legitimate colonial interests and intervention throughout the Middle East; indeed, the development of a unified national identity was seen as an important anticolonial tool (Akçam 81).

There are similarities to the experiences of the Kurdish minority in Turkey. After increasing cultural repression, an independence movement with radical elements emerged in the 1950s, as witnessed by the novel's characters as well. The references to Halid as Chechen, and to other characters as Kurdish, Armenian, and Greek, further challenge the national Turkish narrative of ethnic homogeneity. The enactment of racialized violence via gender violence in *Leyla*—namely, the rape of Emine—serves as a powerful reminder that any form of violence occurs, not only embedded in a historical and sociopolitical moment, but often deeply interconnected with other forms of violence as well. It is further one of the most obvious examples of the fallacy of the thesis that modernizing is necessarily a path to peace; in the turn to a Western style "nation," modernization attempts, during the last days of the Ottoman Empire, led to the expulsion of the Greeks and the massacres of Armenians, while the new Turkish Republic helped to solidify the myths of ethnic homogeneity. The lack of attention to these forms of violence in popular reception and the displacement of political violence in the reception of *Leyla* to domestic violence in in the name of Islam permits a secular narrative of a peaceful West versus a violent Turkey to remain intact and prohibits a recognition of the existence of racialized violence and shared histories of ethnic violence.[5] Careful attention to *Leyla* reveals that it assumes that Kurdish, Armenian, Turkish, and German histories are part of a shared European struggle to achieve multiethnic democratic societies in the face of nationalist and racist violence. To many western European readers, however, the references to genocide may be difficult to recognize, leaving the novel open to the same criticism that had been leveled at Zafer Senocak's *Dangerous Kinship*, another Turkish German novel that makes connections between the Holocaust and the Armenian genocide: namely, that references to genocide are so obscure that they remain tangential to readers unfamiliar with Turkish history (Littler, "Guilt" 366). This level of analysis would be outside the perspective of Leyla in the novel, however. Alternatively, we can read this novel as an invitation to the reader to examine these obscured connections.

The value placed on *Leyla* as genuinely authentic due to its representation of gender violence, rather than racialized political violence, became more obvious when Zaimoglu was briefly accused of having plagiarized from Emine Sevgi Özdamar's novel *Life is a Caravanserai*. A literary scholar from Germany presented a journalist from the *Frankfurter Allgemeine* with a long list of linguistic and narrative similarities between the two novels. Özdamar initially refused to respond but eventually made a public accusation of plagiarism. Although in earlier interviews Zaimoglu insisted that *Leyla* was "99.9% made up" (Hammelehle), he now claimed that the story was that of his mother—which he proved by providing recorded tapes of a series of conversations with his mother, which indeed provide much of the novel's material (Sezgin, "Eine Stimme"). Zaimoglu, ever the provocateur, even argued that his mother and two aunts lived in the same guestworker dorm and that the similarities would almost suggest that Özdamar's "memories" were actually those of Zaimoglu's family (Sezgin, "Eine Stimme"); he insisted that he, in any case, had never read any of Özdamar's novels.

The "truth" value of Zaimoglu's claim is irrelevant here. The discussion around this plagiarism revealed once again the importance a concept of "authenticity" plays in the marketing of Turkish-German work. Zaimoglu's claim is also awkward; after over a decade of positioning himself as the true voice of Turkish Germany against the "Orientalizing" language of other authors, Zaimoglu now suggests that he has never read those authors in the first place. He also shifts his position from being an authentic author precisely because he "made up" most of the story to a position that claims value in the story because of its truth as part of his familial inheritance. In common, however, is the way in which the popular reception has tended to emphasize that both novels were valuable in their authenticity, in particular, in the way in which they represented violence against Muslim women; a scholar has now "worked out how the representations of female suffering share similarities" (Krause). Zaimoglu emerged from this controversy hailed as an important, "serious" literary figure whose "breakthrough" work was now understood to be *Leyla*. And, similar to the boost given to Kelek by her book, Zaimoglu's new prominence led to his also being chosen as a DIK member. Although he considers himself a believing, but not practicing, Muslim, like Kelek, it was precisely his writing of a book that took violence against Muslim women as its subject that gave him this position.

Shortly thereafter, however, Zaimoglu took a controversial stand. The only two women represented as Muslims in the first group of the DIK, Necla Kelek and Seyran Ates, are nonreligious, and Kelek's work in particular can be understood as advocating complete rejection of Islam. Deeply critical of Kelek, Zaimoglu repeatedly offered to give up his place so that it could be taken by a practicing Muslima who wore a headscarf of her own accord and could be considered an independent and confident representative of practicing Muslims outside Muslim institutions. This offer was not accepted; the debates spurred by Zaimoglu's comments led to fractious debates within and about the DIK.

Literature of Turkish German Migration and Secular Violence

Whereas Özdamar writes largely fictionalized but autobiographical works, she makes no claim to an authenticity; on the contrary, she is much more interested in representing shifting and complex subject positions, even as her literary criticism continues to turn to her work as an authentic voice. Zaimoglu's desire to self-represent as authentic and to undo essentialized notions of Islam has led to deeply contradictory results. *Koppstoff,* a book that portrays a range of subject positions that anticipate his public opinions on Islam in the 2000s, has been largely ignored, whereas *Leyla* can be misread as an example of Muslim violence rather than as a revelation of the complex (and gendered) effects of secular violence. Yet when read outside the public desire for authenticity, *Leyla* presents the reader with textual figures that contest the terms of democratic modernity as well as the forms of threat posed to it. The reception of Zaimoglu's literary figures, as well as his public persona, can be read as revealing the imbrications of racialization and Islamophobia in Germany today. So long as he can be (mis)read as authentically describing the plight of oppressed Muslim women today, he has "arrived" in German "Hochkultur." When he undermines that understanding, however, with an attempt to differentiate public perception of Islam and to articulate a specifically European Islam, he becomes, again, the disturbing figure that he was with his earlier work.

Yet when read outside the public desire for authenticity, Özdamar and Zaimoglu, both, in often radically different ways, present the readers with textual figures that contest the terms of democratic modernity as well as the forms of threat that are posed to it. Özdamar does this largely in terms of a consideration of the forms of secular violence that emerged in response to the upheaval of the 1960s and 70s, imagining transnational forms of participation in the political and artistic realms in which women are active. Zaimoglu's figures, as well as his public persona, can be read as revealing the imbrications of racialization and discrimination with a regime of violence through which the Germany of the 1990s and 2000s denies Turkish German women full participation in the realms of cultural and political citizenship.

Conclusion

In the early 2000s I presented work examining Emine Sevgi Özdamar's various engagements with German literary tradition in her own literary texts, at several academic conferences. Inevitably, the conversation during the question-and-answer periods turned to the headscarf debates, despite the fact that this had nothing to do with the work at hand. As the decade continued, whenever presenting or teaching Turkish German literary texts, the "irrelevant" questions evolved, from "But what about the headscarf?" to "But what about forced marriage?," "But what about honor killings?," "But what about the future of feminism and gender equity?," and "But what about promoting human rights?" I saw these questions as inappropriate to the reality of Turkish-German writers and artists and their artistic production. Yet it became clear that trying to divert attention from the "irrelevant questions" was an inadequate strategy. In fact, incessant attention to violence against women was very much a part of the context in which these people produce art. In other words, insisting on thinking about Turkish-German artistic production *as* artistic production was inadequate without a deeper analysis of the context in which it was produced—a part of what Lawrence Grossberg has called "radical contextuality" (Grossberg 20). This context in turn could not be understood without critically examining the discourses around violence against Muslim women, focused as they are on honor killings, forced marriages, headcovering practices, and familial violence.

We can repeat the catalog of problems with the litany of questions above: it assumes that "honor" only exists in Muslim cultures, that familial violence is largely acceptable in Muslim cultures, that there is no potential for Muslim activism against violence, and that

European culture is absent of violence. It belies Muslim and Turkish German participation in the German public and the democratic public sphere.

Scholars have often found themselves divided into two groups vis-à-vis these issues: one interested in examining the question of whether or not Islam promotes violence toward women, the other on insisting that this was the wrong question. And indeed, it is the wrong question. Nevertheless, simply labelling this question as "the wrong question" also seemed to devalue the experiences of domestic violence survivors. Because the difficult issues surrounding how to approach violence against women in Europe from an antiracist perspective are often avoided, the discussion has been dominated by those who either resort to cultural relativism or who accuse the Left of cultural relativism. This project, then, has been an attempt to ask why the issues of familial violence became so important, whereas racism, xenophobia, structural disadvantage, and economic injustice easily recede, and to highlight alternative understandings of violence and Muslim women's participation in German society.

Throughout the 2000s and the various crises of European Union (EU) legitimacy, elite attempts to define the EU relied on a utopian vision of a Europe that could protect human rights in the world (often over and against US militarism) (Habermas and Derrida 6); Europe as the "natural champion of international law, which it often does not obey itself" (Balibar, *We the People* 224; further see El-Tayeb, *European Others* 87). Within this logic, Europe is also the natural protector of women's rights. Islam (and in Germany, Turkey and Turkish culture) provide the border to that Europe, the division between a place of gender equity and gender inequality. From a popular perspective, of course, identification with the EU has remained low, and the Othering of Muslim culture is aligned with continued national and nationalist sentiments.

These developments produced a particular set of contradictions that came to a head at the turn of the decade. Notions of intersectionality and multiple forms of oppression reemerged as a popular topic in special journal issues and conferences throughout Europe (Davis), even as a number of EU initiatives began considering the impact of multiple forms of oppression on women (Koldinská; Lombardo and Verloo). In 2010, Germany's "multicultural" World Cup team was celebrated joyously nationwide and remarked upon positively around the world as the face of a new Germany (Stehle and Weber). Had something approaching a new definition of European and the European citizen taken hold, one that welcomed diverse heritages as part of the New Europe?

At the same time, Muslim women's presence in public space and their engagement in the public sphere was becoming increasingly regulated and constrained. This was evidenced by bans on face veiling in public in France and Belgium, the various headscarf bans in schools in France and Germany, and proposed bans in numerous other locations. In Germany, Thilo Sarrazin's 2010 book *Deutschland schafft sich ab: wie wir unser Land aufs Spiel setzen* [Germany Destroys Itself: How We Are Putting Our Country in Danger] gained tremendous popularity. Advance interviews had generated significant attention when Sarrazin used the inflammatory language of fears of "headscarf girls" and the "constant delivery" of less intelligent "brides from Anatolia," who are having babies at a higher rate than "Germans" ("Was Thilo Sarrazin sagt"). The discovery of a racist terrorist cell in Germany that killed ten people over thirteen years, as well as the xenophobically motivated massacre perpetrated by Anders Behring Breivik in Norway, have called new public attention to ongoing racist violence in Europe. Has the utopia of a Europe supporting human rights failed?

How can we situate a discourse of gender violence in Germany vis-à-vis these most recent developments? The most visible struggles against violence, particularly against gender violence, have often proved to participate in other forms of exclusionary violence, especially racist and Islamophobic violence. In a circular way, these latter forms of violence are not only gendered but prohibit activism that targets violence against women. Yet perhaps this period also demonstrates exciting potential for change, even as it reveals the frightening potential for increased racism. During this same time period (the turn of the decade), a new group called the "Aktionsbündnis muslimischer Frauen" [Action Alliance of Muslim Women; hereafter AMF] was founded. Their mission statement argues that "the Basic Law, human rights, as well as the leading principles founded in Islam of human worth, responsible action before God and people, and the living together of all people in peace and justice are the basis of our activities" (Aktionsbündnis muslimischer Frauen e.V.). On the International Day of Action against Violence against Women, they declared:

> Violence against women has many facets—from verbal attacks to brutal physical attacks, from psychological terror to open violence. Many marginalizations and discriminations are often publicly barely visible, so that for example lack of access to education, politically initiated exclusions from careers and the complication—or even prohibition—of societal participation. The newly founded Action Alliance of Muslim Women in Germany speaks out against all forms of violence against women. (Aktionsbündnis muslimischer Frauen e. V.)

This group represents a growing voice among Muslim women in Germany today, a voice that wishes to express an affiliation with Islam that exists not only alongside their feminist activity (Muslim *and* feminist) but also grounds their feminist activity as *Muslim feminists*. Their work further calls attention to the ongoing complexity of Muslim women's experiences. Although they are still not gaining a tremendous amount of media attention, members of this group have participated in the DIK's 2012 meeting. Their public action and activity has thus begun to gain state validation, which is leading to a number of new recommendations, particularly those around access to employment and education. These recommendations, however, have not yet been institutionalized in new policy.

Fatima El-Tayeb has shown the importance of activist and artistic communities in Europe that are formed outside traditional identity politics, ones that draw on local identifications and communities of shared values, on connections between racialized and minority groups (El-Tayeb, *European Others*). She concludes, however, that

> these alternative networks must communicate with those who continue to discursively erase their voice and thus their very existence as legitimate European subjects. [...] if people with vastly different religious, sexual, and political attachments are to live together peacefully they must master the art of conversation (Appiah 2006). This

claim could be considered a humanist version of Seyla Benhabib's "democratic iterations," the idea that concepts shaping societies' self-representations evolve through constant collective application (Benhabib 2006). Neither statement leaves much to disagree with, so what seems to be at stake here are the conditions under which these conversations and collective applications take place: who is allowed to speak and who is not, what can and cannot be said, from which position(s) are we speaking and with what authority? No honest dialogue is possible until these questions have been addressed. (El-Tayeb 277)

An ongoing interrogation of the open discussion of violence against women is an important part of the dialogues to which El-Tayeb points. Just as future alternative networks must communicate with those who erase their voice, practices of teaching and research must also attend to these erased voices. This is an approach thus somewhat different from that articulated by Žižek in his discussion of resistance to violence. In *Violence* he argues that sometimes the best way to interrupt the patterns of violence is to do "nothing"—but by "nothing" he further means to step back and to take the time and space needed for critique. The moment of critical reflection should not be conflated with "doing nothing." Critique not only reveals the conditions under which ideologies emerge but imagines the conditions for the future and for progressive change. Critical reflection cannot be relegated to a position before action; rather, it should occur in ongoing interaction with conceptions of political change. This is not to say that platforms for change and critical reflection must occur in the same space. The humanities should retain its special function as a space where critical approaches to culture might lead to new imaginations of the future.

Challenges to how we fight gender violence, especially domestic violence and rape, are understandably contentious. The discussions I've had with colleagues and friends while working on this project have often been deeply impassioned. People feel powerfully about fighting violence against women—as do I. Women who haven't experienced some form of sexualized violence themselves likely know somebody who has. That experience leads many feminists of many backgrounds, including myself, to develop a powerful affective identification with the ongoing fight against sexualized violence. This makes challenging the discourse of gender violence difficult. Yet, the insistence on associating gender violence with Islam runs counter to effective resistance to violence. And the insistence on a hierarchal valuation of forms of violence, one that privileges the challenge of gender violence over racism, or vice versa, proves equally counterproductive. Effective action can only occur when the interrelationships between multiple forms of violence are acknowledged and understood and when the potential for change in any community is assumed to be possible. Currently, we might turn our analyses to rethinking the violence of racism, sexism, and Islamophobia as violences that intersect and are sometimes mutually constitutive but always connected by the society that normalizes and enables them. Nurturing a democratic public sphere requires a space not only for religious language and representation, but also for religious identities. This seems particularly important given the powerful way in which many, such as the members of the AMF, define their ethics, values, or motivation to commitment for social justice as inspired by religious or spiritual identifications. Just as a politics of radical listening assumes agency on the part of Muslim women, it also allows us to conceptualize a situation where people may simultaneously occupy subject positions as religious, antiracist, and antigender violence.

I've been reminded, in thinking about the role that secularism plays in our imaginations of the potential for justice, of these words from Audre Lorde:

> Unity implies the coming together of elements which are, to begin with, varied and diverse in their particular natures. Our persistence in examining the tensions within diversity encourages growth toward our common goal. So often we either ignore the past or romanticize it, render the reason for unity useless or mythic. (Lorde 136)

Secularism has played a tremendously contradictory role in the struggles against violence: as the mythologized past, as the reason for unity, and as the very goal to be achieved.

The call to attend to religious identities and representation in the public sphere is not to be misconstrued as a simple equation of women's agency and progressive politics. Although I've focused on the potential for resistance to violence within this book, it is clear that in recognizing the potential for agency on the part of Muslim women, one must also recognize the potential for their agency as conservative political actors. Saba Mahmood's *Politics of Piety*, in exploring the agency that women take as part of Islamist movements in Egypt, seeks to question the "overwhelming tendency within poststructuralist feminist scholarship to conceptualize agency in terms of subversion or resignification of social norms" (Mahmood 14). For this reason I have been careful to focus on possible anti-racist critiques of gender violence rather than hightlight Muslim women's agency.

Finally, I think that a consequence of the strict division between public and private sphere has done something else for scholars. Many of the things that sustain us—whether they be our spirituality, our community, our bodily care, or our service or activism in the name of community—are expected to be excluded from our working lives. In other words, in our teaching and thinking lives. Feminist, queer, and antiracist activists have been able to do significant theorizing about using lived experiences as part of scholarly agendas, though these forms of theorizing are often greeted with immense discomfort outside the fields of gender,, queer, or ethnic studies. Even more discomfort attends similar questionings of the relationships between faith and activist subjectivities, between faith and intellectual projects. Yet faith and spiritualities are experienced as embodied lived relationships as well: whether to a deity, to a community, or to cultural traditions. Just as "setting aside" race, gender, and sexuality in the service of an abstracted public sphere has proven impossible, it is also proving necessary to recognize faith and spiritualities, as well as a range of possible atheist positionings. It is possible that in excluding religious subjectivities from the imagination of feminist, queer, or antiracist subjectivities, that scholars have reinforced a heritage of Western feminism that "produces a 'white' genealogy of both queer and feminist studies by, among other things, leaving to the side the women of color and transnational feminisms whose relationships to religion have historically been far more complex and variegated" (Pellegrini 208).

We move from these diverse positionings in our interactions in a democratic public sphere. Acknowledgment of—even an evaluation of—religious diversity is a precondition for a truly democratic public sphere that has yet to come. This acknowledgment provides a foundation from which common agendas and strategies against violence and for democracy can be articulated and fought for.

NOTES

Introduction: Undoing the Connections between Muslim Violence, "Culture," and Secularism

1. I am using gender violence here in its common usage as an umbrella term for violence that is generally targeted against women, particularly domestic violence, rape, and familial violence. While this term has established itself in political as well as academic discourse, I do consider this a deeply problematic term as well, for it uses "gender" as a screen for "woman" in a way that obscures the existence of violence against men as well as heterosexist violence against gay, lesbian, bisexual, and transgender people.
2. This awkward phrase is frequently used in German language literature to refer to people whose parents or grandparents migrated to Germany since World War II.
3. Seyla Benhabib provides an overview of the history of German immigration law and the 1999 changes that took effect in 2000. One can find a brief summary of guestworker migration and the accompanying questions of citizenship in *Geschichte der Ausländerpolitik in Deutschland* (Herbert 332–34), and *The Guestworker Question* (Chin 1–29). For a broader history of migration to Germany see Bade.
4. Intersectionality emerged as a critical approach to analyzing gender in the late 1980s and the early 1990s in the United States. First formulated by Black feminist theorist Kimberlé Crenshaw and popularized by Patricia Hill Collins, the term has much in common with Audre Lorde's understanding of gender. Intersectionality emphasizes that identity and experiences of oppression are more than the "sum of their parts," that categories such as race and gender complicate and mutually inflect one another.
5. Elsewhere I have expressed this, following Spivak, as "laying the necessary enabling groundwork for collectivities potentially capable of planetary thought and action" (Weber, "Beyond the Culture Trap" 34). There is more to be thought about the notion of planetary collectivities and the undoing of race, though I will not have space to address this here.
6. For an extensive discussion, see Mir-Hosseini; further see Abid.
7. Joyce Cesari's article also provides an interesting explanation of the range of contradictory approaches to modernization and their relationship to a divide within Islam between popular (often mystical or folk) Islam and a more modernized intellectual Islam.

8. Here, for reasons of space, I must leave out the extensive debates about the larger, fundamental feminist critique of the notion of rights and the Enlightenment subject itself. It is interesting to note, however, that this critique has played almost no role for German immigrant women activists, who generally seek to frame their struggles within relatively traditional notions of democracy and rights.
9. The burqa is a specific form of full body veiling that is most common in Afghanistan and parts of Pakistan; the small opening for the eyes is also veiled. However, all forms of face covering are prohibited by the proposed bans.

1 A Regime of Gender Violence: Honor Killings, Familial Violence, and Muslim Women's Subjectivities

1. Sentences for violent crimes are, overall, significantly shorter in Germany than in the United States; minors can receive a maximum term length of ten years. This led to some confusion in the international press, which occasionally interpreted the sentence to be reduced because of the nature of the crime rather than the sentencing maximums.
2. See, for example, Schneider; Fleishman; Diver; Nickerson; Boyes; Cleaver; Ehrkamp.
3. The inability to imagine emancipation for Muslim women without the paternal protection of the state from Islam plays out in an especially contradictory way in the *Spiegel special* "Mystery Islam." This issue includes an article by an Egyptian Muslim feminist but ignores (im)migrant participation in feminist groups in Germany.
4. Katherine Pratt Ewing makes important related points about the scripts this case produces for Turkish masculinity, ones that ignore the everyday experiences of discrimination faced by men of Turkish heritage (Ewing 153–164).
5. See chapter 5 for a discussion of their autobiographies and the role that they played in the visibility of these two women. The controversy over Kelek's rewriting of her dissertation to come to entirely different conclusions (with a new focus on Islam as a primary reason for violence) is also addressed in chapter 5.
6. Unfortunately, this study does not consider violence against men and children, but this is to be a direction for the long-term project under which the study was conducted.
7. Women of Eastern European heritage were classified in a separate group, which means that Muslims from Bosnia and Serbia, a quickly growing segment of the population, were included as Eastern Europeans.

2 Contentious Headscarves: Cleaning Woman, Forbidden Schoolteacher, Hijab Martyr

1. I will use the term *hijab* here as it is popularly used by Muslim women in Germany, namely, to refer to a form of headcovering that covers the hair, though not necessarily the neck, and leaves the face free. Additional meanings for *hijab* elsewhere might be both more general and more specific, referring to a specific way of binding the headscarf, or to modest dress that includes the covering of arms and legs, or even to forms of gender seclusion (I. M. Brown 438).

2. In particular, a 2004 special issue of *Comparative Studies of South Asia, Africa and the Middle East* reconsidered German Orientalisms to show that they reflected a range of political interests and that they existed not merely in elite discourse but "from below" as well (Jenkins 99).
3. Alice Schwarzer was the founder and longtime editor of *EMMA*, a magazine that plays a role in German culture similar to that of *MS* magazine in the United States. Throughout the 1990s and the 2000s, Schwarzer has taken a prominent role in discussions about gender and Islam in Germany.
4. There are two waves of headscarf controversies in France that roughly coincide with the waves of attention to Muslim women in Der Spiegel that I address in the previous chapter, namely the early 1990s and from 1997 on. Norma Moruzzi provides an excellent analysis of the early headscarf debates, which also responds to earlier, less nuanced academic discussions. For an examination of the more recent controversies that eventually led to a national ban on students wearing headscarves in public schools, see Jane Freedman and Rachel Bloul.
5. Zaptçıoğlu's points are further supported by later research. Nilufer Göle's work on the wearing of headscarves in Turkey suggests that for many women it serves as a marker of entrance to or participation in modernity (Göle, *Anverwandlungen* 115–130; Göle, *Forbidden* 4). Alev Çınar points out, however, that these women's choice to enter into the public sphere has been appropriated by conservative Islamist groups, resulting in a return to a status as visible public symbols with little political power (Çınar, "Subversion and Subjugation" 907–908).
6. For a discussion on the French headscarf debates in the context of racist and colonial discourses, see *The Politics of the Veil* (Scott). There has been extensive discussion of the French headscarf debates and the complications of an antiracist position. Some voice a stance that is common in Germany as well, which assumes that antiracist critiques of the headscarf debates are unreflected (see, for example, B. Winter 296), whereas others suggest that the arguments for secularism actually work against integration (Freedman), or that headscarf bans may serve to inhibit antiracist practices (Freedman, "Women, Islam and Rights in Europe" 43).
7. Additional cases involving the headscarf have also come before the courts. Some permit Muslim, but not Christian, girls to be released from swimming education or more general physical education on the basis of their religious beliefs (BVerwG; Wesel; Mückl 99) were partially argued on the basis of Islam's prescriptive laws for women's clothing and the difference of the Muslim girls' culture from Christian culture. In 2003, a federal court ruled that a department store could not fire a woman due to her wearing of the headscarf (LAG Hessen and ArbG Hanau; Hessen). This decision was upheld by the Federal Constitutional Court (BVerfG, *1 BvR 792/03*).
8. Elsewhere, I have discussed in greater detail how notions of visibility in the Ludin case are used to produce the body of the Muslim woman as lying outside the German nation and of Germanness (Weber, "Cloth" 45–47).
9. It is interesting to note that Swiss newspapers expressed outrage that el-Sherbini's case was receiving so much more interest than were violent attacks by youth against Swiss tourists in Munich ("Bluttat").

3 Troubling Headscarves: Covering, Artistic Reconfigurations of Public Space, and the Muslim Woman's Body

1. The connection was also made by a Neo-Nazi youth organization in Germany, which appropriated the ad campaign for their own advertising, adding the tagline "not all advertising is false," until the organization was banned (Wittrock).
2. Thanks to Deepti Misri for suggesting this reading of the press materials.
3. Although there is no evidence of direct intertextuality, it is interesting to note that Berlin-based Japanese Austrian filmmaker and video artist Hito Steyerl has already introduced these contexts to a German-language audience familiar with avant-garde video art. Steyerl takes up the complex implications of bondage in her short film *Lovely Andrea*. For Steyerl, bondage becomes a metaphor for forms of interdependency with complex implications for freedoms: "There is bondage all over the place. Bondage is everywhere. I bind; you bind; we are bound. The art of knot-tying is not just popular in Abu Ghraib and Guantanamo. I spin, you spin; we are connected. Networks and webs, suspense and dependency: we are hooked" (Steyerl).

4 Freedom to Imagine the World: Violence and the Writing of Self

1. Eberhard Seidel's essay is of particular interest in this context. Seidel points out that hundreds of articles have been printed in recent years on honor killings, forced marriages, and other forms of violence against women. Yet few have reported on the recent studies showing how rare these things are, on the similarities between the Turkish German population and the ethnic German population in terms of attitudes about secularism, on the extensive use of fluent German by immigrant populations, or on the high value placed on education and knowledge by Turkish Germans.
2. See, for example, Caldwell; "Turkish Honor Killings in Germany"; Poggioli, "Reporter's Notebook"; Poggioli, "Muslim Women"; Poggioli, "Muslim Activist"; Schneider; Snyder; and Simons. Both Kay Sokolowsky and Elisabeth Beck-Gersheim are critical of the way both national and international press have turned to Necla Kelek as representatives of Turkish German communities and spokeswoman for the plight of the Muslim woman; Sokolowsky also addresses Ateş in this context (Sokolowsky 112–132; Beck-Gernsheim 76–79).
3. Numerous additional narratives in the same vein were published in the mid-2000s, including: *Wir sind eure Töchter, nicht eure Ehre* by Serap Çileli (We are Your Daughters, Not Your Honor, published in 2002 and republished in 2006 by Blanvalet, a Random House publisher); *Mich hat keiner gefragt. Zur Ehe gezwungen—eine Türkin in Deutschland erzählt*, (Nobody Asked Me. Forced into Marriage—a Turkish Woman in Germany Tells Her Story, published under the pseudonym Ayşe, Blanvalet 2005), *Erstickt an euren Lügen. Eine Türkin erzählt*, (Choke on Your Lies. A Turkish Woman Tells Her Story, published under the pseudonym Inci, Piper 2005), Hülya Kalkan, *Ich wollte nur frei sein. Meine Flucht vor der Zwangsehe* (I Only Wanted My Freedom. My Flight from Forced Marriage, Ullstein 2005). Also on the market are

translations such as Ayaan Hirsi Ali's *Ich klage an. Plädoyer für die Befreiung der muslimischen Frauen* (original title *De Maagdenkooi*, 2004, published in English as *The Caged Virgin: An Emancipation Proclamation for Women and Islam*).
4. The German here is as awkward as this translation suggests.
5. For an early example of this, see this discussions at a 1984 conference documented in *Sind wir uns denn so fremd?* (Arbeitsgruppe Frauenkongreß). These tensions are further discussed in a work by Sara Lennox and Encarnación Gutiérrez Rodríguez (Lennox, "Divided Feminism: Women, Racism and German National Identity"; and Rodríguez, "Migrantinnenpolitik").
6. Phillip also assumes a unified "southern" masculinity that will contribute to violence. Having spent time in Italy, he considers himself an expert on Italian culture and is certain that Alanyali's brother will enforce sexual mores "like in Sicily" (208–209).
7. As Spivak herself points out, the two women she describes in her famous essay "Can the Subaltern Speak," the Rani of Sirmur and Bhubaneswari Bhaduri can hardly be called subaltern, as they have already moved into the path of upward mobility (Spivak, *A Critique* 308–309).

5 Violent Authenticities: The Work of Emine Sevgi Özdamar and Feridun Zaimoglu

1. It is unclear to which deaths she is referring here; this conversation does not reappear in the text. The infamous May 1 demonstration that led to dozens killed and over a hundred injured took place a year later, in 1977, at Taksim Square. This is further significant because it was the site of the first monument built in a public square in the new Turkish Republic, inaugurating a significant turn to a public politics of national space (Baykan and Hatuka).
2. For an overview of the events, see (Varon 196–198).
3. Schleyer was at the time president of the Employers' Association of West Germany and of the Federation of Germany Industry; he was also a former SS officer under Reinhard Heydrich, one of the architects of the "Final Solution."
4. She seems unaware of her former flatmate, Gundula Bahro's, cooperation with the Stasi investigation of Rudi Bahro (Herzberg and Seifert 162–164).
5. Taner Akçam proposes that understanding Kurdish, Armenian, and Turkish histories as the same history rather than as separate histories is a necessary precondition to a future based on democratic principles (Akçam, *From Empire to Republic* x–xi). *Leyla* might suggest that a recognition of shared and connected histories of violence, which includes German history, is equally valuable. In Turkey, the distancing from religion was intimately connected to the rise in ethnic identities. Modernization in Turkey was in turn founded on a process of collective identity, not individual rights and identities, which some see as a hindrance to democratic futures. In any case, it shows that modernization doesn't equal democracy (Akçam, *From Empire to Republic* 124). This is a point of similarity rather than of difference to the German case, in which a process of modernity, rooted in nationalism, also led to genocide. Indeed, a declaration of human rights was part of pre-Republican treaties with the West, which were voided after the establishment of the Republic.

Works Cited

Abid, Lise. "Die Debatte um Gender und Menschenrechte im Islam." *Facetten islamischer Welten. Geschlechterordnungen, Frauen- und Menschenrechte in der Diskussion.* Eds. Mechtild Rumpf, Ute Gerhard, and Mechtild M. Jansen. Bielefeld, Germany: Transcript, 2003. 143–162. Print.
Ackermann, Irmgard. "Emine Sevgi Özdamar." *Kritisches Lexikon der Deutschsprachigen Literatur.* Ed. Heinz Ludwig Arnold. Vol. 7. edition text and kritik, 1999. Print.
Adelson, Leslie A. *The Turkish Turn in Contemporary German Literature: Toward a New Critical Grammar of Migration.* New York: Palgrave Macmillan, 2005. Print.
"Afghan Daily Condemns Silence over Action Against Uighurs in China." *BBC Monitoring South Asia* 12 Jul. 2009. Web. 7 Sep. 2009.
Ahmed, Leila. "The Discourse of the Veil." *Veil: Veiling, Representation and Contemporary Art.* Eds. David A. Bailey and Gilane Tawadros. Cambridge, MA: The MIT Press, 2003. 42–55. Print.
Akçam, Taner. *A Shameful Act: The Armenian Genocide and the Question of Turkish Responsibility.* New York: Metropolitan Books, 2007. Print.
———. *From Empire to Republic: Turkish Nationalism and the Armenian Genocide.* New York: Zed Books, 2004. Print.
Akgün, Lale. "Null Toleranz für die Doppelmoral." *Die Zeit.* 12 Apr. 2006: 4. Web. 03 Aug. 2010.
Akkent, Meral. "Sind deutsche Frauen emanzipiert und türkische Frauen unterdrückt?" *Die Schwierigkeit, nicht rassistisch zu sein.* Eds. Annita Kalpaka and Nora Räthzel. Berlin: EXpress, 1986. 20–31. Print.
Akkent, Meral, and Gaby Franger. *Das Kopftuch: Ein Stückchen Stoff in Geschichte und Gegenwart = Başörtü: Geçmişte ve Günümüzde Bir Parça Kumaş.* Frankfurt am Main: Dağyeli, 1987. Print.
———. *Kopftuchkulturen.* Nürnberg: Frauen in der einen Welt, 2000. Print.
Aktionsbündnis muslimischer Frauen e. V. "Internationaler Tag zur Beseitigung von Gewalt gegen Frauen [Presseerklärung zum 25.11.09]." *Aktionsbündnis muslimischer Frauen e. V.* 25 Oct. 2009. Web. 14 Sep. 2011.
———. "Über uns." *Aktionsbündnis muslimischer Frauen e. V.* Web. 30 Aug. 2011.
Akyün, Hatice. *Ali zum Dessert: Leben in einer neuen Welt.* Munich: Goldmann, 2008. Print.
———. *Einmal Hans mit scharfer Sosse.* Munich: Goldmann, 2005. Print.

Akyün, Hatice, and Alexander Smoltczyk. "Die verlorenen Töchter." *Der Spiegel* 47 (2004): 79–88. Print.

Alanyali, Iris. *Die blaue Reise: und andere Geschichten aus meiner deutsch-türkischen Familie.* Reinbek bei Hamburg: Rowohlt, 2006. Print.

———. "Ihr seid nichts als mein verströmter Samen." *Die Welt* 24 Apr. 2006: 23. Web. 07 Jul. 2012.

Ali, Ayaan Hirsi. *Ich klage an: Plädoyer für die Befreiung der muslimischen Frauen.* Trans. Anna Berger and Jonathan Krämer. Munich: Piper Verlag, 2006. Print.

———. *Mein Leben, meine Freiheit: Die Autobiographie.* Trans. Anne Emmert and Heike Schlatterer. Munich: Piper Verlag, 2006. Print.

Al-Aswany, Alaa. "Western Hostility to Islam Is Stoked by Double Standards and Distortion." *The Guardian* 21 Jul. 2009: 25. Web. 07 Jul. 2012

Am Orde, Sabine. "Frauen wie Seyran Ates haben mir mein Leben erschwert." *taz. die tageszeitung* 4 Sep. 2008: 13. Web. 06 May 2009.

Arbeitsgruppe Frauenkongreß, ed. *Sind wir uns denn so fremd? Ausländische und deutsche Frauen im Gespräch.* 2nd ed. Berlin: Subrosa Frauenverlag, 1985. Print.

Asad, Talal. "Europe Against Islam: Islam in Europe." *The Blackwell Companion to Contemporary Islamic Thought.* Ed. Ibrahim M. Abu-Rabi'. Malden, MA: Blackwell, 2006. 302–312. Print.

———. *Formations of the Secular: Christianity, Islam, Modernity.* Stanford University Press, 2003. Print.

———. *On Suicide Bombing.* New York: Columbia University Press, 2007. Print.

Ataman, Ferda. "Die verlorene Ehre der Familie Sürücü." *Der Tagesspiegel* 06 Feb. 2010. Factiva. Web. 05 Nov. 2010.

Ateş, Seyran. *Grosse Reise ins Feuer: die Geschichte einer deutschen Türkin.* Berlin: Rowohlt, 2003. Print.

"Ates wieder Anwältin; deutsch-türkische Frauenrechtlerin arbeitet wieder als Anwältin. Dies sei ein Signal für alle bedrohten Frauen." *Taz, die Tageszeitung* 07 Sep. 2007: 24. Web. 06 Aug. 2010.

Avenarius, Tomas. "Empörung in Alexandria; Proteste nach Mord an Ägypterin in Deutschem Gerichtssaal." *Süddeutsche Zeitung* 07 Jul. 2009: 10. Web. 06 Aug. 2010.

Ayim, May. *Blues in schwarz weiß.* Berlin: Orlanda Frauenverlag, 1995. Print.

Ayşe, with Renate Eder. *Mich hat keiner gefragt: Zur Ehe gezwungen: Eine Türkin in Deutschland erzählt.* 2005. Print.

Bade, Klaus J. *Deutsche im Ausland, Fremde in Deutschland: Migration in Geschichte und Gegenwart.* München: C. H. Beck, 1992. Print.

Bader, Johann. "Darf eine muslimische Lehrerin in der Schule ein Kopftuch tragen?" *Verwaltungsblätter für Baden-Württemberg* 19.10 (1998): 361–365. Print.

Bahners, Patrick. *Die Panikmacher: Die deutsche Angst vor dem Islam: eine Streitschrift.* Munich: C. H.Beck, 2011. Print.

———. "Feridun Zaimoglu: Kritiker der Islamkritikerinnen." *Frankfurter Allgemeine Zeitung* 26 Apr. 2007: 40. Print.

Bakirdögen, Ayhan, and Tanja Laninger. "Lebte Hatun Sürücü zu modern?" *Die Welt* 10 Feb. 2005: 35. Web. 02 Feb. 2010.

———. "War Hatun Sürücü zu modern?" *Berliner Morgenpost* 10 Feb. 2005: 21. Web. 02 Feb. 2010.

Balibar, Etienne. *We, the People of Europe?: Reflections on Transnational Citizenship.* Princeton UP, 2003. Print.
Balibar, Etienne, and Immanuel Maurice Wallerstein. *Race, Nation, Class: Ambiguous Identities.* New York: Verso, 1991. Print.
Bartsch, Matthias et al. "Haben wir schon die Scharia?" *Der Spiegel* 26 Mar. 2007: 22. Web. 18 Jun. 2010.
Baumgartner-Karabak, Andrea, and Gisela Landesberger. *Die verkauften Bräute: türkische Frauen zwischen Kreuzberg und Anatolien.* Reinbek bei Hamburg: Rowohlt, 1978. Print.
Baykan, Aysegul, and Tali Hatuka. "Politics and Culture in the Making of Public Space: Taksim Square, 1 May 1977, Istanbul." *Planning Perspectives* 25.1 (2010): 49–68. Web. 13 Jul. 2012.
BayVGH. "Ausländerrechtliche Anordnung zur Vorlage eines Lichtbilds." *Die öffentliche Verwaltung* 53.13 (2000): 559–560. Print.
Beck-Gernsheim, Elisabeth. *Wir und die Anderen.* Frankfurt am Main: Suhrkamp Verlag GmbH, 2007. Print.
Bednarz, Dieter. "Allah-Mania." *Spiegel special* 1 (1998): 106–112. Print.
Behr, Alfred. "Muslimin beschäftigt den Stuttgarter Landtag." *Frankfurter Allgemeine Zeitung* 11 Jul. 1998: 4. Web. 08 Oct. 2008.
Beicht, Ursula, and Mona Granato. *Prekäre Übergänge vermeiden–Potenziale nutzen. Junge Frauen und Männer mit Migrationshintergrund an der Schwelle von der Schule zur Ausbildung.* Bonn: Abteilung Wirtschafts- und Sozialpolitik der Friedrich-Ebert-Stiftung, 2011. Web. 26 Mar. 2012.
Benhabib, Seyla. "Citizens, Residents, and Aliens in a Changing World: Political Membership in the Global Era." *Social Research* 65 (1999): 709–744. Print.
Berghahn, Sabine. "Deutschlands konfrontativer Umgang mit dem Kopftuch der Lehrerin." *Der Stoff, aus dem Konflikte sind. Debatten um das Kopftuch in Deutschland, Österreich und der Schweiz.* Eds. Sabine Berghahn, Petra Rostock, and Alexander Nöhring. Bielefeld, Germany: Transcript, 2009. 33–71.
———. "Ein Quadratmeter Stoff als Projektionsfläche. Gesetzliche Kopftuchverbote in Deutschland und anderen europäischen Ländern." *Gender...politik...online* (2009): n. pag. Web. 19 Jun. 2011.
Berlant, Lauren Gail. *The Queen of America Goes to Washington City: Essays on Sex and Citizenship.* Durham, NC: Duke UP, 1997. Print.
Bertrams, Michael. "Lehrerin mit Kopftuch? Islamismus und Menschenrecht." *Deutsches Verwaltungsblatt* 19 (2003): 1225–1234. Web. 08 Oct. 2008.
Bhabha, Homi K. *The Location of Culture.* London: Routledge, 1994. Print.
Bielefeldt, Heiner. "'Westliche' versus 'islamische' Menschenrechte? Zur Kritik an kulturalistischen Vereinnahmungen der Menschenrechtsidee." *Facetten islamischer Welten. Geschlechterordnungen, Frauen-und Menschenrechte in der Diskussion.* Ed. Mechtild Rumpf, Ute Gerhard, and Mechtild M. Jansen. Bielefeld, Germany: Transcript, 2003. 123–142. Print.
Bloul, Rachel. "Engendering Muslim Identities. Deterritorialization and the Ethnicization Process in France." *Making Muslim Space in North America and Europe.* Ed. Barbara Daly Metcalf. Berkeley: U of California P, 1996. 235–250. Print.
"Bluttat mit internationalen Konsequenzen; Ein Mord in Dresden erregt Empörung in der muslimischen Welt." *Neue Zürcher Zeitung* 14 Jul. 2009: 3. Web. 11 Nov. 2009.

Böckenförde, Ernst-Wolfgang. "'Kopftuchstreit' auf dem richtigen Weg?" *Neue Juristische Wochenschrift* 54.10 (2001): 723–728. Print. 8 Oct. 2008.
Booth, Heather. *The Migration Process in Britain and West Germany.* Aldershot, UK: Avebury, 1992. Print.
Boran, Erol. "Faces of Contemporary Turkish-German Kabarett." *Text & Presentation* (2005): 172–186. Print.
Borowczyk, Ulrike. "Frauenpower." *Berliner Morgenpost* 28 Jan. 2008: 21. Web. 30 Jun. 2010.
Boyes, Roger. "Teenager Killed His Sister for Living a Western Life." *The Times* 14 Apr. 2006: 53. Web. 30 Jun. 2010.
Von Braun, Christina, and Bettina Mathes. *Verschleierte Wirklichkeit. Die Frau, der Islam und der Westen.* Berlin: Aufbau-Verlag, 2007. Print.
Breger, Claudia. "'Meine Herren, spielt in meinem Gesicht ein Affe?' Strategien der Mimikry in Texten von Emine S. Özdamar und Yoko Tawada." *AufBrüche: kulturelle Produktionen von Migrantinnen, Schwarzen und jüdischen Frauen in Deutschland.* Ed. Kader Konuk, Peggy Piesche, and Cathy S. Gelbin. Königstein/Taunus: Ulrike Helmer, 1999. 30–59. Print.
———. "Religious Turns: Immigration, Islam, and Christianity in Twenty-First-Century German Cultural Politics." *Konturen* 1.1 (2008): n. pag. Web. 16 Nov. 2009.
Brown, Indre Monjezi. "Muslimische Frauen und das Kopftuch–Hijab und Islamischer Feminismus." *Der Stoff, aus dem Konflikte sind: Debatten um das Kopftuch in Deutschland, Österreich und der Schweiz Unter Mitarbeit von Alexander Nöhring.* Eds. Sabine Berghahn and Petra Rostock. Bielefeld, Germany: Transcript, 2009. 437–464. Print.
Brown, Wendy. "Introduction." *Is Critique Secular? Blasphemy, Injury, and Free Speech.* Berkeley: U of California P, 2009. 7–19. Web. 14 Jan. 2011.
———. *Regulating Aversion: Tolerance in the Age of Identity and Empire.* Princeton UP, 2008. Print.
Brozska, Ina. "Wo sind die Mitbürger?–Bei der ersten Langen Nacht der Deutschtürken bleibt man unter sich." *Berliner Zeitung* 08 Jun. 2009: 22. Web. 30 Jun. 2010.
Bruns, Tissy. "5 Jahre Sürücü-Mord." *Der Tagesspiegel* 07 Feb. 2010: 001. Web. 30 Jun. 2010.
Buchbinder, Sascha. "Ehrenmorde rütteln Deutschland auf." *Der Tageszanzeiger* 07 Mar. 2005: 8. Web. 30 Jun. 2010.
Bukow, Wolf-Dietrich, and Roberto Llaryora. *Mitbürger aus der Fremde: Soziogenese Ethnischer Minoritäten.* Opladen: Westdeutscher Verlag, 1988. Print.
Bullion, Constanze von. "In den Fängen einer türkischen Familie." *Süddeutsche Zeitung* 26 Feb. 2005: 3. Web. 30 Jun. 2010.
———. "Mord im Namen der Ehre." *Süddeutsche Zeitung* 14 Sep. 2005: 12. Web. 30 Jun. 2010.
———. "Mord und Sühne." *Süddeutsche Zeitung* 28 Aug. 2007. Web. 04 Aug. 2010.
Bundesministerium des Innern. "Deutsche Islam Konferenz (DIK) Muslime in Deutschland–Deutsche Muslime." *Bundesministerium des Innern.* Web. 24 Sep. 2008.
Bundesverband der Migrantinnen in Deutschland. "Abschlußerklärung." *Bundesverband der Migrantinnen in Deutschland e.V.* 20 Mar. 2005. Web. 02 Aug. 2010.

BurkaBondage. Dir. Helena Waldmann. Haus der Berliner Festspiele, Berlin. 20 Oct. 2009. Performance.

"BurkaBondage–No Ordinary Experience. Pressemitteilung." Oct. 2009. Web. 30 Oct. 2009.

Butler, Judith. "Critique, Coercion, and Sacred Life in Benjamin's 'Critique of Violence'." *Political Theologies: Public Religions in a Post-Secular World.* New York: Fordham UP, 2006. 201–219. Print.

———. *Undoing Gender.* New York: Routledge, 2004. Print.

BVerfG. *2 BvR 1436/02 vom 3.6.2003.* Bundesverfassungsgericht, 2003. Web. 07 Feb. 2011.

———. *1 BvR 792/03vom 30.07.2003.* Bundesverfassungsgericht, 2003. Web. 08 Oct. 2008.

BVerwG. "Befreiung einer Schülerin islamischen Glaubens vom Sportunterricht. Urt. v. 25.8.1993–6 C 8/91 (Münster)." *Neue Zeitschrift für Verwaltungsrecht* 13.6 (1994): 578–581. Print.

———. "BVerwG 2 C 45.03." 24 Jun. 2004. Web. 13 Dec. 2010.

———. "Die Einstellung als Lehrerin an Grund- und Hauptschulen im Beamtenverhältnis." *Die Öffentliche Verwaltung* 55 (2002): 997–999. Print.

Çağlar, Ayşe. "Das Kulturkonzept als Zwangsjacke in Studien zur Arbeitsmigration." *Zeitschrift für Türkeistudien* 1 (1990): 93–105. Print.

Caldwell, Christopher. "Where Every Generation Is First-Generation." *The New York Times* 27 May 2007. Web. 8 Jun. 2011.

Casanova, José. "Religion, European Secular Identities, and European Integration." *Religion in an Expanding Europe.* Eds. Timothy Byrnes and Peter J. Katzenstein. Cambridge: Cambridge UP, 2006. 65–92. Print.

Celik, Ipek Azime. *Realism, Violence and Representation of Migrants and Minorities in Contemporary Europe.* 2009. New York University.

Cerha, Birgit. "Die Wut Ägyptens; Islamische Welt über Bluttat entsetzt." *Frankfurter Rundschau* 13 Jul. 2009: 6. Print.

Cesari, Jocelyne. *When Islam and Democracy Meet: Muslims in Europe and in the United States.* New York: Palgrave Macmillan, 2004. Print.

Cesari, Joyce. "Modernisation of Islam or Islamisation of Modernity? Muslim Minorities in Europe and the Issue of Pluralism." *Muslims in Europe: From the Margin to the Centre.* Ed. Jamal Malik. Münster: Lit Verlag, 2004. 93–99. Print.

Chakrabarty, Dipesh. *Provincializing Europe: Postcolonial Thought and Historical Difference.* Princeton, NJ: Princeton UP, 2000. Print.

Cheesman, Tom. "Akçam–Zaimoğlu–'Kanak Attak': Turkish Lives and Letters in German." *German Life and Letters* 55.2 (2002): 180–195. Print.

———. *Novels of Turkish German Settlement: Cosmopolite Fictions.* Camden House, 2007. Print.

Chin, Rita et al. *After the Nazi Racial State: Difference and Democracy in Germany and Europe.* Ann Arbor: U of Michigan P, 2009. Print.

Chin, Rita. *The Guest Worker Question in Postwar Germany.* Cambridge: Cambridge UP 2009. Print.

Chin, Rita, and Heide Fehrenbach. "German Democracy and the Question of Difference, 1945–1995." *After the Nazi Racial State: Difference and Democracy in Germany and Europe.* Ed. Rita Chin et al. Ann Arbor: U of Michigan P, 2009. 102–136. Print.

Çileli, Serap. *Wir sind eure Töchter, nicht eure Ehre.* Munich: Blanvalet, 2006. Print.

Çınar, Alev. *Modernity, Islam, and Secularism in Turkey: Bodies, Places, and Time.* Minneapolis: U of Minnesota P, 2005. Print.

———. "Subversion and Subjugation in the Public Sphere: Secularism and the Islamic Headscarf." *Signs: Journal of Women in Culture and Society* 33.4 (2008): 891–913. Print.

Cizmecioglu, Aygül. "Feridun Zaimoglu: Leyla. ARTS.21 Book Browser: Our New Favourites." *DW-WORLD.DE.* News. Web. 24 Jun. 2011.

Cleaver, Hannah. "Outrage as Family of 'Honour Killing' Victim Tries to Adopt Her Son." *The Daily Telegraph* 19 Apr. 2006: 013. Web. 15 Jun. 2010.

Connolly, Kate, and Jack Shenker. "Racism Row: The Headscarf Martyr: Murder in German Court Sparks Egyptian Fury at West's 'Islamophobia'." *The Guardian* 08 Jul. 2009: 17. Web. 15 Jun. 2010.

Cziesche, Dominik, et al. "Das Kreuz mit dem Koran." *Der Spiegel* 40 (2003): 82–97. Print.

Dadrian, Vahakn N. *The History of the Armenian Genocide: Ethnic Conflict from the Balkans to Anatolia to the Caucasus.* New York: Berghahn Books, 2003. Print.

Davis, Kathy. "Intersectionality as Buzzword: A Sociology of Science Perspective on What Makes a Feminist Theory Successful." *Feminist Theory* 9.1 (2008): 67–85. Web. 30 Apr. 2010.

Debus, Anne. "Der Kopftuch-Streit in Baden Württemberg." *Kritische Justiz* 32.3 (1999): 430–448. Print.

———. "Machen Kleider wirklich Leute?–Warum der 'Kopftuch-Streit' so 'spannend' ist." *Neue Zeitschrift für Verwaltungsrecht* 20.12 (2001): 1355–1360. Print.

Deckwerth, Sabine. "Ein angekündigter Tod." *Berliner Zeitung* 27 Oct. 2005: 26. Web. 30 Jun. 2010.

———. "Opfer ihrer Brüder?–Hatun Sürücü wurde mit drei Schüssen ermordet–nun wird auch wegen Vergewaltigung ermittelt." *Berliner Zeitung* 15 Jul. 2005: 16. Web. 30 Jun. 2010.

"Der Zorn der Muslime." *Neue Zürcher Zeitung* 22 Jul. 2009: 2. Web. 30 Jun. 2010.

Dernbach, Andrea. "Marwa S., Ein Fall wie der Karikaturenstreit?" *Der Tagesspiegel* 20 Jul. 2009: 5. Web. 30 Jun. 2010.

———. "Weiße Rosen Für Marwa." *Der Tagesspiegel* 12 Jul. 2009: 5. Web. 30 Jun. 2010.

"Die Deutschlandtür geht auf und gleich wieder zu. Eine fiktive Biographie nach Gesprächen mit Emine Sevgi Özdamar." *Volksbühne am Rosen-Luxemburg-Platz.* 2002. Web. 22 Nov. 2002.

"Die unvergessene Tat. Mahnwache für Hatun Sürücü." *Der Tagesspiegel* 08 Feb. 2010: 012. Web. 30 Jun. 2010.

"DIK–Muslimische Verbände: Neue Zahlen, aber kein Ende der Diskussion." Web. 28 Mar. 2012.

Dirlik, Arif. "Culturalism as Hegemonic Ideology and Liberating Practice." *Cultural Critique* 6 (1987): 13–50. Print.

———. "Race Talk, Race, and Contemporary Racism." *PMLA* 123.5 (2008): 1363–1379. Web. 18 Feb. 2011.

Diver, Krysia. "Author Backs Forced-marriage Ban." *The Guardian* 01 Aug. 2005: 11. Web. 15 Jun. 2010.
Drucksache 13/3091. Gesetz Zur Änderung Des Schulgesetzes. Landtag von Baden-Württemberg, 2004. Print.
"Egyptian Fury at Dresden Murder: Protestors Accuse Germany of Racism." *Spiegel online.* 07 Jul. 2009. Web. 08 Sep. 2009.
"Ehrenmord-Prozess: Die Frage der Ehre." *Zeit online.* Newspaper. 28 Aug. 2007. Web. 03 Aug. 2010.
Ehrkamp, Patricia. "The Limits of Multicultural Tolerance? Liberal Democracy and Media Portrayals of Muslim Migrant Women in Germany." *Space & Polity* 14.1 (2010): 13. Print.
El Tayeb, Fatima. "Dangerous Liaisons: Race, Nation and German Identity." *Not So Plain as Black and White. Afro-German Culture and History, 1890–2000.* Ed. Patricia Mazon and Reinhild Steingröver. Rochester, NY: U of Rochester P, 2005. 27–60. Print.
———. *European Others: Queering Ethnicity in Postnational Europe.* U of Minnesota P, 2011. Print.
Eley, Geoff. "The Trouble with 'Race': Migrancy, Cultural Difference, and the Remaking of Europe." *After the Nazi Racial State: Difference and Democracy in Germany and Europe.* Ed. Rita Chin, et al. U of Michigan P, 2009. 137–181. Print.
"'Er konnte gar nicht anders handeln.' Gewalt in Einwandererfamilien–Tatmotiv: Kulturschock." *Der Spiegel* 06 Mar. 1989: 96. Print.
Erel, Umut et al. "Intersektionalität oder Simultaneität?!–Zur Verschränkung und Gleichzeitigkeit mehrfacher Machtverhältnisse." *Heteronormativität. Empirische Studien zu Geschlecht, Sexualität und Macht—eine Einführung.* Ed. Jutta Hartmann and Christian Klesse. Wiesbaden: VS Verlag für Sozialwissenschaften, 2007. 239–249. Print.
Ewing, Katherine Pratt. "Legislating Religious Freedom: Muslim Challenges to the Relationship Between 'Church' and 'State' in Germany and France." *Daedalus* 129.4 (2000): 31. Print.
———. *Stolen Honor: Stigmatizing Muslim Men in Berlin.* Stanford, CA: Stanford UP, 2008. Print.
Fanizadeh, Andreas. "Aufstand der Anständigen?" *Taz, Die Tageszeitung* 18 Jul. 2009: 10. Web. 30 Jun. 2010.
Farrokhzad, Schahrzad. "Bildungs- und Berufschancen von Frauen mit Migrationshintergrund in der Bundesrepublik Deutschland." *Beiträge zur feministischen Theorie und Praxis* 63/64 (2003): 41–58. Print.
———. "Erfahrungen, Strategien und Potenziale von Akademikerinnen mit Migrationshintergrund." *Migrations-und Integrationsforschung in der Diskussion: Biografie, Sprache und Bildung als zentrale Bezugspunkte.* 2nd ed. Eds. Gudrun Hentges, Volker Hinnenkamp, and Almut Zwengel. Wiesbaden: VS Verlag, 2010. 305–324. Print.
Farrokhzad, Schahrzad et al. *Verschieden-Gleich-Anders?: Geschlechterarrangements im intergenerativen und interkulturellen Vergleich.* Wiesbaden: VS Verlag, 2011. Print.
Fertig, Gudrun. "Serpil Pak Stand Up Comedy." *AVIVA-Berlin.* 11 May 2008. Web. 23 Jun. 2010.

"Fessel und Befreiung. Helena Waldmanns BurkaBondage." *Kulturzeit*. 3SAT, 11 May 2010. Television.

Fietz, Kathleen. "Ehrenmord: Eine Straße zum Gedenken." *Taz.de*. 02 Jul. 2010. Web. 03 Aug. 2010.

Filiz, Şahin, and Tahir Ucuç. "Contemporary Turkish Thought." *The Blackwell Companion to Contemporary Islamic Thought*. Ed. Ibrahim M. Abu-Rabi'. Malden, MA: Blackwell, 2006. 23–38. Print.

Fleishman, Jeffrey. "'Honor Killings' Show Culture Clash in Berlin." *Los Angeles Times* 20 Mar. 2005: A.10. Web. 26 Jun. 2010.

Forouhar, Parastou. "Veiled–Unveiled." *Parastou Forouhar*. 2004. Web. 02 Jul. 2010.

Foucault, Michel. "Truth and Power." *Power/Knowledge: Selected Interviews and Other Writings* 1977 (1972): 109–133. Print.

Franck, Julia. "Schriftstellerin Julia Franck über den Berliner Religionsstreit." *Der Spiegel* 19 Jan. 2009: 124. Web. 30 Jun. 2010.

Fraser, Nancy. "Rethinking the Public Sphere: A Contribution to the Critique of Actually Existing Democracy." *Social Text* 25/26 (1990): 56–80. Print.

Freedman, Jane. "Secularism as a Barrier to Integration? The French Dilemma." *International Migration* 43.3 (2004): 5–28. Print.

———. "Women, Islam and Rights in Europe: Beyond a Universalist/Culturalist Dichotomy." *Review of International Studies* 33.01 (2007): 29–44. Web. 07 May 2009.

Gamper, Markus. *Islamischer Feminismus in Deutschland*. Bielefeld, Germany: Transcript Verlag, 2011. Print.

Gerigk, Helga. "Grusswort." *Literatur der Migration*. Ed. Nasrin Amirsedghi and Thomas Bleicher. Mainz: Donata Kinzelbach Verlag, 1997. 17–18. Print.

Giordano, Ralph. "Lachen, bis der Doktor kommt." *Die Welt* 29 Nov. 2008: 5. Web. 06 May 2009.

Göçmen Kadınlar Birliği–Bundesverband der Migrantinnen in Deutschland e.V. "Menschenrechtsverletzungen Gemeinsam Bekämpfen–Vorurteile Und Diskriminierungen Abbauen!" *Göçmen Kadınlar Birliği–Bundesverband der Migrantinnen in Deutschland e.V.* Web. 10 Nov. 2008.

———. "Presserklärung zum jüngst beschlossenen Gesetzespaket gegen Zwangsverheiratung des Bundeskabinetts." *Göçmen Kadınlar Birliği–Bundesverband der Migrantinnen in Deutschland e.V.* 03 Nov. 2010. Web. 06 Jun. 2011.

———. "Verband." Web. 06 Jun. 2011.

Goerlich, Helmut. "Distanz und Neutralität im Lehrberuf–zum Kopftuch und anderen religiösen Symbolen." *Neue Juristische Wochenschrift* 40 (1999): 2929–2933. Print.

———. "Religionspolitische Distanz und kulturelle Vielfalt unter dem Regime des Art. 9 EMRK." *Neue Juristische Wochenschrift* 54.39 (2001): 2862–2863. Print.

Göktürk, Deniz. "Kennzeichen: weiblich / türkisch / deutsch. Beruf: Sozialarbeiterin / Schriftstellerin / Schauspielerin." *Frauen Literatur Geschichte*. Eds. Hiltrud Gnüg and Renate Möhrmann. Stuttgart: Metzler, 1999. 516–532. Print.

———. "Migration und Kino–Subnationale Mitleidskultur oder transnationale Rollenspiele?" *Interkulturelle Literatur in Deutschland: ein Handbuch*. Ed. Carmine Chiellino. Stuttgart: Metzler, 2000. 329–347. Print.

———. "Strangers in Disguise: Role-Play Beyond Identity Politics in Anarchic Film Comedy." *New German Critique* 92 (2004): 100–122. Print.
Göle, Nilüfer. *Anverwandlungen*. Berlin: Klaus Wagenbach Verlag, 2008. Print.
———. *The Forbidden Modern: Civilization and Veiling*. Ann Arbor: U of Michigan P, 1996. Print.
Graves, Peter J. "Karen Duve, Kathrin Schmidt, Judith Hermann: 'Ein literarisches Frauleinwunder'?" *German Life and Letters* 55.2 (2002): 196–207. Web. 23 Aug. 2010.
Grewal, Inderpal. "Postcoloniality, Globalization, and Feminist Critique." *American Anthropologist* 110.4 (2008): 517–520. Web. 27 Mar. 2012.
"Grimmelshausen-Preis 2007: Feridun Zaimoglu für sein Werk geehrt." *Zeit Online*. 04 Jul. 2007. Web. 02 Jul. 2011.
Grossberg, Lawrence. *Cultural Studies in the Future Tense*. Durham, NC: Duke UP Books, 2010. Print.
Gümen, Sedef. "Das Soziale des Geschlechts. Frauenforschung und die Kategorie 'Identität'." *Gegen-Rassismen: Konstruktionen, Interaktionen, Interventionen*. Ed. Brigitte Kossek. Argument Sonderband Neue Folge 265. Hamburg: Argument, 1999. 220–241. Print.
———. "Die sozialpolitische Konstruktion 'kultureller' Differenzen in der bundesdeutschen Frauen- und Migrationsforschung." *Beiträge zur feministischen Theorie und Praxis* 19.43 (1996): 77–89. Print.
———. "Frauen, Arbeitsmarkt und Einwanderungsgesellschaft–(k)ein Thema für die Frauenforschung?" *Migration, Gender, Arbeitsmarkt*. Eds. María del Mar Castro Varela and Dimitria Clayton. Königstein/Taunus: Ulrike Helmer Verlag, 2003. 30–57. Print.
Güngör, Dilek. *Das Geheimnis meiner türkischen Großmutter: Roman*. Munich: Piper, 2007. Print.
———. *Ganz schön Deutsch: Meine türkische Familie und ich*. Munich: Piper Taschenbuch, 2007. Print.
———. *Unter Uns*. Berlin: Edition Ebersbach, 2004. Print.
Ha, Kien Nghi. "Hybridität und ihre deutschsprachige Rezeption. Zur diskursiven Einverleibung des 'Anderen'." *Doing Culture. Neue Positionen zum Verhältnis von Kultur und sozialer Praxis*. Bielefeld, Germany: Transcript, 2004. 221–238. Print.
———. *Hype um Hybridität: kultureller Differenzkonsum und postmoderne Verwertungstechniken im Spätkapitalismus*. Bielefeld: Transcript, 2005. Print.
Haase, Arwen. "Serpil Pak: Psychologin, Passdeutsche, Sexkoryphäe." *Siegessäule.de–queer Berlin*. Web. 27 Jul. 2010.
Habermas, Jürgen. "Notes on a Post-Secular Society." *Signandsight.com*. 18 Jun. 2008. Web. 06 Oct. 2008.
———. "Religion in the Public Sphere." *European Journal of Philosophy* 14.1 (2006): 1–25. Print.
———. "The Public Sphere: An Encyclopedia Article (1964)." *New German Critique* 3 (1974): 49–55. Print.
Habermas, Jürgen, and Jacques Derrida. "February 15, or, What Binds Europeans Together: Plea for a Common Foreign Policy, Beginning in Core Europe." *Old Europe, New Europe, Core Europe: Transatlantic Relations after the Iraq War*. Eds. Daniel Levy, Max Pensky, and John Torpey. Verso, 2005. 3–13. Print.

Hajjar, Lisa. "Religion, State Power, and Domestic Violence in Muslim Societies: A Framework for Comparative Analysis." *Law & Social Inquiry* 29.1 (2004): 1–38. Web. 05 Jul. 2011.

Halfmann, Ralf. "Der Streit um die 'Lehrerin mit Kopftuch'." *Neue Zeitschrift für Verwaltungsrecht* 19.8 (2000): 862–868. Print.

Halle, Randall. *German Film After Germany: Toward a Transnational Aesthetic.* Urbana, IL: U of Illinois P, 2008. Print.

Hammelehle, Sebsatian. "Meine Leute sind die Deutschen." *Welt am Sonntag* 26 Feb. 2006: 61. Web. 12 Aug. 2010.

Hauschild, Thomas. "Ehrenmord, Ethnologie und Recht." *Wider den Kulturenzwang: Migration, Kulturalisierung und Weltliteratur.* Eds. Özkan Ezli, Dorothee Kimmich, and Annette Werberger. Bielefeld, Germany: Transcript Verlag, 2009. 23–46. Print.

Häußler, Ulf. "Religion Und Integration." *Zeitschrift für Ausländerrecht und Ausländerpolitik* 19.1 (1999): 32–37. Print.

Heine, Hannes. "Am Start für den Staat Opfer der Hetze. Die offenbar rassistische Messerattacke auf eine Ägypterin im Landgericht Dresden wird zunehmend zu einem Politikum. Warum ist die Tat so brisant?" *Der Tagesspiegel* 09 Jul. 2009: 2. Web. 30 Jun. 2010.

Henkel-Waidhofer, Brigitte-Johanna. "'Man könnte meinen, die Türken stehen wieder vor Wien.' Hitzige Debatte im Südwesten über Lehrerin mit Kopftuch; Landesregierung muss entscheiden." *AP Worldstream–German* 08 Jul. 1998. Web. 01 Dec. 2002.

Herbert, Ulrich. *Geschichte der Ausländerpolitik in Deutschland: Saisonarbeiter, Zwangsarbeiter, Gastarbeiter, Flüchtlinge.* München: Beck, 2001. Print.

Herzberg, Guntolf, and Kurt Seifert. *Rudolf Bahro.* Ch. Links Verlag, 2002. Print.

Hessen, L. A. G. "Kündigung einer Kaufhausangestellten wegen religiös motivierten Tragen eines Kopftuchs." *Neue Juristische Wochenschrift* 54.49 (2001): 3650–3652. Print.

LAG Hessen, and ArbG Hanau. "Tragen eines religiös motivierten Kopftuchs einer Kaufhausangestellten als Kündigungsgrund." *Neue Zeitschrift für Verwaltungsrecht–Rechtsprechung* 6.12 (2001): 632–635. Print.

Hillgruber, Christian. "Der deutsche Kulturstaat und der muslimische Kulturimport." *Juristenzeitung* 11 (1999): 538–547. Print.

Hügel-Marshall, Ika. *Invisible Woman: Growing up Black in Germany.* New York: Continuum, 2001. Print.

Huhnke, Brigitta. *Macht, Medien Und Geschlecht: Eine Fallstudie zur Berichterstattungspraxis der Dpa, Der Taz sowie der Wochenzeitungen Die Zeit und Der Spiegel Von 1980–1995.* Opladen: Westdeutscher Verlag, 1996. Print.

Huth-Hildebrandt, Christine. *Das Bild von der Migrantin: Auf den Spuren eines Konstrukts.* Frankfurt am Main: Brandes & Apsel, 2002. Print.

———. "Ethnisierungsprozesse re-visited. Die Relevanz der Kategorie Geschlecht im Umgang mit Fremdheit." *Die Erfindung der Fremdheit: zur Kontroverse um Gleichheit und Differenz im Sozialstaat.* Eds. Doron Kiesel, et al. Frankfurt a.M.: Brandes & Apsel, 1998. 185–202. Print.

"Iranians Protest Killing of Veiled Egyptian Woman in Germany." *BBC Monitoring Trans Caucasus Unit Supplied by BBC Worldwide Monitoring* 11 Jul. 2009. Web. 07 Sep. 2009.

Jankowsky, Karen. "German Literature Contested: The 1991 Ingeborg-Bachmann-Prize Debate, 'Cultural Diversity,' and Emine Sevgi Özdamar." *German Quarterly* 70.3 (1997): 261–276. Print.

Janz, Norbert, and Sonja Rademacher. "Das Kopftuch als religiöses Symbol oder profaner Bekleidungsgegenstand?—BayVGH, NVwZ 2000, 952 und VG Stuttgart, NVwZ 2000, 959." *Juristische Schulung* 5 (2001): 440–444. Print.

Jarausch, Konrad. *After Hitler: Recivilizing Germans, 1945–1995*. Oxford UP, USA, 2006. Print.

Jenkins, Jennifer. "German Orientalism: Introduction." *Comparative Studies of South Asia, Africa and the Middle East* 24.2 (2004): 97. Print.

Kalkan, Hülya. *Ich wollte nur frei sein: meine Flucht vor der Zwangsehe*. Berlin: Ullstein, 2005. Print.

Kalpaka, Annita, and Nora Räthzel, eds. *Die Schwierigkeit, nicht rassistisch zu sein*. Berlin: EXpress Edition, 1986. Print.

Kant, Immanuel. *Observations on the Feeling of the Beautiful and Sublime*. Trans. John T. Goldthwait. Berkeley: U of California P, 2004. Print.

Kaplan, Caren, Norma Alarcón, and Minoo Moallem, eds. *Between Woman and Nation: Nationalisms, Transnational Feminisms, and the State*. Durham, NC.: Duke UP, 1999. Print.

Kaplan, Caren, and Inderpal Grewal. "Transnational Feminist Cultural Studies: Beyond the Marxism/Poststructuralism/Feminism Divides." *Between Woman and Nation: Nationalisms, Transnational Feminisms, and the State*. Eds. Caren Kaplan, Norma Alarcón, and Minoo Moallem. Durham, NC: Duke UP, 1999. 349–363. Print.

Kappert, Ines. "Sibel Kekilli in 'Die Fremde': Der Türke als Zeitbombe." *Taz.de*. 11 Mar. 2010. Web. 03 Aug. 2010.

Kaufman, Bettina, Michèlle Jacobsohn, and Asgedech Ghirmazion, eds. *Blick Zurück Im Zorn. Dokumentation des Kongresses: "Frauen gegen Nationalismus-Rassismus/Antisemitismus–Sexismus." 16.–18. November 1990 in Köln*. Köln: Sozialwissenschaftliche Forschung und Praxis für Frauen e.V., 1990. Print.

Kelek, Necla. "Anwälte einer Inszenierung." *Zeit Online*. Newspaper. 17 Sep. 2005. Web. 03 Aug. 2010.

———. *Die Fremde Braut: Ein Bericht aus dem Inneren des türkischen Lebens in Deutschland*. Köln: Kiepenheuer & Witsch, 2008. Print.

———. "Ein Verstoß gegen die Menschenwürde!" *EMMA* Oct. 2009. Web. 06 Apr. 2010.

———. "Eure Toleranz bringt uns in Gefahr." *Die Welt* 26 Feb. 2005: 9. Web. 03 Aug. 2010.

———. "Glück gibt es nur ohne den Vater." *Berliner Zeitung Archiv*. 25 Mar. 2006. Web. 10 Nov. 2008.

———. "Reifeprüfung. Der Fall Sürücü wird neu verhandelt." *Frankfurter Allgemeine Zeitung* 30 Aug. 2007: 33. Web. 03 Aug. 2010.

Kelek, Necla, and Monika Maron. "Nicht Sarrazin, sondern die Diskussion spaltet das Land." *Welt Online* 09 Feb. 2010. Web. 26 Aug. 2011.

Kerscher, Helmut. "Ein Stück Stoff und seine Folgen." *Süddeutsche Zeitung* 04 Jun. 2003: 2. Web. 08 Oct. 2008.

Keyman, E. Fuat. "Modernity, Secularism and Islam." *Theory, Culture & Society* 24.2 (2007): 215–234. Web. 30 Aug. 2010.

Kirschstein, Gisela. "Gewalt in der Ehe: Richterin verweist auf Züchtigungsrecht im Koran–Nachrichten Politik." *WELT online.* 21 Mar. 2007. Web. 05 Aug. 2010.

Kiyak, Mely. "Und was ist mit uns?" *Die Zeit* 03 Jul. 2008. Web. 27 Sep. 2008.

Klimke, Martin. *The Other Alliance: Student Protest in West Germany and the United States in the Global Sixties.* Princeton UP, 2011. Print.

Klimke, Martin, and Wilfried Mausbach. "Auf der äusseren Linie der Befreiungskriege. Die RAF und der Vietnamkonflikt. Die RAF und der Vietnamkonflikt." *Die RAF und der linke Terrorismus.* Ed. Wolfgang Kraushaar. Hamburger Edition, 2006. 620–643. Print.

"Knüppel im Kreuz, Kind im Bauch." *Der Spiegel* 44 (1990): 98–113. Print.

Kofman, Eleonore, et al. *Gender and International Migration in Europe: Employment, Welfare, and Politics.* New York: Routledge, 2000. Print.

Kogacioglu, Dicle. "The Tradition Effect: Framing Honor Crimes in Turkey." *differences* 15.2 (2004): 118–151. Web. 15 Jun. 2010.

Koldinská, Kristina. "Institutionalizing Intersectionality" *International Feminist Journal of Politics* 11.4 (2009): 547. Web. 18 Oct. 2010.

Konuk, Kader. *Identitäten im Prozess: Literatur von Autorinnen aus und in der Türkei in deutscher, englischer und türkischer Sprache.* Vol. 28. Essen: Die Blaue Eule, 2001. Print.

———. "'Identitätssuche ist ein [sic!] private archäologische Graberei': Emine Sevgi Özdamar's inszeniertes Sprechen." *AufBrüche: Kulturelle Produktionen Von Migrantinnen, Schwarzen und jüdischen Frauen in Deutschland.* Eds. Cathy S Gelbin, Kader Konuk, and Peggy Piesche. Königstein/Taunus: Ulrike Helmer, 1999. 60–74. Print.

Konuk, Kader, Peggy Piesche, and Cathy S Gelbin, eds. *AufBrüche: Kulturelle Produktionen von Migrantinnen, Schwarzen und Jüdischen Frauen in Deutschland.* Königstein/Taunus: Ulrike Helmer. Print.

Korteweg, Ann, and Gökçe Yurdakul. "Islam, Gender, and Immigrant Integration: Boundary Drawing in Discourses on Honour Killing in the Netherlands and Germany." *Ethnic and Racial Studies* 32.2 (2009): 218–238. Print.

Kramer, Stephan J. "In Solidarity with All Muslims." *Qantara.de.* 13 Jul. 2009. Web. 06 Apr. 2010.

Krause, Tilman. "Immer Romane?" *Welt Online* 17 Jun. 2006: 2. Web. 07 Mar. 2011.

Krause-Burger, Sibylle. "Ein Unbehauster in seinem dumpfen Drang." *Stuttgarter Zeitung* 15 Jul. 2009: 4. Web. 19 Jul. 2010.

Kreye, Andrian. "Kampf der fremden Kulturen; Die Multikulturalismus-Frage im Messermord von Dresden." *Süddeutsche Zeitung* 14 Jul. 2009: 9. Web. 07 Sep. 2009.

Landtag von Baden-Württemberg. *Drucksache 12/1140. Antrag der Abg. Helmut Rau u. a. CDU und Stellungnahme des Ministeriums für Kultus, Jugend und Sport Islamische Lehrkraft im Vorbereitungsdienst Islamischer Religionsunterricht in deutscher Sprache.* 1997. Web. 11 Feb. 2004.

———. *Plenarprotokoll 12/23 20.03.97.* 1997. Print.

Langenbach, Sascha. "Hatun S., Rukiye Und Derya P., Morsal O … " *Berliner Kurier* 25 May 2008: 21. Web. 07 Aug. 2010.

Laninger, Tanja, and Dirk Banse. "Mord an einer Türkin–Ermordet, weil sie frei sein wollten." *Berliner Morgenpost* 16 Feb. 2005: 20. Web. 03 Aug. 2010.

Lau, Jörg. "Kulturbedingte 'Ehrenmorde'." *Die Zeit* 03 Mar. 2005. Web. 03 Aug. 2009.

———. "Wie eine Deutsche." *Die Zeit* 24 Feb. 2005. Web. 18 Feb. 2006.

Lehnhard, Ulrich. "Zwischen zwei Stühlen." *Berliner Morgenpost* 20 Aug. 2008: 28. Web. 03 Aug. 2009.

Lennox, Sara. "Divided Feminism: Women, Racism and German National Identity." *German Studies Review* 18 (1995): 481–502. Print.

———. "Feminisms in Transit: American Feminist Germanists Construct a Multicultural Germany." *Multiculturalism in Transit: A German-American Exchange.* Eds. Klaus J Milch and Jeffrey M. Peck. Providence, RI: Berghahn, 1998. 77–92. Print.

Lentin, Alana. "Europe and the Silence About Race." *European Journal of Social Theory* 11.4 (2008): 487–503. Web. 04 Jan. 2009.

———. "Replacing 'Race', Historicizing 'Culture' in Multiculturalism." *Patterns of Prejudice* 39.4 (2005): 379–396. Print.

Leveringhaus, Peter. "'Wie eine Deutsche Gelebt'–Prozessbeginn im Mordfall Hatun Sürücü." *ddp-Wirtschaftsdienst* 13 Sep. 2005: n. pag. Web. 03 Aug. 2009.

Littler, Margaret. "Diasporic Identity in Emine Sevgi Özdamar's Mutterzunge." *Recasting German Identity: Culture, Politics, and Literature in the Berlin Republic.* Eds. Stuart Taberner and Frank Finlay. Rochester, NY: Camden House, 2002. 217–234. Print.

———. "Guilt, Victimhood, and Identity in Zafer Şenocak's 'Gefährliche Verwandtschaft'." *The German Quarterly* 78.3 (2005): 357–373. Print.

———. "Intimacies Both Sacred and Profane." *Encounters with Islam in German Literature and Culture.* Eds. James Hodkinson and Jeffrey Morrison. New York: Camden House, 2009. 221–235. Print.

Lombardo, Emanuela, and Mieke Verloo. "Institutionalizing Intersectionality in the European Union?" *International Feminist Journal of Politics* 11.4 (2009): 478. Web. 30 Apr. 2010.

Lorde, Audre. *Sister Outsider: Essays and Speeches.* Berkeley: Crossing P, 2007. Print.

Ludin, Fereshta. "Marwa." *Islam.de.* 05 Aug. 2009. Web. 19 Aug. 2010.

Lutz, Helma. "Rassismus und Sexismus, Unterschiede und Gemeinsamkeiten." *"Ein Herrenvolk von Untertanen": Rassismus, Nationalismus, Sexismus.* Ed. Andreas Foitzik. Duisburg: Duisburger Institut für Sprach- und Sozialforschung, 1992. 57–79. Print.

———. "Sind wir un simmer noch fremd? Konstruktionen von Fremdheit in der weißen Frauenbewegung." *Entfernte Verbindungen: Rassismus, Antisemitismus, Klassenunterdrückung.* Ed. Ika Hügel. Berlin: Orlanda Frauenverlag, 1993. 138–156. Print.

———. "Unsichtbare Schatten? Die 'Orientalische' Frau in westlichen Diskursen– zur Konzeptualisierung einer Opferfigur." *Peripherie* 37 (1989): 51–65. Print.

Lutz, Helma, and Christine Huth-Hildebrandt. "Geschlecht im Migrationsdiskurs. Neue Gedanken über ein altes Thema." *Das Argument* 40.1/2 (224/225) (1998): 159–173. Print.

Luzina, Sandra. "Ich lasse mir meine Sprache nicht verbieten." *Der Tagesspiegel.* 07 Oct. 2009. Web. 03 Aug. 2010.

MacMaster, Neil. *Racism in Europe, 1870–2000.* New York: Palgrave, 2001. Print.
Mahmood, Saba. *Politics of Piety: The Islamic Revival and the Feminist Subject.* Pinceton: Princeton UP, 2005. Print.
Mahmoody, Betty. *Nicht ohne meine Tochter.* Cologne: Lübbe Bastei Verlag, 1987. Print.
Mahrem, Footnotes on Veiling. Tanas, Berlin. 2008. Art exhibition.
Mani, B. Venkat. *Cosmopolitical Claims: Turkish-German Literatures from Nadolny to Pamuk.* U of Iowa P, 2007. Print.
Marcus, Sharon. "Fighting Bodies, Fighting Words: A Theory and Politics of Rape Prevention." Eds. Constance L. Mui and Julien S. Murphy. *Gender Struggles: Practical Approaches to Contemporary Feminism* (2002): 166–185. Print.
Mardorossian, Carine M. "Toward a New Feminist Theory of Rape." *Signs* 27.3 (2002): 743–775. Print.
Marion, George. "Un Nouveau 'Crime D'honneur' Scandalise l'Allemagne." *Le Monde* 08 Mar. 2005: 7. Web. 26 Jun. 2010.
Michael, Lothar. "Anmerkung. Die Einstellung als Lehrerin an Grund- und Hauptschulen im Beamtenverhältnis auf Probe." *Juristen Zeitung* 58.5 (2003): 256–258. Print.
Minkmar, Nils, and Volker Weidermann. "Zwei Leben, ein Geheimnis; Wem gehört die Geschichte der Einwanderer: Emine Sevgi Özdamar und Feridun Zaimoglu Streiten." *Frankfurter Allgemeine Sonntagszeitung* 04 Jun. 2006: 21. Print.
Mir-Hosseini, Ziba. "Neue Überlegungen zum Geschlechterverhältnis im Islam–Perspektiven Der Gerechtigkeit und Gleichheit für Frauen." *Facetten islamischer Welten. Geschlechterordnungen, Frauen- und Menschenrechte in Der Diskussion.* Eds. Mechtild Rumpf, Ute Gerhard, and Mechtild M Jansen. Bielefeld, Germany: Transcript, 2003. 53–81. Print.
Morlok, Martin, and Julian Krüper. "Auf dem Weg zum 'forum neutrum'?–Die 'Kopftuch-Entscheidung' des BVerwG." *Neue Juristische Wochenschrift* 56.14 (2003): 1020–1021. Print.
Moruzzi, Norma. "A Problem with Headscarves: Contemporary Complexities of Political and Social Identity." *Political Theory* (1994): n. pag. Web. 11 Oct. 2008.
Mouffe, Chantal. "Religion, Liberal Democracy, and Citizenship." *Political Theologies: Public Religions in a Post-Secular World.* Eds. Hent de Vries and Lawrence E. Sullivan. New York: Fordham UP, 2006. 318–326. Print.
———. *The Democratic Paradox.* New York: Verso, 2000. Print.
Mückl, Stefan. "Religionsfreiheit und Sonderstatusverhältnisse–Kopftuchverbot für Lehrerinnen?" *Der Staat* 40.1 (2001): 96–127. Print.
Müller, Reinhard. "Freisprüche im Ehrenmordfall Sürücü aufgehoben." 29 Aug. 2007: 4. Web. 03 Aug. 2010.
Müller, Ursula et al. "Lebenssituation, Sicherheit und Gesundheit von Frauen in Deutschland." 2004. Web. 01 Nov. 2008.
Müller-Gerbes, Heidi. "Schande, keine Ehre." *Frankfurter Allgemeine Zeitung.* Sec. Rhein-Main-Zeitung 30 Sep. 2006: 61. Print.
"Murder of Egyptian Woman and Islamophobia." *Korea Times* 19 Jul. 2009. LexisNexis Academic. Web. 07 Sep. 2009.
Narayan, Uma. *Dislocating Cultures: Identities, Traditions, and Third-World Feminism.* New York: Routledge, 1997. Print.

Nickerson, Colin. "For Muslim Women, a Deadly Defiance: 'Honor Killings' on Rise in Europe." *Boston Globe* 16 Jan. 2006: A.1. Web. 03 Aug. 2010.
Nökel, Sigrid. *Die Töchter der Gastarbeiter und der Islam: Zur Soziologie alltagsweltlicher Anerkennungspolitiken: Eine Fallstudie.* Bielefeld: Transcript, 2002. Print.
———. "Migration, Islamisierung und Identitätspolitiken: zur Bedeutung der Religiosität junger Frauen in Deutschland." *Religion und Geschlechterverhältnis.* Eds. Ingrid Lukatis, Regina Sommer, and Christof Wolf. Opladen, Germany: Leske Budrich, 2000. 261–278. Print.
O'Brien, Traci S. "A 'Daughter of the Occident' Travels to the 'Orient': Ida Von Hahn-Hahn's The Countess Faustina and Letters From the Orient." *Women in German Yearbook: Feminist Studies in German Literature & Culture* 24 (2008): 26–48. Print.
Oestrich, Heide, and Sabine Am Orde. "Eine Lust am Schaudern. [Interview]." *Taz, Die Tageszeitung* 17 Oct. 2005: 4. Web. 03 Aug. 2010.
Okin, Susan Moller. *Is Multiculturalism Bad for Women?* Eds. Joshua Cohen, Matthew Howard, and Martha Craven Nussbaum. Princeton, NJ: Princeton UP, 1999. 7–25. Print.
Onis, Ziya. "Turkey, Europe and the Paradoxes of Identity." *Mediterranean Quarterly* 10.3 (1999): 107–136. Print.
Oswald, Andreas. "Scharia in Deutschland?" *Der Tagesspiegel.* Newspaper. 21 Mar. 2007. Web.05 Aug. 2010.
OVG Lüneburg. "Tragen eines Kopftuches im staatlichen Schuldienst als Eignungsmangel (Nds. OVG, Urteil Vom 13.3.2002–2 LB 2171/01)." *Deutsches Verwaltungsblatt* 55.14 (2002): 995. Print.
Özdamar, Emine Sevgi. *Seltsame Sterne Starren zur Erde.* Köln: Kiepenheuer & Witsch, 2003. Print.
"Özdamar im Interview. Manche denken, Türken können nicht schreiben." *Die Berliner Literaturkritik.* News. 04 Apr. 2009. Web. 11 Jul. 2012.
Özyürek, Esra. *Nostalgia for the Modern: State Secularism and Everyday Politics in Turkey.* Durham, NC: Duke UP, 2006. Print.
Pelinka, Anton. "Zu den Fallstricken des Multikulturalismus." *Demokratie und das Fremde: Multikulturelle Gesellschaften als demokratische Herausforderung des 21. Jahrhunderts.* Ed. Erna Appelt. Vol. 1. Innsbruck: Studien Verlag, 2001. 153–195. Print.
Pellegrini, Ann. "Feeling Secular." *Women & Performance:Aa Journal of Feminist Theory* 19.2 (2009): 205. Web. 21 Jan. 2011.
Pfeiffer, Ida. *Visit to the Holy Land, Egypt, and Italy.* Trans. H. W Dulcken. Ingram, Cooke and Co., 1853. Web. 06 Dec. 2010.
Pinn, Irmgard, and Marlies Wehner. *EuroPhantasien: Die islamische Frau aus westlicher Sicht.* Duisburg: Duisburger Institut für Sprach- und Sozialforschung, 1995. Print.
Plarre, Plutonia. "Nach Anzeige von Alice Schwarzer: Betrugs-Ermittlungen gegen Frauenprojekt."–*Taz.de*. 18 Feb. 2010. Web. 03 Aug. 2010.
Plenarprotokoll 13/62. Landtag von Baden-Württemberg, 2004.
Poggioli, Sylvia. "Issues for Muslim Women in Europe Evolve: NPR." *Reporter's Notebook: NPR.* 20 Jan. 2008. Web. 06 May 2009.
———. "Muslim Activist Critical of 'Multicultural Mistake': NPR." Exploring the Status of Muslim Women in Europe. *National Public Radio*, 22 Jan. 2008. Web.

Poggioli, Sylvia. "Muslim Women Behind Wall of Silence in Germany: NPR." *Exploring the Status of Muslim Women in Europe. National Public Radio*, 21 Jan. 2008. Web.
Pressemitteilung Nr. 119/98. Ministerium für Kultus, Jugend und Sport Baden-Württemberg, 1998. Print.
Ranze, Michael. "Mord–Niemals Eine Frage Der Ehre." *Hamburger Abendblatt* 11 Mar. 2010. Web. 12 Nov. 2010.
"'Raus mit dem Volk.' Bomben und Heztparolin–in der Bundesrepublik wächst der Haß gegen die Ausländer." *Der Spiegel* 12 Sep. 1980: 19–36. Print.
Reimer, Wulf. "Kopftuchstreit in Plüderhausen. Eine muslimische Pädagogin verwirrt Baden-Württemberg." *Süddeutsche Zeitung* 08 Jul. 1998: 1. Print.
Rodríguez, Encarnación Gutiérrez. "Fallstricke des Feminismus: Das Denken 'Kritischer Differenzen' ohne Geopolitische Kontextualisierung. Einige Überlegungen zur Rezeption antirassistischer und postkolonialer Kritik." *Polylog* 4 (1999): n. pag. Web. 04 Oct. 2010.
———. *Intellektuelle Migrantinnen: Subjektivitäten im Zeitalter von Globalisierung*. Opladen: Leske + Budrich, 1999. Print.
———. "Migrantinnenpolitik jenseits des Differenz- und Identitätsdiskurses." *Beiträge zur feministischen Theorie und Praxis* 19.42 (1996): 99–111. Print.
———. "Repräsentation, Subalternität und postkoloniale Kritik." *Spricht Die Subalterne Deutsch? Migration und postkoloniale Kritik*. Eds. Hito Steyerl and Encarnación Gutiérrez Rodríguez. Münster: UNRAST-Verlag, 2003. 17–37. Print.
Rommelspacher, Birgit. *Anerkennung und Ausgrenzung: Deutschland als Multikulturelle Gesellschaft*. Frankfurt am Main: Campus, 2002. Print.
———. "Islamkritik und antimuslimische Positionen am Beispiel von Necla Kelek und Seyran Ateş." *Islamfeindlichkeit: wenn die Grenzen der Kritik verschwimmen*. Ed. Thorsten Gerald Schneiders. Wiesbaden: VS Verlag für Sozialwissenaften, 2009. 433–456. Print.
Rottmann, Susan B., and Myra Marx Ferree. "Citizenship and Intersectionality: German Feminist Debates About Headscarf and Antidiscrimination Laws." *Social Politics: International Studies in Gender, State & Society* 15.4 (2008): 481–513. Print.
Roy, Olivier. *Secularism Confronts Islam*. Columbia UP, 2007. Print.
Rüdenauer, Ulrich. "Sich herausnehmen, was sonst nur Jungs tun." *Frankfurter Rundschau* 15 Mar. 2006: 4. Web. 03 Aug. 2010.
Rux, Johannes. "Das Kopftuch als Missionsinstrument? [Religiös motiviertes Kopftuch im öffentlichen Schuldienst (VGH Bad.–Württemberg vom 26.6.2001–4 S 1439/00)]." *Deutsches Verwaltungsblatt* 116.19 (2001): 1542–1546. Print.
Said, Edward W. *Orientalism*. New York: Vintage Books, 1994. Print.
Sarıgöz, Fatma. "Die Multikulturelle Gesellschaft im Spiegel der Medien." *Medien und multikulturelle Gesellschaft*. Eds. Christoph Butterwege, Gudrun Hentges, and Fatma Sarıgöz. Opladen, Germany: Leske + Budrich, 1999. 9–28. Print.
Sarrazin, Thilo. *Deutschland schafft sich ab: Wie wir unser Land aufs Spiel setzen*. 19th ed. Munich: Deutsche Verlags-Anstalt, 2010. Print.
Scheinhardt, Saliha. *Frauen, die sterben, ohne dass sie gelebt hatten*. Berlin: EXpress, 1983. Print.

Schießl, Michaela, and Caroline Schmidt. "Augen fest verschlossen. [Interview mit Alice Schwarzer]." *Der Spiegel* 15 Nov. 2004: 70. Web. 03 Aug. 2010.
Schiffauer, Werner. "Schlachtfeld Frau." *Süddeutschen Zeitung* 25 Feb. 2005. Web. 02 Feb. 2010.
Schirrmacher, Christine. "Ehrenmorde zwischen Migration und Tradition.– Rechtliche, soziologische, kulturelle und religiöse Aspekte." *Internationale Gesellschaft für Menschenrechte.* Web. 16 Jul. 2012.
Schmidt, Wolf. "Vorwärts und vergessen?; Viele Dresdner wollen nichts mehr von der Bluttat hören. Was bleibt, ist die Abneigung gegen das Fremde." *Taz, Die Tageszeitung* 24 Jul. 2009: 05. Web. 03 Aug. 2010.
Schmitt, Cosima. "Oft erziehen Frauen zum Ehrenmord." *Taz. die Tageszeitung* 25 Feb. 2005: 6. Web. 03 Aug. 2010.
Schmitz, Thorsten. "Kein Stoff für die Schule. Der Fall Ludin: wer steckt unter dem Tuch?" *Süddeutsche Zeitung* 23 Jul. 1998: 3. Web. 10 Aug. 2008.
Schneider, Peter. "The New Berlin Wall." *The New York Times* 04 Dec. 2005. Web. 06 May 2009.
Schöbener, Burkhard. "Die 'Lehrerin mit dem Kopftuch'—Europäisch Gewendet!" *Juristische Ausbildung* 3 (2001): 186–191. Print.
Schönberger, Irene. "Gedanken zur türkischen Kleidung." *Spagat mit Kopftuch.* Ed. Jürgen Reulecke. Hamburg: Körber-Stiftung, 1997. 120–153. Print.
Schröder, Christoph. "Unser Mann in Rom." *Frankfurter Rundschau* 27 Jul. 2007 : 37. Print.
Schröttle, Monika. "Gewalt gegen Frauen mit türkischem Migrationshintergrund in Deutschland. Diskurse zwischen Skandalisierung und Bagatellisierung." *Islamfeindlichkeit: wenn die Grenzen der Kritik verschwimmen.* Ed. Thorsten Gerald Schneiders. Wiesbaden: VS Verlag für Sozialwissenaften, 2009. 269–287. Print.
Schulz, Dagmar. "Unterschiede zwischen Frauen–Ein kritischer Blick auf den Umgang mit 'den Anderen' in der feministischen Forschung weißer Frauen." *Beiträge zur feministischen Theorie und Praxis* 13.27 (1990): 45–57. Print.
Schulz-Ojala, Jan. "Familientragödie: 'Die Fremde' auf der Flucht." *Der Tagesspiegel.* 12 Mar. 2010. Web. 13 Nov. 2010.
Schwarzer, Alice. *Die Gotteskrieger und die falsche Toleranz.* Köln: Kiepenhauer & Witsch, 2002. Print.
———. *Die Große Verschleierung: Für Integration, gegen Islamismus.* Köln: Kiepenheuer & Witsch, 2010. Print.
———. "Eine Offene Antwort an '60 Migrationsforscher'." *Die große Verschleierung.* Ed. Alice Schwarzer. Köln: Kiepenheuer & Witsch, 2010. 154–161. Print.
———. "Kein Kopftuch in der Schule!" *EMMA* Oct. 2009: 78–81. Print.
———. *Krieg. Was Männerwahn anrichtet und wie Frauen Widerstand leisten.* Frankfurt am Main: Fischer, 1992. Print.
Scott, Joan Wallach. *The Politics of the Veil.* Princeton UP, 2007. Print.
Seidel, Eberhard. "Ihr und Wir." *taz. die tageszeitung* 18 Apr. 2009: 14. Web. 07 May 2009.
Seils, Christoph. "Morde im Namen der Ehre entsetzen Berlin." *Frankfurter Rundschau* 23 Feb. 2005: 4. Print.
Sen, Purna. "'Crimes of Honour,' Value and Meaning." *Honour: Crimes, Paradigms and Violence Against Women.* Eds. Sara Hossain and Lynn Welchman. London: Zed Books, 2005. 42–63. Print.

Senocak, Zafer. "Ganze Stadtteile verwandeln sich in anatolische Provinznester." *WELT online.* 07 Oct. 2011. Web. 17 Jul. 2012.

———. *War Hitler Araber?: IrreFührungen an den Rand Europas: Essays.* Berlin: Babel Verlag Hund & van Uffelen, 1994. Print.

Şenocak, Zafer. *Deutschsein: Eine Aufklärungsschrift.* Hamburg: Edition Körber Stiftung, 2011. Print.

Seyhan, Azade. "Lost in Translation: Re-Membering the Mother Tongue in Emine Sevgi Özdamar's Das Leben Ist Eine Karawanserei." *The German Quarterly* 69.4 (1996): 414–426. Print.

———. *Writing Outside the Nation.* Princeton, NJ.: Princeton UP, 2001. Print. Translation/Transnation.

Sevindim, Asli. *Candlelight Döner.* Berlin: Ullstein, 2005. Print.

Sezgin, Hilal. "Das reine deutsche Gewissen." *Taz.de.* Newspaper. 22 Jul. 2009. Web. 04 Mar. 2010.

———. "Das Schlagloch: Feminismus ist unteilbar." *Taz.de.* 23 Sep. 2008. Web. 25 Sep. 2008.

———. "Eine Stimme, ein Unschuldsbeweis." *Zeit Online.* News. 22 Jun. 2006. Web. 02 Jul. 2011.

———. *Typisch Türkin?: Porträt einer neuen Generation.* Freiburg: Herder, 2006. Print.

Shafi, Monika. "Talkin"Bout My Generation: Memories of 1968 in Recent German Novels." *German Life and Letters* 59.2 (2006): 201–216. Web. 01 Jul. 2009.

Shepherd, Laura J. "'Victims, Perpetrators and Actors' Revisited." *British Journal of Politics & International Relations* 9.2 (2007): 239–256. Web. 31 Jan. 2010.

Sieg, Katrin. "Ethnic Drag and National Identity: Multicultural Crises, Crossings, and Interventions." *The Imperialist Imagination: German Colonialism and Its Legacy.* Eds. Sara Friedrichsmeyer, Sara Lennox, and Susanne Zantop. Ann Arbor: U of Michigan P, 1999. 295–315. Print.

Simons, Marlise. "Muslim Women in Europe Claim Rights and Keep Faith." *New York Times* 29 Dec. 2005. Web. 08 Jun. 2011.

Simpson, Patricia. "Brechtian Specters in Contemporary Fiction: Emine Sevgi Özdamar and Rohinton Mistry." *Brecht Yearbook / Das Brecht-Jahrbuch.* Eds. Jürgen Hillesheim, Mathias Mayer, and Stephen Brockmann. Vol. 32. Madison: U of Wisconsin P. 388–404. Print.

Snyder, Donald. "Turkish Women in Germany Lose an Advocate." *Foxnews.com.* 05 Jan. 2007. Web. 06 May 2009.

Sokolowsky, Kay. *Feindbild Moslem.* Hamburg: Rotbuch, 2009. Print.

Sorge, Helmut. "Grenzen der Toleranz." *Spiegel special* 1 (1998): 125–126. Print.

Spiegel, Hubert. "Der Tag, an dem der Teufel sich die Beine brach." *Frankfurter Allgemeine Zeitung* 15 Mar. 2006: L1. Web. 06 Jun. 2010.

Spies, Axel. "Verschleierte Schülerinnen in Frankreich und Deutschland." *Neue Zeitung für Verwaltungsrecht* 12.7 (1993): 637–640. Print.

Spivak, Gayatri Chakravorty. *A Critique of Postcolonial Reason: Toward a History of the Vanishing Present.* Cambridge, MA: Harvard UP, 1999. Print.

———. "A Note on the New International." *Parallax* 7.3 (2001): 12–16. Print.

———. "Cultural Talks in the 'Hot Peace': Revisiting the Global Village." *Cosmopolitics: Thinking and Feeling Beyond the Nation.* Eds. Pheng Cheah and Bruce Robbins. Minneapolis: U of Minnesota P, 1998. 329–348. Print.

———. *Death of a Discipline*. New York: Columbia UP, 2003. Print.
———. *Imperatives for Re-Imagining the Planet–Imperative zur Neuerfindung des Planeten*. Vienna: Passagen, 1999. Print.
———. *Other Asias*. Malden, MA: Blackwell, 2008. Print.
———. *Outside in the Teaching Machine*. New York: Routledge, 1993. Print.
———. "Righting Wrongs." *Human Rights, Human Wrongs: The Oxford Amnesty Lectures, 2001*. Ed. Nicholas Owen. Oxford: Oxford UP, 2003. 164–227. Print.
Stehle, Maria. "Narrating the Ghetto, Narrating Europe: From Berlin, Kreuzberg to the Banlieues of Paris." *Westminster Papers in Communication and Culture* 3.3 (2006): 48–70. Print.
———. "White Ghettos: The 'Crisis of Multiculturalism' in Post-Unification Germany." *European Journal of Cultural Studies* 4.Questioning the European Crisis of Multiculturalism (2012): 167–181. Print.
Stelzig, Eugene L. *The Romantic Subject in Autobiography: Rousseau and Goethe*. Charlottesville: U of Virginia P, 2000. Print.
Steyerl, Hito. *Lovely Andrea*. Hito Steyerl (Self-distributed), 2007. DVD.
Steyn, Mark. "Honor, and Shame–The Corner–National Review Online." *National Review Online*. Magazine. 17 Jun. 2010. Web. 02 Aug. 2010.
"Struktur der Deutschen Islam Konferenz in der zweiten Phase." Web. 21 Jun. 2011.
Sunder, Madhavi. "Piercing the Veil." *Yale Law Journal* 112 (2003): 1399–1472. Print.
Teraoka, Arlene Akiko. *East, West, and Others: The Third World in Postwar German Literature*. Lincoln, Neb.: U of Nebraska P, 1996. Print.
Terkessidis, Mark. "Global Culture in Germany or: How Repressed Women and Criminals Rescue Hybridity." *Communal/Plural* 8.2 (2000): 219–235. Web.
———. "Globale Kultur in Deutschland oder: Wie unterdrückte Frauen und Kriminelle die Hybridität retten." *Kultur-Medien-Macht. Cultural Studies und Medienanalyse*. Ed. Andreas Hepp and Rainer Winter. Vol. 2. VS Verlag für Sozialwissenaften, 1999. 237–252. Print.
———. "Wir selbst sind die Anderen. Globalisierung, multikulturelle Gesellschaft und Neorassismus." *Zuwanderung im Zeichen der Globalisierung. Migrations-, Integrations- und Minderheitenpolitik*. Ed. Christoph Butterwege and Gudrun Hentges. Opladen, Germany: Leske + Budrich, 2000. 188–209. Print.
Treibel, Matthias. "Kopftuch und staatliche Neutralität." *Bayrische Verwaltungsblätter* 20.20 (2002): 624–627. Print.
"Turkish Honor Killings in Germany." *CNN Insight*. CNN, 22 Jun. 2005. Television.
Varela, María do Mar Castro. "Zur Skandalisierung und Politisierung eines bekannten Themas: 'Migrantinnen auf dem Arbeitsmarkt'." *Migration, Gender, Arbeitsmarkt. Neue Beiträge zu Frauen und Globalisierung*. EdS. María do Mar Castro Varela and Dimitria Clayton. Königstein/Taunus: Ulrike Helmer Verlag, 2003. 8–29. Print.
Varon, Jeremy. *Bringing the War Home: The Weather Underground, the Red Army Faction, and Revolutionary Violence in the Sixties and Seventies*. Berkeley: U of California P, 2004. Print.
VG Berlin. "Einbürgerung eines iranischen Staatsangehörigen." *Neue Zeitschrift für Verwaltungsrecht–Rechtsprechung* 9.2 (1990): 108–110. Print.

VG Lüneburg. "1 A 98/00 VG Lüneburg Urteil vom 16.10.2000. Einer Lehrerin kann nicht deshalb die Eignung als Pädagogin abgesprochen werden, weil sie im Unterricht ein Kopftuch tragen will." *Verwaltungsgericht Lüneburg.* 16 Oct. 2000. Web. 14 Dec. 2010.

VGH Mannheim. "Religiös motiviertes Tragen eines Kopftuchs als Eignungskriterium für Lehramtsbewerberin. Urt. v. 26.6.2001-4 S 1439/00." *Neue Juristische Wochenschrift* 54.39 (2001): 2899–2905. Print.

VG Stuttgart. "Tragen eines Kopftuchs im Unterricht durch Lehrerin. Urt. v. 24.3.2000-15 K 532/99." *Neue Zeitschrift für Verwaltungsrecht* 19.8 (2000): 959–961. Print.

"Von der Kunst der Einfühlung." *Frankfurter Allgemeine Zeitung* 04 Oct. 2007: 59. Print.

De Vries, Heinrich. *Religion and Violence: Philosophical Perspectives from Kant to Derrida.* Johns Hopkins UP, 2001. Print.

Wahba, Annabel. "Schwestermord: Der Fluch der bösen Tat." *Die Zeit* 23 Jul. 2009. Web. 03 Aug. 2010.

Waidhofer, Brigitte J. "Lehrerin mit Kopftuch." *AP Worldstream–German* 13 Jul. 1998. Web. 10 Oct. 2006.

Waltz, Viktoria. "Muß das Kopftuch herunter? Zur Situation der Migrantinnen in unseren Städten." *Durch die Wand! Feministische Konzepte zur Raumentwicklung.* Eds. Christine Bauhardt and Ruth Becker. Vol. 7. Pfaffenweiler: Centaurus-Verlagsgesellschaft, 1997. 123–145. Print. Stadt, Raum und Gesellschaft.

"Was Thilo Sarrazin sagt: 'Ständig neue kleine Kopftuchmädchen'." *Frankfurter Allgemeine Zeitung* 04 Apr. 2009. Web. 15 Jul. 2012.

"WDR-Fun(k)haus." WDR, 16 Aug. 2009. Television.

Weber, Beverly M. "Beyond the Culture Trap: Immigrant Women in Germany, Planet-Talk, and a Politics of Listening." *Women in German Yearbook: Feminist Studies in German Literature & Culture.* Eds. Helga Kraft and Marjorie Gelus. Vol. 21. 2005. 16–38. Print.

———. "Cloth on Her Head, Constitution in Hand: Germany's Headscarf Debates and the Cultural Politics of Difference." *German Politics and Society* 22.3 (2004): 33–63. Print.

———. "Work, Sex, and Socialism: Reading Beyond Cultural Hybridity in Emine Sevgi Özdamar's Die Brücke Vom Goldenen Horn." *German Life and Letters* 63.1 (2010): 37–53. Print.

Weber, Beverly M, and Maria Stehle. "German Soccer, the 2010 World Cup, and Multicultural Belonging." *German Studies Review* 36.1 (2013). Forthcoming.

Weickmann, Dorion. "Buch im Gespräch: Inländer und Ausländer." *Die Zeit* 15 Jul. 2004. Web. 19 Jul. 2012.

Weitz, Eric D. *A Century Of Genocide: Utopias Of Race And Nation.* Princeton UP, 2005. Print.

"'Wenn je ein Problem voraussehbar war.' Einwanderungsland Bundesrepublik (IV): Reizthema Ausländerkriminalität–was ist wirklich dran?" *Der Spiegel* 43.10 (1989): 88–104. Print.

Wesel, Uwe. "Turnvater Jahn und der Bart des Propheten." *Neue Juristische Wochenschrift* 47.21 (1994): 1389–90. Print.

Westphal, Manuela. "Arbeitsmigrantinnen im Spiegel westdeutscher Frauenbilder." *Beiträge zur feministischen Theorie und Praxis* 19.42 (1996): 17–28. Print.
Windfuhr, Volkhard, and Bernhard Zand. "Egyptian Author on Murdered Muslim Woman: 'The Reaction of the German Government Was Not Fair'." *spiegel online*. 20 Jul. 2009. Web. 08 Sep. 2009.
Winter, Bronwyn. "Secularism Aboard the Titanic: Feminists and the Debate over the Hijab in France." *Feminist Studies* 32.2 (2006): 279–298. Print.
Winter, Irene. "Iris Alanyali." *WIR online–Magazin für die Ehemaligen der freien Universität*. 07 Dec. 2007. Web. 10 Sep. 2010.
Winter, Steffen. "Justiz: 'Bloßer Hass'." *Spiegel online*. 31 Aug. 2009. Web. 08 Sep. 2009.
Wittrock, Philipp. "HDJ-Verbot: Rechtsextreme Kinderfänger organisieren sich neu." *Spiegel online*. 31 Mar. 2009. Web. 15 Oct. 2010.
Wölk, Florian. "Spagat mit Kopftuch. Muslimische Mädchen im deutschen Sportunterricht." *Spagat mit Kopftuch*. Ed. Jürgen Reulecke. Hamburg: Körber-Stiftung, 1997. 491–525. Print.
Wright, Michelle Maria. "Others-from-Within from Without: Afro-German Subject Formation and the Challenge of a Counter-Discourse." *Callaloo* 26.2 (2003): 296–305. Web. 17 May 2011.
Y, Inci. *Erstickt an euren Lügen: Eine Türkin in Deutschland erzählt*. Munich: Piper, 2007. Print.
Yavuz, M. Hakan, and John L. Esposito. *Turkish Islam and the Secular State: The Gülen Movement*. Syracuse, NY: Syracuse UP, 2003. Print.
Yeğenoğlu, Meyda. *Colonial Fantasies. Towards a Feminist Reading of Orientalism*. Cambridge, England: Cambridge UP, 1998. Print.
Yeşilada, Karin. "'Nette Türkinnen von nebenan'–Die neue deutsch-türkische Harmlosigkeit als literarischer Trend." *Von der nationalen zur internationalen Literatur; Transkulturelle deutschsprachige Literatur im Zeitalter globaler Migration*. Vol. 69. Amsterdam: Rodopi, 2009. 117–142. Print. Amsterdamer Beiträge zur neuren Germanistik.
Yıldız, Yasemin. "Turkish Girls, Allah's Daughters, and the Contemporary German Subject: Itinerary of a Figure." *German Life and Letters* 62.4 (2009): 465–481. Print.
Young, Iris Marion. "Impartiality and the Civic Public: Some Implications of Feminist Critiques of Moral and Political Theory." *Praxis International* 4 (1985): 381–401. Print.
Yücel, Kübra. "Seit dem Mord reden wir offener." *taz.de*. 31 Jul. 2009. Web. 06 Apr. 2010.
Yurtsever-Kneer, Selcuk. "Strategien feministischer Migrantinnenpolitik." *FeMigra*. 15 Sep. 2002. Web. 10 Jul. 2005.
Zaimoglu, Feridun. *Kanak Sprak: 24 Mißtöne vom Rande der Gesellschaft*. Hamburg: Rotbuch Verlag, 1995. Print.
———. *Leyla*. Köln: Kiepenheuer & Witsch, 2006. Print.
Zaptçıoğlu, Dilek. "Widerstand im blauen Chiffon." *Kopftuchkulturen*. Eds. Meral Akkent and Gaby Franger. Nürnberg: Frauen in der einen Welt, 1999. 153–156. Print.
Žižek, Slavoj. "Multiculturalism, or, the Cultural Logic of Multinational Capitalism." *New Left Review* 225 (1997): 28–51. Print.
———. *Violence*. New York: Picador, 2008. Print.

INDEX

Action Alliance of Muslim Women, *see Aktionsbündnis muslimischer Frauen*
activism
   and Afro-German women, 13–14
   alliances, 10, 20, 36, 38, 47–48, 68, 74, 142, 183
   and gender violence, 50–52, 144, 201
   against headscarf ban, 133
   queer, 205
   against racism, 3, 13–16, 48–49, 104, 108, 120, 139, 189–190, 200, 204–205
   against rape, 50–51
   against violence, 23, 36–37, 42–43, 47–49, 50–52, 68, 138–139, 199–206
Adelson, Leslie, 15–16, 177–178, 182–183, 188
Afro-Germans, 144, 199
agency, 10, 14, 17–23, 48–49, 57, 74, 84, 127–128, 130, 134, 142, 166, 188, 204, 205
Ahmed, Leila, 19, 47, 85
Akgün, Lale, 70–71
Akkent, Meral, 86, 89–90
Aktionsbündnis muslimischer Frauen (AMF), 201–202, 204
Akyün, Hatice, 103, 140, 143, 152–155, 165–166
Alanyali, Iris, 140, 155–162, 166, 176, 193
An Order of Hans with Hot Sauce, see *Einmal Hans mit scharfer Soße*
anticolonial movements, 19, 21, 49, 195

antidemocratic, 22, 66, 76
antiracism, 3, 13–16, 48–49, 104, 108, 120, 139, 189–190, 200, 204–205, 209
anti-Semitism, 13, 85, 87, 124
archive, alternative, 9, 53, 83, 114–116
Armenian genocide, 192, 194–196, 211
art
   Özdamar's conception of, 174, 186–187
   and representations of covering, 115–116, 133–135
Asad, Talal, 22, 24, 30–32
Ataman, Kutluğ, 64, 133–134
Ateş, Seyran, 68, 70, 72, 75–76, 139–140, 143–147, 150, 169–170, 210
authenticity, 8, 38, 56, 140, 145–146, 152, 155, 161, 167, 171, 173–198, 211
autobiographical works, 137–172

Baba, Acci, 126–129
Baden-Württemberg, 77, 80, 93–98, 100
Bahners, Patrick, 72, 193–194
Bahro, Gundula, 182, 186, 211
Bahro, Rudolf, 180, 182, 186, 211
Balibar, Étienne, 5, 7, 53, 200
Berlin, 7, 14, 39–40, 54, 62, 67, 81, 86, 92, 94, 112–113, 115–118, 121, 125–126, 131, 133, 135, 160, 168, 173, 175, 179–180, 182–185
Biermann, Wolf, 180, 185–186

Blue Journey, The, see *Die blaue Reise*
Brown, Wendy, 35, 43, 45
Bundesverband der Migrantinnen in Deutschand (BdMD), see *Göçmen Kadınlar Birliği*
Bundesverfassungsgericht, 78, 94, 96–98, 100–102, 209
BurkaBondage, 116, 126–135
burqa, 27, 60, 88, 116, 126–128, 130, 133–135, 208
Butler, Judith, 23, 42

Celik, Ipek, 190–191, 194
chador, 92
Chakrabarty, Dipesh, 20–21
Christianity, 13, 24, 27, 30–31, 33, 44, 64, 70, 76–77, 81, 87–88, 93–102, 137, 139, 141, 157, 162–163, 194, 209
Çınar, Alev, 27–28, 34, 59, 82, 86, 209
citizenship, 5, 23, 27–28, 42, 51, 58, 73, 81–82, 92, 102, 198
  jus sanguinis, 5
  and multiculturalism, 23
  and Muslim women, 28, 42, 51, 81–82, 92, 102
clash of cultures, 7, 64, 99
class, 6, 11, 13–14, 33, 54, 58, 89–91, 118, 158
colonial fantasies, 5–7, 84–85
colonial narratives, 5–7, 47, 209
colonialism, 8, 29, 31, 43, 83, 112, 172, 195
  and racism, 5, 7
  and women, 19–20, 209
community identities, 19, 29, 40–41, 48, 51–52, 62–63, 125, 142, 145–146, 160–163, 166–168, 194, 204–205
constitution
  European, 34
  German, 32, 45, 59, 64, 77, 82, 95, 97–99, 101, 150–151

criminality
  and Turkish German men, 51, 54–55, 117, 119
Ctrl+Alt+Del, 113–114
cultural difference, 4–17, 53–54, 58, 74
  and gender, 11–17, 64–65, 79, 89–93, 125, 174
  and public sphere, 26
  in research, 7, 9, 11–14, 123–124
  and space, 66
cultural racism, 10–11, 18, 139
cultural studies, 4, 15, 37, 172
  and feminism, 4, 172
  transnational, 4, 37
culture
  conceptualization of, 4–17
  and multiculturalism, 4–17
  and race, 5–8, 11–14, 53, 85

Das Leben ist eine Karawanserai, 176–177, 196
Debus, Ann, 95, 99, 101
democracy
  and colonialism, 22–23, 195
  and gender, 27–28, 44–45
  and Islam, 22, 60, 78–79, 86, 90, 96–98, 109, 132
  and the Left, 133, 183–184, 187
  and the public sphere, 26–30, 102–103, 200, 204–206
  and racism, 6, 80–81, 87–88, 109, 112, 196
  and religion, 2, 22, 26–29, 60, 76
  and secularism, 6, 23–30, 60, 76, 90
democratic subjectivities, 10, 15, 22–23, 37–38, 44–45, 61, 66, 78, 81–82, 111–112, 115, 133, 135, 137, 164–165
Der Hof im Spiegel, 173
Deutsche Islam Konferenz (DIK), 19, 25–26, 28, 137–139, 170–171, 189, 191, 197, 202
Deutschland schafft sich ab, 2, 165, 201

Die Große Verschleierung: Für Integration, gegen Islamismus, 87–88
Die blaue Reise, 140, 152, 155–161, 176
Die Deutschlandtür geht auf und gleich wieder zu, 173–174
Die fremde Braut, 132, 138, 145, 148–151
Die Gotteskrieger und die falsche Toleranz, 87
DIK, *see* Deutsche Islam Konferenz
domestic violence, 1, 13, 28, 32, 40, 44–76, 83, 120, 138, 145, 196

Einmal Hans mit scharfer Soße, 152–155, 166–167
El-Sherbini, Marwa, 37, 77–83, 104–112, 114, 209
El-Tayeb, Fatima, 5, 6, 21, 53, 200, 202–203
Enlightenment, 16, 18, 21, 24, 30–32, 43, 45, 55, 60, 81, 95–96, 110–111, 143, 184, 208
eroticization, 84–85, 110, 129
ethnic difference, 12–13, 35, 106–107, 122, 148, 150
ethnic violence, *see* Armenian genocide; Holocaust
ethnicity
  and gender, 12, 14, 41, 150
  and interethnic alliances, 36, 48
  narratives of homogeneity, 33, 111–112, 161, 194
ethnicization
  of culture, 7, 12
  of sexism, 12
Eurocentrism, 8, 20, 22, 31, 47
  and human rights, 18, 20–23, 30, 44, 57, 80, 96–98, 143, 199–201, 211
Europe
  colonial legacies, 5, 8, 19–20, 22–23, 29, 31, 43, 47, 83–85, 112, 117, 195, 209
  and diversity, 111–112
  and multiculturalism, 8–9
  and race, 5–6, 8–9, 11–12, 53–54
  and secularism as path to peace, 23–30
European Court of Human Rights, 95
European public, 35–36
European Union, 2, 33, 35, 76, 79–80, 94–95, 160, 200
  antidiscrimination laws, 80
Europeanness, 64, 76, 148, 149

familial violence, 17, 32, 39, 41–42, 44–76, 78, 83, 115, 156, 160, 171, 191, 193–194, 199–200, 207–208
Farbe Bekennen, 14
Federal Constitutional Court of Germany, *see* Bundesverfassungsgericht
FeMigra, 13
feminism, 3–4, 12–17, 20–23, 29–30, 40, 44, 48–50, 62, 66, 69, 81, 85, 87–88, 90, 101–102, 105, 108, 115, 122, 125, 128, 137, 142, 145, 148–151, 164, 166, 168, 170–172, 182, 199, 202–208
  and antiracism, 12–15, 108, 205–206
  Eurocentric, 148, 170, 205
  and the German headscarf debates, 101–102
  global, 17
  and immigrant women, 12–13, 15
  and intersectionality, 11–12
  and Islam, 19–22, 48, 90, 148–151
  and multiculturalism, 40
  and racism, 29, 211
  and scholarship, 14, 16, 22, 172–173
  transnational, 205–206
  and whiteness, 170
feminist transnational cultural studies, 3–4, 172–173

Ferree, Myra Marx, 80
forced marriage, 2, 42, 48, 52, 63–65, 71–72, 100, 120, 143, 149, 154, 156, 163, 168–169, 199, 210
Foreign Bride, The, see *Die fremde Braut*
Forouhar, Parastou, 131–133
France, 5, 14, 24, 27, 32, 53, 79, 88, 92–93, 95, 104, 145, 180, 201, 209
freedom, 22–23, 32, 55, 66–67, 69, 71, 77, 82, 94, 97–99, 103, 116, 120, 127–130, 137, 139, 145, 147, 166–167, 210

Gastarbeiter, see guestworkers
gender
  gender violence, 2–4, 9–10, 12, 16–17, 20, 23–24, 28, 31, 36–37, 39–76, 127, 138–139, 154–155, 160, 165–167, 174, 182, 189, 191, 194–196, 201, 203–205, 207, 208
  and race, 12–14, 23
genocide, 182, 192, 194–196, 211, 213, 218, 232
German Democratic Republic, 180, 182–185
German Islam Conference, see Deutsche Islam Konferenz (DIK)
German unification, 36–37, 42, 53–55, 58, 75, 88, 188
Germanness, 55, 57, 66, 107, 121, 146, 179, 189, 209
Germany Does Away with Itself, see *Deutschland schafft sich ab*
Ghadirian, Shadi, 113–114
ghetto, 59–60, 118–119, 162
globalization, 7–8, 10–11, 15, 43, 52, 70–71, 188
Göçmen Kadınlar Birliği, 48, 71, 168–170
Göktürk, Deniz, 7, 52, 55–56, 117, 146, 176
Göle, Nilüfer, 33, 86, 113–116, 131–135, 209

Große Reise ins Feuer, 139–140, 143–147
guestworkers, 5–6, 12, 53, 86, 193
Gümen, Sedef, 11–14
Güngör, Dilek, 140, 166

Habermas, Jürgen, 26, 29–30, 200
Halle, Randall, 146
headscarf debates, 113–135
headscarves, 2, 27–28, 37, 39, 41, 44, 46, 52, 54, 58–62, 64, 66, 75–135, 139, 150, 152, 154, 156, 163–165, 173–174, 197, 199, 201, 208–209
  in academic studies, 86–87
  and art, 113–135
  bans, 81, 86, 94–96, 98–99, 108, 201
hijab martyr, 77–78, 111, 208
Hirsi Ali, Ayaan, 145, 211
Holocaust, 6, 35, 88, 100, 150, 183, 196
honor, 39–76, 78, 86, 120, 143, 150, 158, 193, 199, 208, 210
  in academic studies, 46—48
  honor crimes, 40–42, 46–49, 52, 61, 63–72, 75, 143, 199
human rights, 18, 20–23, 30–31, 44, 57, 80, 95–98, 103, 108, 112, 143, 171, 195, 199–201, 211
hybridity, 7–8, 122–123, 174, 189–190
  and activism, 8
  depoliticizing, 7–8

In Schleier Haft, 115–117
In Veil Prison, see *In Schleier Haft*
integration, 9, 11–12, 18, 30, 39, 41, 52, 59, 61–63, 65, 103, 105, 108, 120–122, 138, 141–142, 145, 150, 152, 160, 168, 170–171, 209
  failure of, 9, 11, 39
  and gender issues, 11–12, 18, 30, 41, 62, 65, 108, 171
intersectionality, 11–15, 23, 42, 80, 171, 200, 207
intimate violence, 17, 30, 32, 129, 130

Islamist, 33–34, 77, 86, 108, 150, 158, 165, 205, 209
Islamophobia, 3, 36, 40, 47, 70, 78, 82–83, 87, 104–110, 112, 139, 171, 198, 201, 204

Judaism, 24, 81, 96, 100, 182
and the German state, 25
jus sanguinis, 5

Kanak Attak, 190
kanak movement, 152, 189–190
Kanak Sprak, 189–191, 193
Karakaşoğlu, Yasemin, 90
Kawaguchi, Yui, 126–130
Kelek, Necla, 11, 46, 64, 68–72, 75, 102, 108, 132, 137–140, 143, 145–146, 148–151, 153, 168–170, 197, 208
Kiyak, Mely, 169–170
Konuk, Kader, 13, 176–177
Koran, 1, 59–60, 93, 150, 153
Krieg. Was Männerwahn anrichtet und wie Frauen Widerstand leisten, 87
Kurdish heritage, 42, 48, 75, 147–148, 159–160, 182, 192, 195–196
Kurdish region, 211
Kurdish resistance movement, 33, 192–194

laïcité, 32, 79, 95
Lentin, Alana, 5–6, 8, 54
Leyla, 175, 189–198, 211
Life is a Caravanserai, see *Das Leben ist eine Karawanserai*
Littler, Margaret, 177, 186–187, 196
Lorde, Audre, 14, 204, 207
Ludin, Fereshta, 58–59, 76–83, 90, 92–112

Mahmood, Saba, 205
Mahrem. Footnotes on Veiling, 113–116, 131–135
masculinity, 52, 54, 149, 152, 190, 208, 211

modernity
and colonialism, 7, 31
and Eurocentrism, 7
and gender, 43–45, 56, 63–66, 144–146
and individualism, 7
and Islam, 29–32, 63–66, 80, 111, 132–133
non-Western, 21, 34
and racism, 8, 79
and secularism, 32–34, 98
and violence, 31, 191–198
modernization
of Turkey, 21, 159, 194–195, 207, 211
Mortazavi, Mohammad Reza, 126–129
Mother Tongue, see *Mutterzunge*
multiculturalism, 4, 7–9, 11, 15, 23, 35, 40, 53, 57, 65, 71, 92, 107, 119, 121, 138, 155, 201
radical, 9
Mutterzunge, 176–181

Narayan, Uma, 47, 49, 51, 67
National Federation of Immigrant Women in Germany, see Göçmen Kadınlar Birliği
Nationaldemokratische Partei Deutschlands (NPD), 77
nationalism, 13, 177, 195–196, 200, 211
Neo-Nazi, 31, 91, 124, 149, 157, 159, 210
Neukölln, 117–119, 121–123

Orientalism, 7, 58, 84–85, 110, 121, 123, 128, 209
OVG Lüneburg, 99, 101
Özdamar, Emine Sevgi, 15, 38, 173–188, 196–199, 211, 213

Pak, Serpil, 89, 115–125, 134–135
political theater, 177
post-secular, 29

public sphere, 2–3, 16, 20–24, 26–30, 32, 35, 37, 41–44, 46, 48–49, 51, 59, 62, 66, 68, 72, 74–76, 78–80, 82–83, 85, 95, 102–103, 105, 107–108, 110, 112, 114–116, 122, 125, 130–131, 133–135, 138–143, 146, 152–155, 165–167, 169, 188, 191, 200–201, 204–206, 209

race, 5–6, 8, 11–12, 14, 23, 53, 80, 85, 106, 108, 135, 195, 205, 207, 215, 218–219, 225, 232
  biological concept, 11, 85, 137, 150
  and culture, 5–8, 11–14, 53, 85
  and purity, 120
  as taboo, 5–6, 11, 80
racialization, 53, 107, 123, 198
racialized violence, 10, 17, 20, 32, 36, 38, 42, 78, 110–111, 116, 135, 140–141, 155, 157, 160, 172, 195, 201
racism
  and democracy, 6, 80–81, 87–88, 109, 112, 196
  and feminism, 29, 211
  and gender, 12–14, 23
  and the murder of Marwa el-Sherbini, 105–108
regime of gender violence, 3, 28, 36, 39–76
religion
  and the public sphere, 26–30
religious violence, 31, 32
Republikaner, 65, 80, 92–93, 96
Rodríguez, Encarnación Gutiérrez, 14, 211
Rommelspacher, Birgit, 93, 138
Rote Armee Fraktion (RAF), 180, 183–185, 188
Rottmann, Susan B., 80
Rovisco, Vania, 126–130
Russlanddeutscher, 106–107

sacred, 23, 187
Sarrazin, Thilo, 2, 4, 8, 10–11, 28, 137, 139, 165, 201

Schäuble, Wolfgang, 137
Schiffauer, Werner, 63–64, 66–67
Schwarzer, Alice, 62, 87–88, 102–104, 209
secularism, 6, 16, 21, 23–24, 26–27, 29–35, 38, 44–45, 52, 58, 60, 62, 67, 69, 76, 79–81, 86, 88, 90, 95–96, 98–99, 105–112, 114–115, 131–135, 139, 142, 160, 162, 166, 172, 175, 179, 186–188, 194–195, 197–198, 204, 207, 209–210
  European, 44, 96–98, 112
  German, 24–25
  Turkish, 32–35
Seltsame Sterne starren zur Erde, 175, 177–188, 197–198
Şenocak, Zafer, 64–65, 176, 196
Seyhan, Azade, 144, 177–179, 187–188
Sezgin, Hilal, 109, 111, 140, 161–170, 172, 196
Showing Our Colors, see *Farbe bekennen*
Sokolowsky, Kay, 72, 111, 147, 149, 210
Spivak, Gayatri, 4, 9–10, 17–19, 22–23, 47, 171, 207, 211
Stehle, Maria, 66, 118, 201
Strange Stars, see *Seltsame Sterne starren zur Erde*
student movement
  Federal Republic of Germany, 179, 183
  Turkey, 183
Sürücü, Hatun, 39–42, 48, 61–71, 73–78

Tanas, 113, 115, 131–132
Terkessidis, 8, 26, 52–53, 58, 103, 146
Terrorism
  and Islam, 47, 134, 163
  left, 180, 183–185, 188
theater, 173–175, 177, 179–180, 182, 186, 187
tolerance, 31, 35, 40, 43, 57, 59, 69, 79, 87, 98–101, 109, 111–112, 150
transgender, 133, 173, 207

transnational feminism, 4, 21–22, 205
transnational feminist cultural studies, 4, 205
Turkey
  and the European Union, 34
  modernization of, 21, 159, 194–195, 207, 211
  secularism in, 21, 32–34, 104
  Typisch Türkin, 152, 161–166

United Kingdom, 14, 24, 36, 79, 105, 176
Unter uns, 140

VG Lüneburg, 99, 101
VG Stuttgart, 94, 96, 100
victim narratives, 137–151, 152, 157, 162, 167
violence against women, 3, 16, 23, 30, 36–37, 40–41, 43, 47–49, 51–52, 54, 56–57, 65, 67–69, 72–76, 140–142, 168, 172, 180, 182, 193, 199–203, 210

Waldmann, Helena, 116, 126–130
Western historicism, 20–21
whiteness, 17, 19, 76–102, 120

Wiens, Alex, 77, 81–82, 104–108, 111
women of color, 11, 13, 23, 47, 114, 151
women of immigrant heritage in Germany
  employment and working lives, 4, 8, 11–12, 48, 69, 75, 82, 93, 119, 170–171
  excluded from scholarship, 11–14
  organizations against violence, 48, 71, 168
  in the public sphere, 36, 68–69, 110, 116, 119, 139, 144–146
  writing by, 15–16
Women Who Wear Wigs, 133–135
women's rights, 10–13, 15–16, 20, 36, 41, 53–54, 58, 62, 68, 74, 83, 119, 139, 144, 169, 171

xenophobia, 3, 5, 13, 70, 89, 99, 107, 112, 188, 200

Yeşilada, Karin, 140, 151–154

Zaimoglu, Feridun, 38, 173–175, 188–194, 196–198
Zaptçıoğlu, Dilek, 90, 92–93
Žižek, Slavoj, 8, 35–36, 43, 203

Printed in the United States of America